HOW TO CONQUER YOUR ALCOHOLISM

– MADE SIMPLE!

The *Practical* Way to Get and STAY Sober

D.H. WILLIAMS

Conquer Your Addiction LLC

Saint Louis, Missouri

The information in this book is designed to provide helpful information on the subjects discussed. This book is not meant to be used, nor should it be used, to diagnose or treat any medical condition. For the diagnosis or treatment of any medical problem, consult your own physician or practitioner. The author is not responsible for any specific health needs that may require medical attention or supervision and is not liable for any damages or negative consequences from any treatment, action, application, or preparation given to any person reading or following the information in this book. References are provided for informational purposes only and do not constitute endorsement of any websites or other sources. Readers should be aware that the websites listed in this book may change.

Conquer Your Addiction LLC
P.O. Box 220442
Saint Louis, Missouri 63122
www.ConquerYourAddiction.com

ISBN: 978-0-9991915-0-7

Printed in the United States of America

To My Children:

Adam, Anna, Michael, and Maria, who continue to be fantastic adults despite a "challenging" childhood. Well done! I Love You!

To My Parents:

You Did Good!

To Robin:

For being there for the rest of my life!

CONTENTS

PREFACE

My name is D.H. Williams. I am not a doctor, psychologist, or any professional service provider. What I am is someone who was an active alcoholic for over 20 years, tried everything you are supposed to try to overcome it, and failed. This book is a (greatly) condensed and simplified version of the program I developed to finally get and *stay* sober in *How to Conquer Your Alcoholism—A Complete and Useable Reference Guide to Getting & Staying Sober*. Everything you need to know to get and stay sober is described in *this* book. However, if you would like much more detail on any aspect of the program and/or would like a complete reference guide on all aspects alcoholism, I would encourage you to consider the complete reference. More information can be found at www.ConquerYourAddiction.com.

DH Williams, July 2017

INTRODUCTION

You've tried to get sober before. You've tried rehab, Alcoholics Anonymous (AA), therapy, and/or maybe some lesser known approaches. You've stayed sober for weeks or months at a time, but eventually you always go back to drinking. Nothing sticks!

You feel that something (besides the alcoholism) must be wrong with you. You hear about people coming "clean" out of rehab (and incorrectly assume they stay that way) and wonder why it didn't work for you. Or AA old-timers say "just work the steps" and you do, but it doesn't take. In the back of your mind you feel these approaches are simplistic and cookie-cutter, that they don't acknowledge your unique situation, but you grit your teeth and try anyway-to no avail!

Perhaps you have read a few alcoholism self-help books that are interesting but their lessons seem to fade quickly. Or they are so academic or high level that they border on worthless when applied to everyday life. They just are not practical!

You may have also encountered "bait-and-switch" type programs that profess to be secular, but then try and ram religion down your throat!

The program described in this book—The Conquer Program—addresses all these obstacles to staying sober. It is a comprehensive yet intuitive program, focused on your particular situation and history. It is neither a cookie-cutter, spirituality-based step program, nor a one-size-fits-all approach that ignores the practical realities of everyday alcoholic life. It consists of a unique mix of the best-of-the-best existing treatments, combined with brand new approaches invented and tested by the author, integrated in a new and highly effective way.

In a nutshell, The Conquer Program is a personalized, multi-level approach designed to have multiple safety nets to prevent a drinking relapse, so when one technique isn't working well one day, there are others to back it up. Its emphasis on drinking "triggers" ensures that the defenses *you* select to defend against alcohol are the best for *your* situation. And the defense options are all <u>practical</u>—tested and used by alcoholics to successfully combat the everyday pressures that alcohol puts on us every day, every hour of our life. In total, I believe The Conquer Program is far superior to any other program in the alcoholism treatment world, and believe you will too!

* * * * *

For additional help associated with this book, consider acquiring the comprehensive, unabridged edition of The Conquer Program as well as its comprehensive reference guide on all aspects of alcoholism titled *How to Conquer Your Alcoholism*, available on <u>Amazon</u>[1] and <u>iTunes</u>[2]. Key excerpts, descriptions of the program, and breaking alcoholism news are available for free at <u>www.ConquerYourAddiction.com</u>.

One last thought: reading self-help books are often as fun as watching paint dry. How can you expect to really embrace a treatment program if you can't stay awake while learning about it? This book is described in a way that is engaging, even entertaining. Enjoy it while you get your life on track!

THE 10 KEYS TO UNDERSTANDING YOUR ALCOHOLISM

Alcoholism to an outsider seems like a straightforward problem: you drink too much and need to stop. So, they start nagging you to do the seemingly "simple" solutions that everybody knows. Go to Rehab! Go to Therapy! Go to AA! Or worst of all: "just" stop- like it's just a question of willpower, intelligence, effort, or even morals. Non-addicts do NOT understand addiction, including many addiction "professionals".[1]

In the meantime, you get frustrated and angry, which doesn't help your relationships and certainly doesn't help you get or stay sober. Even when you are past your denial stage (*every* alcoholic goes through denial), and have tried the "treatments" you are supposed to, your resentment grows. Nothing is more frustrating and in turn anger-inducing then to do what you're supposed to, for it not to work, and then have people blame you for it not working!

Before we get into the specifics of The Conquer Program and address your specific reasons for drinking, it is essential that you understand dimensions of alcoholism that are common to all alcoholics. This will provide you with the foundation of understanding how you got to where you are today. It will also be very helpful for anyone helping you get sober (see Level 4—Engage Friends and Family) to understand these dimensions or "keys", as it is likely that most of your friends and family are mystified by your drinking (most non-addicts have no idea what happens in addiction). These 10 keys listed are introduced in roughly the chronological order they are encountered, with many building off previous ones. They are:

The 10 Keys to Understanding an Alcoholic

1. Alcoholics can't control alcohol. *At all.*

2. Becoming an alcoholic is a *process*. It didn't happen overnight—it snuck up on you and your loved ones.

3. Alcoholism is both a physical *and* mental addiction.

4. *Every* alcoholic goes through denial.

5. Until the alcoholic *truly* admits a problem, no treatment will work.

6. The longer an alcoholic drinks, the more *complicated* staying sober becomes.

7. The fear of quitting drinking outweighs the fear of *not* quitting.

8. Alcoholics often do not understand *why* they drink like they do.

9. Alcohol "attacks" in many ways, from *many* different directions and forms.

10. Most treatments do a *very* poor job of addressing 1-9.

As you might imagine there is a lot of detail behind each one of these keys.[2] But admitted alcoholics recognize the truth of each one and don't need convincing, particularly those having tried various methods and are still struggling. Even if you don't believe you are an alcoholic (yet), the inherent truths of these statements should seem intuitive. Any successful treatment needs to incorporate these 10 keys into the details of their program, otherwise they *will* fail.

The results of these 10 keys can be defined in the following treatment principles at the heart of The Conquer Program:

Essential Alcoholism Treatment Principles

- If you don't *truly* believe you have an alcohol problem, *no* treatment will help. Forcing a treatment down a non-believer's throat is pointless.

- An alcoholic has to understand *why* they drink. Otherwise you are treating symptoms, not causes.

- Alcoholics no longer have (or never had) any effective defenses against alcohol—new ones have to be built. This argues against the effectiveness of a few small-scale "adjustments" in an alcoholic's mindset and behavior. *Large* changes are needed. That said, it doesn't mean you have to completely reinvent your life—you can do so with a large number of small adjustments.

- No one defense can defend against all the ways alcohol can attack you all the time. You need multiple, layered defenses so if one fails there are others to back it up. Simple, "one-level" treatments rarely work.

- General, high-level, feel-good ideas for staying sober fade with time. You need *practical, specific* guidance on what to do (and not to do) in everyday life to stay sober long-term.

With that as the setup, let's get into The Conquer Program.

THE CONQUER PROGRAM OVERVIEW

The 13 Levels of The Conquer Program are organized in a logical, intuitive, and above all *practical* way through the methodically building of multiple defenses against the attacks of alcohol. Visualize that you will be building a fortress, Level-by-Level, similar to the fortress below, with you safely inside.

Figure 1: Alcoholism Defense "Fortress"

This defense fortress can't be built all at once of course. Instead, we will build it one level at a time, just like any major structure.

The 13 Levels are organized into 3 Phases. They are:

PHASE 1—*Lay the Foundation* for your sobriety (Levels 1-3)

> **LEVEL 1**—Admit You Have an Addiction to Alcohol
> **LEVEL 2**—Know Your Triggers
> **LEVEL 3**—Listen to Your Body!

PHASE 2—*Build New Defenses* using the best-of-the-best of existing treatment methods (Levels 4-9)

> **LEVEL 4**—Engage Friends and Family
> **LEVEL 5**—Detox
> **LEVEL 6**—Rehab and Therapy
> **LEVEL 7**—Join a Community
> **LEVEL 8**—Break Bad Habits
> **LEVEL 9**—Develop New Hobbies

PHASE 3—*Complete Your Fortifications* for repelling alcohol attacks (Levels 10-13)

> **LEVEL 10**—Consider Spirituality (Optional)
> **LEVEL 11**—Make Yourself Sick of Alcohol (Optional)
> **LEVEL 12**—The LAST Detox
> **LEVEL 13**—Develop Your Defense Progressions

The figures above illustrate the 3 Phases and the Levels in each Phase. The term "Levels" is used purposely; it is intended to show a progressive building up of defenses, like the progressive building of new floors in a building. It is also a deliberate avoidance of the term "Steps"—a word that can imply small, short-term, reversible movements, whereas "Levels" is about long-term *building*—a new permanent foundation, for a new life.

Figure 1 illustrates the Levels of Defense and fortress concepts, with the result being an extremely strong, multilevel fortress built on a rock-solid foundation that together can enable you to successfully withstand the multitude of ways that alcohol can attack you, all day, every day.

Let's now look at each phase in more detail:

Phase 1— Lay the Foundation for Sobriety

Phase 1 looks to lay a rock-solid foundation for sobriety through a combination of self-admission (*truly* admitting you are an alcoholic), self-understanding (*thoroughly* understanding what causes you to drink) and physical assessment (*completely* determining the toll that alcohol is taking on your body). Figure 2 below illustrates this multiple Level foundation building approach with Levels 1 through 3.

PHASE 1 – Lay The Foundation for Sobriety

LEVEL 3 — LISTEN TO YOUR BODY! — **COMPLETE** *Knowledge of What it is Doing To Your Body*

LEVEL 2 — KNOW YOUR TRIGGERS — **FULL** *Understanding of What Makes You Drink*

LEVEL 1 — ADMIT YOU ARE AN ALCOHOLIC — **TRULY** *Admitting You Have an Addiction*

Figure 2: The Three Levels of Phase 1—Lay the Foundation for Sobriety

Why is this so important? Well, just as trying to erect a building on a sandy foundation is doomed to have it crumble around you, so is trying to build a solid fortress against alcohol doomed if it is built on a foundation of ignorance, self-delusion, and outright lies. <u>Nothing</u> is going to help you if you don't truly admit deep in your heart and mind that you have a problem.

Such insight may seem obvious (particularly if you are a nonalcoholic), but getting to that state of clarity is *very* hard for most alcoholics. Why? The answer is easy: <u>no one</u> wants to admit that they are flawed, have a major weakness, or are (negatively) different from most other people. Sure, nobody is perfect, but who wants to seemingly be <u>that</u> imperfect? No one, thus laying the core of denial for the addict. This core must be removed for any treatment to be truly effective, replaced instead by a solid foundation of acceptance, self-knowledge, mental and physical readiness to be helped.

Phase 1 consists of 3 Levels:

Level 1— (Getting you to) ***Admit You Have an Addiction to Alcohol*** is the first (and mentally hardest) part of conquering alcoholism: admitting you have a problem in the first place! Instead of using a handful of simplistic, highly subjective questions to "test" whether you are an alcoholic, we've developed a much more objective, comprehensive, yet easy-to-answer questionnaire that focuses on your day-to-day behaviors and end results.

Level 2— (Getting to truly) ***Know Your Triggers*** is where you will learn more about *why* you want to drink in the first place. If you are past your mid-20s and still drink heavily, you are not drinking for "fun" anymore; you are drinking to "deal with" life's pressures. But odds are you don't really understand the details of what these pressures are really about. If you believe you drink because of "Stress" for example, what does that really mean? There are so many sources of stress (your job, kids, money, relationships, etc.) complicated individually, and often mixed up. Think about it: if you don't know, at a deep, detailed level, the source(s) of a problem, how can you be expected to solve it?

Level 3— (Understand your health situation by) *Listening to Your Body* looks to understand your current and likely physical health situation with respect to alcohol. Too often an alcoholic's health plays little or no role in his or her thinking about their alcoholism (which is very ironic if you think about it). When attention finally turns that way, sometimes years into the descent into alcoholism, they often find a great deal of unpleasantness awaiting them.

When you have completed Phase 1, you will have a foundation for sobriety that will underlay and support all the subsequent Levels of defenses that you will build in Phases 2 and 3. Of all the Phases, Phase 1 will be the fastest to complete, possibly in as little as a few hours, as it is primarily reading and taking time to think through your triggers.

Phase 2—Build New Defenses

Phase 2 builds on the Level 1 foundation by taking the best of existing approaches to achieving sobriety and integrating them together in a logical yet intuitive manner, continuing to build up a solid and united set of defenses against alcohol. Figure 3 below illustrates how these Levels "stack" together. The Levels with different shades (Levels 5, 6 & 8) indicate a significant physical aspect to that Level's activities.

Phase 2 covers the importance of building various types of support networks, as well as "traditional" methods such as rehabilitation programs, therapy, and alcoholic community–type meetings, and discusses areas such as alcohol-related bad habits and the importance of developing new hobbies.

One key difference in these topics versus other programs is that they are discussed and analyzed in a different and <u>more practical light</u>. One of my biggest complaints I experienced with other programs was how few of the methods discussed were actually *useful* on a daily basis in combating my alcoholism. Much of it was general "ear candy" that sounded good at the time, but gradually became a memory (often within days), and often little help when it came to helping me *practically* change my thinking or actions.

PHASE 2—Build New Defenses

LEVEL 9 — DEVELOP NEW HOBBIES — *Fill Your Newfound Time*

LEVEL 8 — BREAK BAD HABITS — *Clean Out The Garbage*

LEVEL 7 — JOIN A COMMUNITY — *Expand Your Support Network*

LEVEL 6 — REHAB AND THERAPY — *Learn Techniques, Tips, and Yourself*

LEVEL 5 — DETOX — *Understand Detoxification*

LEVEL 4 — ENGAGE FRIENDS AND FAMILY — *Start Building Your Support Network*

Figure 3: The Six Levels of Phase 2—Build New Defenses

Phase 2 consists of six Levels:

- **Level 4**—*Engage Friends and Family* to develop your support network
- **Level 5**— (Understanding and making the most out of) *Detox*
- **Level 6**— (Getting the most out of) *Rehab and Therapy*
- **Level 7**—*Join a Community* of fellow alcoholics to extend your support network
- **Level 8**—*Break Bad Habits* that developed while you were drinking
- **Level 9**—*Develop New Hobbies* to fill the new free time you have from not drinking.

By the end of Phase 2 you will have used the best-of-the-best of "traditional" methods to help you get and stay sober. If it gets you all the way there, wonderful! If not, then it is time to apply the new, unconventional defenses of Phase 3.

Phase 3—Complete Your Fortifications

Phase 3 looks to add some unconventional defenses to those you built in Phases 1 and 2. Phase 3 recognizes that "traditional" methods, no matter how well structured and integrated, may not be enough for some of you. *Phase 3 is not a standalone approach! Completing Phases 1 and 2 are absolutely critical for the success of Phase 3.*

Phase 3 is <u>unorthodox, perhaps even radical</u> in some ways, as it builds those final levels of defense needed for alcoholics who just haven't been able to "get over the hump" and get traditional methods to succeed, no matter how well-crafted and executed. Figure 4 below has a variety of shading/coloring indicating the variety of physical, mental, and even spiritual dimensions that come into play in new ways to help even those most challenging of alcoholics.[1]

PHASE 3 – Complete Your Fortifications

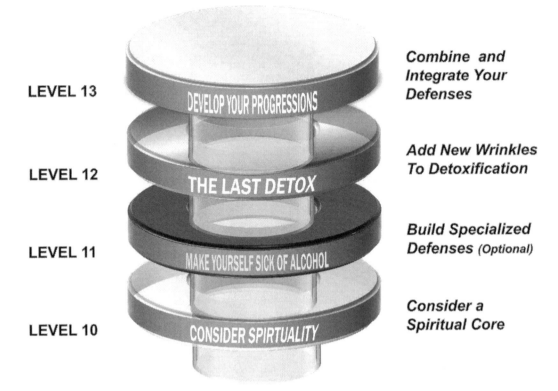

LEVEL 13 — DEVELOP YOUR PROGRESSIONS — *Combine and Integrate Your Defenses*

LEVEL 12 — THE LAST DETOX — *Add New Wrinkles To Detoxification*

LEVEL 11 — MAKE YOURSELF SICK OF ALCOHOL — *Build Specialized Defenses (Optional)*

LEVEL 10 — CONSIDER SPIRTUALITY — *Consider a Spiritual Core*

Figure 4: The Four Levels of Phase 3—Complete Your Fortifications

Phase 3 consists of four Levels:

- **Level 10**—*Consider Spirituality* as a core defense to your sobriety (Optional),
- **Level 11**—*Make Yourself Sick of Alcohol*, particularly to its proximity, smell, and taste (Optional),
- **Level 12**— (Make this) *The LAST Detox* by approaching it in unconventional ways, and
- **Level 13**—*Develop Your Defense Progressions* that combine and structure all the defenses you have built.

It is Level 13 that provides the unique power of The Conquer Program, through integrating and layering multiple defenses in a series of *safety nets* so that if one does not work that day, there are others ready to go to prevent an alcohol attack causing a relapse or worse. Again, one level of defense will not be enough to stop *all* alcohol attacks, *all* the time!

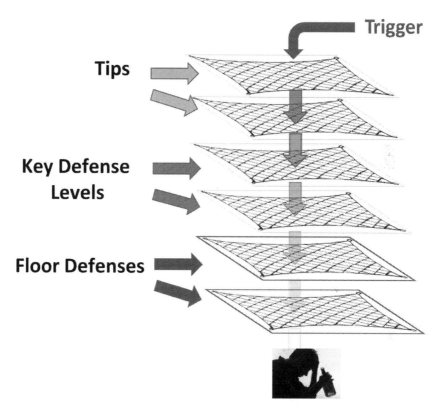

Figure 5: The Conquer Program Safety Nets

Figure 5 illustrates the end result of the multi-Level, multiple safety net nature of The Conquer Program. In a nutshell, for each of your major triggers, you will build a new series of defenses (safety nets) to either catch you before you descend into a relapse, or at least slow your descent (illustrated by the diminishing red arrows) enough so one of the subsequent levels/safety nets will stop you before you take a drink. The makeup of and process for creating these levels/safety nets—Tips, Key Defense Levels, and Floor Defenses—are described in more detail throughout this book.

How Long Will The Conquer Program Take?

How fast you can incorporate the full Conquer Program into your life is completely dependent on the individual. It will depend on: how much chaos your life is currently in; whether you have already done and are "up-to-date" on some of the Levels (e.g. Detox); and most of all how much effort you are prepared to invest mentally and even physically into following the program. Table 1 provides some guidelines on the time required by Level.

The good news is once you achieve a basic understanding of the overall Conquer Program, *you will begin to see positive results in some areas almost immediately*. In addition, some portions of several Levels can be done in

Table 1:   Time Required by Level

Phase	Level	Time	Comments
1	Level 1 – *Admit You Have an Addiction*	Immediately	As soon as immediately, if you are already convinced about your problem or are after taking The Conquer Quiz in this book.
1	Level 2 – *Know Your Triggers*	Varies – Several hours to several days	This may take many hours or even days—as much time as is needed to *accurately* and *in detail* identify what your major triggers are, as well as key related triggers. It will also take time to identify the key tips and defenses you want to employ to defend against those triggers.
1	Level 3 – *Listen To Your Body!*	Time needed for Doctor visit	Immediately, or as soon as you can arrange a frank discussion with your doctor.
2	Level 4 – *Engage Friends and Family*	Few Hours	Odds are high you can immediately identify who meets the criteria described in this Level, then a few hours of conversation with them.
2	Level 5 – *Detox*	2-3 days at least.	Longer however if it is part of a broader Rehabilitation effort. DO UNDER MEDICAL SUPERVISION
2	Level 6 – *Rehab and Therapy*	Several weeks	A rule of thumb for an inpatient Rehab session is about a month; it can be shorter or longer. Outpatient is generally one or more days a week for several weeks. Therapy is generally a weekly session over 12-16 weeks.
2	Level 7 – *Join A Community*	Immediately	Immediately by finding a community online.
2	Level 8 – *Break Bad Habits*	Varies	Can begin almost immediately, though often takes weeks/months of practice to fully overcome deeply entrenched bad habits.
2	Level 9 – *Develop New Hobbies*	Varies	New hobbies may also be easily identifiable, but take some time to get into a rhythm of doing.

parallel. Time for Phases 1 and 2 are show above, Phase 3 next.

Table 1   (Continued)

Phase	Level	Time	Comments
3	Level 10 – *Consider Spirituality*	Varies	Spirituality doesn't come instantly, if at all. But this Level may plant seeds that will grow over time into something resembling reality. So, don't expect immediate results; it can be done in parallel with other Levels.
3	Level 11 – *Make Yourself Sick of Alcohol*	0-6 weeks	Since this is an optional Level, it may not take any time at all. If you choose to do it in the manner that the author did, it may take several weeks. (OPTIONAL)
3	Level 12 – *The Last Detox*	2-3 days	The activities described here do not necessarily take any more time than a "regular" detox, though some may require some planning depending on what "wrinkles" you choose to add to this last attempt to get sober.
3	Level 13 – *Develop Your Progressions*	A few hours to create; a few days testing & tweaking. Periodic updating.	Designing your progressions for all your triggers may take a few hours; adjusting, modifying, and perfecting them could take several weeks. Indeed, this is a set of activities that you will need to revisit every few months for the rest of your life to make sure they are aligned with what else is going on in your life.

Bottom Line: While it is impossible to predict exactly how long it will take you to get sober, the open-minded and motivated alcoholic will see results very quickly. However, since many of us usually have somewhat impaired brains at the start, result timeframes may vary widely. But it will work with perseverance!

However, the first, most critical step in the process is to convince yourself you have a problem, the point of the first Level of The Conquer Program: Level 1—Admit You Have an Addiction to Alcohol.

LEVEL 1—ADMIT YOU HAVE AN ADDICTION TO ALCOHOL

No one thinks they will grow up to be an alcoholic, and the vast majority of us certainly don't do it deliberately. Usually, the road to alcohol abuse is a long one, often taking years. That long transition is why _all_ alcoholics experience some form of denial, as seen in the below diagram. The changes came bit-by-bit, a day at a time, making them very hard to see and even harder to admit!

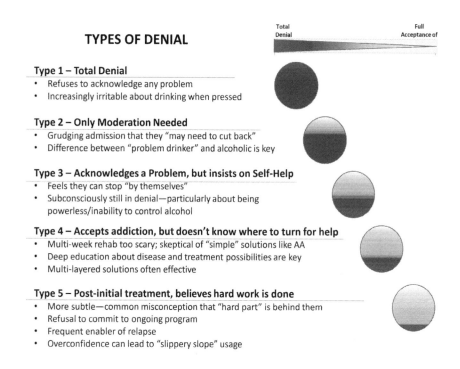

TYPES OF DENIAL

Total Denial — Full Acceptance of

Type 1 – Total Denial
- Refuses to acknowledge any problem
- Increasingly irritable about drinking when pressed

Type 2 – Only Moderation Needed
- Grudging admission that they "may need to cut back"
- Difference between "problem drinker" and alcoholic is key

Type 3 – Acknowledges a Problem, but insists on Self-Help
- Feels they can stop "by themselves"
- Subconsciously still in denial—particularly about being powerless/inability to control alcohol

Type 4 – Accepts addiction, but doesn't know where to turn for help
- Multi-week rehab too scary; skeptical of "simple" solutions like AA
- Deep education about disease and treatment possibilities are key
- Multi-layered solutions often effective

Type 5 – Post-initial treatment, believes hard work is done
- More subtle—common misconception that "hard part" is behind them
- Refusal to commit to ongoing program
- Frequent enabler of relapse
- Overconfidence can lead to "slippery slope" usage

Figure 6: The Five Types of Denial

It helps to overcome this denial by viewing the change from a "normal" person to a "potential" alcoholic as a _process_. That you or your loved ones didn't see it coming doesn't make you or them an idiot; changes that occur over a long period of time are often _very_ hard to detect. These changes didn't happen all at once; instead they were incremental, day-by-day, week-by-week. Changes in your drinking habits so small—a drink more here, another excuse for a binge there—that the incremental differences were almost undetectable, and minimally not a cause for alarm, particularly when much of it was done in the context of "having fun".

★ ★

The Three Basic Stages in the Road to Alcoholism

1. *Drinking for "Fun"* – Basically drinking with your friends, at key events, holidays, etc. It seemed there were an ever-increasing number of "fun" events. Eventually you found "fun" and drinking were inseparable.

2. *Drinking to "Deal With" Life's Pressures* – This is when you began drinking to cope with stress, pressures of everyday life, and major upheavals. It started with one or two pressures, then kept growing, until almost any negative situation (and some positive ones) required drinks to "deal with" them.

3. *Drinking to Compensate for Physical Dependency* – Once you have reached the point of physical addiction, your body and brain chemistry demands alcohol. You started noticing shaking when you stopped drinking for a day or two, "hair of the dog" to "calm your nerves" became more frequent, and you became irritable if you went a day without consuming.

★ ★

In the meantime, life was happening, particularly getting older and dealing with the associated stresses, e.g. jobs, relationships, worries and disappointments. Understanding the alcoholism process in this life context can really help alcoholics overcome their denial and admit their addiction—the first and most critical level in The Conquer Program, or *any* program!

Alcoholism has been greatly studied over the last few decades. While many "findings" are really still theory, researchers generally agree on key aspects of alcoholism, particularly its four key characteristics of Craving, Loss of Control, Tolerance, and Physical Dependency.

★ ★

The Four Cornerstones of Alcoholism

The National Institute on Alcohol Abuse and Alcoholism[1] believes there are four key characteristics to alcoholism. They are:

- **Craving**—A strong need, or urge, to drink.
- **Loss of control**—Not being able to stop drinking once drinking has begun.
- **Tolerance**—Having to drink greater alcohol amounts to feel the same effect.
- **Physical dependence**—Withdrawal symptoms, such as nausea, sweating, shakiness, and anxiety after stopping drinking.

★ ★

Most alcoholics would probably nod their head in agreement with the above "Stages of Life" and "Cornerstones" descriptions. However, it is only when they are *combined* to tell a story that it really starts to sink in about how they became an alcoholic. Figure 7 below puts them all together to illustrate *The Alcoholism Process*.

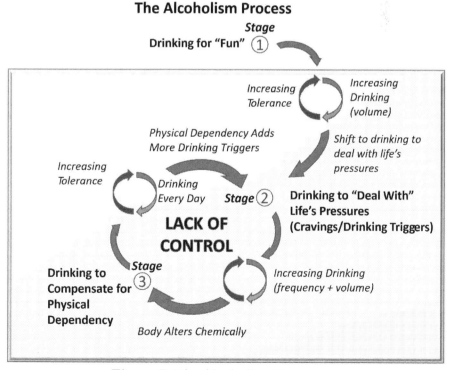

Figure 7: The Alcoholism Process

Figure 7 illustrates several key points. One is that there are several "sub-processes" or cycles within each "Stage of Life". For example, Stage 1—"Drinking for Fun", is when the future alcoholic is building tolerance, resulting in having to drink even more to achieve the same effect.[2] In Stage 2, mental "cravings" increase as the soon-to-be alcoholic starts using alcohol to "deal with" more of life's pressures by increasing the frequency and volume of alcohol consumption. With Physical Dependency in Stage 3, another sub-process starts with ever increasing tolerance and in turn volume as the alcoholic continually chases a feeling that seems to require ever more drinks to achieve.

Underlying all the stages is that alcoholics *cannot control alcohol*. This total *lack of control* underlies the entire process and each sub-process. But the process doesn't end after the first cycle around the circle; it continues into a new cycle of cravings and ever-worsening dependency. All too often it results in an Alcoholism Death Spiral, show next in Figure 8.

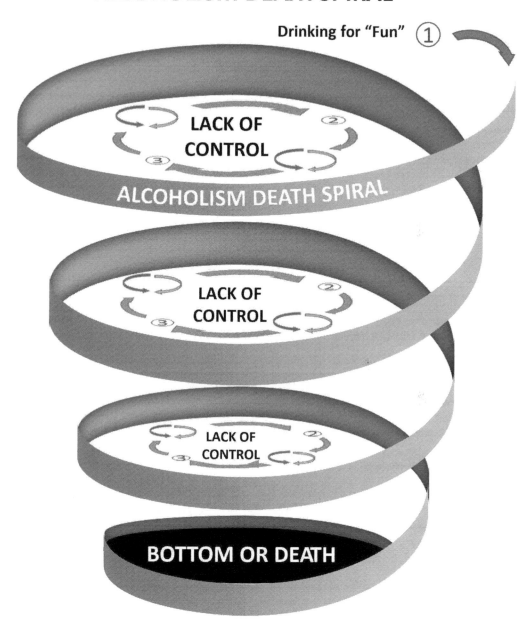

ALCOHOLISM DEATH SPIRAL

Figure 8: The Alcoholism Death Spiral

This "death spiral" is another illustration of why so many people don't recognize alcoholism until it has deeply embedded itself in the person and family. It's not until the 2nd or 3rd pass through the cycle when the "symptoms" of alcoholism really start to be visible. Then it's too late.

Are You an Alcoholic? Take The Conquer Quiz

You now better understand how it is possible for alcoholism to sneak up on you and your loved ones. Now it is time to figure out if *you* are an alcoholic.

This is not as easy as it sounds, for two reasons. Just drinking a lot is *not* definitive. Many drinkers go through periods of heavy indulging. Even physical dependency is not conclusive, as successive binges can cause short-term dependency that causes the non-alcoholic to successfully self-correct.

Unfortunately, there are many so called "experts" who have created simplistic, often (very) subjective psychologically-oriented "tests" that ask questions like "Have you ever felt guilty about your drinking?" *Who hasn't?* These tests are widely used despite their issues, primarily because of inertia and there hasn't been anything better, until now.

★ ★

The Problem with So-Called Scientific Alcoholism "Tests"

Some well-known "tests" include the <u>Short Michigan Alcohol Screening Test</u>[3] (SMAST) and the <u>Drug Abuse Screening Test (DAST)</u>[4], which more broadly seeks to identify all forms of chemical dependency. But there are major problems with these kinds of tests, particularly the ones within articles starting with some variation of "Are You an Addict?"

For example, the SMAST illustrates the subjective and presumptive attitude about what constitutes an addict. Copyright laws prohibit showing the list verbatim. But 8 of the 12 questions start with "Have you ever...?" Do you ever...?" or "Has your drinking ever...?" The other four questions are also highly subjective, such as the one that asks if you *feel* you are a "normal" drinker, or another that asks if your friends or relatives *think* you are or not.[5]

Answered at face value, it means you would have to answer "Yes" if you only did the action once, such as feeling guilty about your drinking. Who hasn't at one time or another, particularly after some embarrassing incident? If you reasonably decided to replace the word "ever" with "often" or "frequently," then it becomes a question as to what defines those new thresholds, by replacing the "ever" part of the question with one with a far more subjective phrasing. And the whole purpose and integrity of the test starts to break down. Most alcoholics can detect bias in these tests, and thus dismiss them entirely, further delaying them admitting they have a problem.

★ ★

Unlike these subjective approaches, the test developed for The Conquer Program, called *The Conquer Quiz*, relies on the principle <u>that actual behavior and end results are the only reliable indicators of alcoholism</u> available, at least right now. There are 25 questions, worth a total possible 45 points, with no one question worth more than 3 points. You will need to exhibit several distinct alcoholism behaviors and/or end results to accumulate enough points to be considered a potential alcoholic. Answering Yes/I Agree to one or even several questions will not necessarily accumulate enough points to qualify you as an alcoholic.

You really need to have a great deal of and variety of "evidence" to build up enough points to become concerned. Take The Conquer Quiz in Table 2.

Table 2: The Conquer Quiz

#	Sign of Alcoholism	Yes/ Agree	Points Possible	Points Awarded	Comments/Explanation
1	Personality Changes (Nasty Drunk)		1, 2 or 3 points		1 point if once a month; 2 if twice a month; 3 points if more than twice a month, OR police have been called in response to arguments you are involved with.
2	Personality Changes (Other)		1		When you drink you act very uncharacteristically, e.g., very loud when you are normally quiet, aggressive vs. passive, etc.
3	• You plan your Day/Night around Drinking; • You drink every day of the week		1		• Includes drinking frequently replacing non-drinking plans. • 1 point if you drink at least 6 out of 7 days or nights of the week regardless of amount.
4	You rotate place of alcohol purchases		1		You do this deliberately, and regularly
5	You are a Binge Drinker		1, 2 or 3 points		When you drink, you drink very heavily (more than 4-5 drinks in 2-3 hours, depending on gender/body weight). 2 times a month is 1 point; 3-4 times a month is 2 points; 5 or more times a month is 3 points.
6	• You say "I can stop anytime I want" frequently; • Defensive when people comment on usage		1		• Usually comes up in "you are drinking too much" arguments. 1 point if you say at least once every 2 months. • People comment "why are you so defensive?"
7	You drink in the morning		1 or 2		Meaning you drink before lunch. 2 points if at least once a month.

#	Sign of Alcoholism	Yes/ Agree	Points Possible	Points Awarded	Comments/Explanation
8	• Strong desire to drink alone. OR • Can't drink alone		1		Depends on personality; indicator of social extremes and personality changes
9	• You become Irritable as drinking time nears/goes by • You always drink at certain times		1		These are strong signs of physical dependency, indicating your body has been chemically altered to expect a "dose" of alcohol at certain times and/or in certain intervals.
10	You hide booze		1 or 2		2 points if you start forgetting where you hide them
11	You smell from alcohol		1, 2, or 3		Once a week, 1 Point. Twice a week, 2 points. Pretty much all the time: 3 points.
12	You sneak and lie about booze		1		You do this more than twice a month
13	You can't sleep without alcohol		1		Consider counting as 1 point if you can sleep but usually have very bad nightmares
14	Usually last to leave bar/party		1		You do this more often than you don't
15	You have alcoholism in your family		1 or 2		Parents 1 point; plus grandparents 2 points
16	You think you do certain things "better" drunk. You are more fun and interesting.		1		Particular emphasis on the word "think." It is subjective, so be honest (if you can). Examples: I drive better, I speak better. I am more sociable/fun.
17	Your appearance has changed dramatically		1		This is subjective, but compare recent photos with photos of parent(s) at your age.
18	Not drinking is a major occasion or accomplishment		1		You go to bed pleased with yourself that you didn't drink that day.
19	Poor airplane behavior with respect to drinks		1		Regularly (more often than you don't). Typically having 2 drinks or more on one flight counts as well.
20	Spend time planning/ getting alcohol "fix" when you are out-of-town		1 or 2		2 points if you pre-plan your alcohol purchase before you leave town.
	THE BIG FIVE				
21	2 or more DUIs		3		Counts even if you get case dismissed for non-alcohol causes or technicalities.
22	Job Loss due to alcohol		3		Definite Yes if on-the-job drinking is cited as cause. Can be subjective but be honest.
23	Marriage Loss due to alcohol		3		Definite Yes if cited in divorce documents.
24	Financial Loss due to alcohol		3		Includes spending over $300/month on alcohol purchases that you consume.
25	Health Problems due to alcohol		3		See Listen to Your Body! list – Check if you have an alcohol-related medical issue.
	TOTAL		45		

Interpreting Your Quiz Results

Total up all the points you recorded on a piece of paper or the online questionnaire. The guidelines for interpreting the results are as follows:

- **7 Points or more**—A problem drinker, at least. Considered a wake-up call that you may be on the road to alcoholism.

- **12 Points or more**—Very likely have an addiction to alcohol. If you haven't crossed that line yet you are very, very close.

- **20 Points or more**—Absolutely no doubt about addiction, with extremely serious problems in your life very soon if not already.

- **30+ Points**—If you don't find a way to stop drinking *immediately* you are headed to disastrous results within months.

What Should You Do with The Results?

You've taken the quiz. Now what? While individuals may react differently to an unpleasant score, my first suggestion is to step back and reflect on it for a while. If you've been thinking in the back of your mind that you *might* have a problem, your score may not come as a complete shock, but disturbing nonetheless. If you are (were), in complete denial, a high score may be far more of one. In both cases thinking about the results for a day or two, might be the best way to come to terms with the reality of your situation. You might even take the test again, though I would caution you to not change any of your initial answers unless there are clear-cut reasons to do so. Above all, *be honest*. You have worked up the strength and courage to take the test, so why lie now?

If you already *knew* you were an alcoholic going into the test, use the results to validate how you came to that conclusion. More importantly you can use the results to fortify your determination when times get tough in later Levels where you may wonder if you really are an alcoholic. The best (worst) of us will wonder this occasionally, even if all the evidence in the world to the contrary is beating us on the head.

If you scored in the "Problem Drinker" territory, from about 7 points to 12, then I would strongly suggest taking the quiz again being as honest as you possibly can be. The big danger is that this can be a gray area, where you say "yes I drink a lot but I can control it if I need to." That would be fine if you actually *did* control it, but those who can yet don't are little different than actual alcoholics. The real tragedy would be using a low score to justify continued heavy drinking.

If your score was very low, say 5 or less, then again the first thing you should do is ask yourself is if you were honest when taking the quiz. While it was very deliberately designed to avoid subjectivity (e.g. being able to weasel out of an honest answer), some questions are unavoidably so, such as the questions about job loss, marriage breakup, and financial problems. Since those questions are worth many points, answering "No" when reality shouts "Yes!" will make a big difference in your total score.

It is _very_ possible the direction you take in your life depends on how you answer the questions, so why not be honest?

If you do believe a low score is accurate, then congratulations! But if you scored *some* points, use it as an early-warning mechanism and start to pay more attention to how much and why you drink, in the process avoiding the spiraling descent into alcoholism many of us have already taken. This is particularly true for younger people, since they haven't necessarily accumulated enough life experiences (such as failed marriages) for some questions to be applicable.

Finally, in all scoring scenarios, you might talk over the results with a close friend or family member (in essence getting a jump on Level 4—Engage Friends and Family). You might even ask them to take the test acting like they were you, then comparing the results. It will set off an interesting conversation, I promise you, particularly if you scored yourself low and they do not.

* * *

This concludes the first and *most critical* Level of The Conquer Program. Again, any program *will* fail if you do not <u>truly</u> admit in your heart that you have a serious problem and need help. Next is to understand *why* you drink like you do, the goal of Level 1.

LEVEL 2—KNOW YOUR TRIGGERS

This Level is the key to all subsequent levels. Without knowing your drinking triggers, _specifically_ and _in detail_, you will _not_ be able to stay sober long-term. Conversely, once you have precisely identified your triggers and built your new defenses for them (the focus of Phases 2 and 3), you _will_ find it progressively easier to resist those triggers.

First, however, you've got to identify and understand your triggers in detail, which is the goal of this Level.

★ ★

Why is Knowing Your Triggers So Important?

Alcoholism is like a deep body wound, and that your drinking triggers are infections that keep the wound from healing. Most alcohol treatment programs take a "Band-Aid" approach to the alcoholism wound; focusing on covering-up the wound but not doing an adequate job of treating the underlying infection and its root causes.

War is another good analogy. Think of yourself as the king or queen of a great city, one being under constant attack by the temptations and cravings for alcohol. The _specific_ attacks—your drinking triggers—come in many ways, shapes, and forms. Your alcoholic city (brain and body) has little in the way of "natural" walls to form a fortress defense against these different attacks; such a fortress either never existed or was destroyed over time by your drinking. A _new_ fortress has to be built, by building new walls, level-by-level, tailored against the types of specific attacks (triggers) to which you are most vulnerable.

Truly knowing your major triggers in detail is essential to your _long-term_ defense against alcoholism, and is a cornerstone of The Conquer Program. Thus, as you go through the rest of this book/program beyond this Level, triggers will repeatedly come up in various ways: understanding their nuances, how to avoid them or minimize their impact, and even using them to your advantage. Once you master all aspects of your triggers, you will have a far better chance of living your life without having to obsess or even think about alcohol. But first you have to specifically, and in detail, understand all the types of attacks (triggers) that make you want to drink.

★ ★

As Figure 9 below illustrates, there are dozens of triggers that can attack an alcoholic over the course of their day, week, month, and life. For different people, some of the triggers may not be applicable at all; other times they may only occasionally occur; and for still others the alcoholic may feel they are constantly under attack. <u>Triggers will vary *greatly* person by person.</u>

The Trigger Wheel – A to Z

Figure 9: The Conquer Program Trigger Wheel

The above is just a partial list; we will get into a more complete list shortly. However, there are several important things you should draw from the above diagram, including:

- There are literally *dozens* of individual ways alcohol can attack you, e.g. "trigger" a strong desire or craving to drink.

- Any one trigger can attack anywhere, anytime.

- A trigger can affect you in different ways. Some <u>always</u> create a major craving to drink, called *major* triggers. Some may only occasionally cause a craving, or the craving can be mild, called *minor* triggers. A trigger can also cause another trigger to "activate", such as

Frustration leading to Anger, or Boredom to Loneliness. These are called "*related*" triggers.

- Every person is unique; what triggers you will be very different than what triggers the next alcoholic. In other words, your triggers are very personalized to you—your history, your living (and working) situations and environment, even your genetics. *Every person's triggers are unique.*

- More than one trigger can attack at the same time.

Most alcoholics will have somewhere between 5 and 12 very significant or "major" triggers. These are triggers that <u>really</u> make you want to drink, <u>more often than not</u>. They can make you want to drink <u>all by themselves</u>, e.g. independently of anything else going on in your life, but they also can set off a number of "related" triggers.

★ ★

More on Related Triggers

Even when traditional treatment programs go through some degree of trigger discussion, they nearly always "treat" triggers as "standalone", the effects that trigger has on your drinking habits is due to that trigger <u>all by itself</u>.

Unfortunately, the pressures of daily life rarely line up single file. Certain situations in an alcoholic's daily, historical, or ongoing life can "activate" or trigger other triggers! These are called *related* triggers. For example, Boredom can make you Lonely, which in turn might make you want to go out with friends who drink (causing direct or indirect Peer Pressure), which may take you to a place where Proximity and Smell of nearby alcohol has you drooling for a Taste of alcohol to help you Escape from other problems in your life. It is <u>incredibly</u> difficult to defend against alcohol in all of these simultaneous circumstances! Figure 10 below illustrates some of the possible relationships between triggers. There are hundreds, even thousands of possible combinations.

★ ★

What makes determining your triggers so difficult is that many triggers often "attack" at the same time, and/or occur so often in conjunction with related triggers that it sometimes becomes impossible to sort out the different triggers involved, and what is a "cause" and what is "effect".

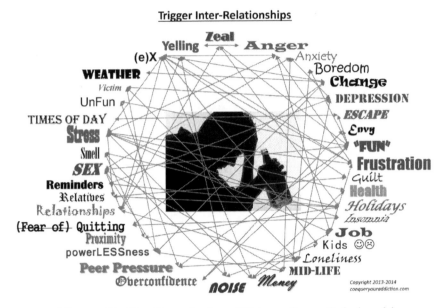

Figure 10: The Complexity of Trigger Inter-Relationships

Figure 10 above illustrates how complex trigger inter-relationships can be, either in multiple major triggers occurring simultaneously or in combination with related triggers. Most of us can come up with past situations where nearly all of the triggers and trigger combinations listed here have occurred in some form or another. Thus sorting out which ones <u>really</u> drive you to drink can be *extremely* challenging.

To add to the complexity, an alcoholic's defenses may be weaker for some triggers than others. Worse still the strength of the defense may vary depending on the hour of the day, day of the week, personal living environment at any given time, how their day at the job went, and so on.

In total, this complexity of trigger relationships and variability of how and when they attack makes it almost impossible to build one set of defenses that works against all alcohol attack. Instead, a <u>multi-level</u> defense for each major trigger is essential to deal with all the possible attacks all of the time in all possible situations and circumstances.

Your Drinking Triggers from A to Z

Table 3 below provides an alphabetical synopsis of the triggers covered much more extensively in the first *How to Conquer Your Alcoholism*[1] book. That book dedicates several pages to each trigger: what it is (and is not), what medical research has to say about their causes, and in particular how to defend against those triggers without alcohol. Similar information is available at www.ConquerYourAlcoholism.com.

This book, particularly Table 3 below, provides the core trigger description, their most common Related Triggers, key "Tips" for dealing with the trigger, and at least one "Key Defense Level" that should form the basis of that trigger's overall defenses. Appendix A provides an example of the full range of possible tips for a trigger. The process for identifying and "structuring" your defenses will be discussed in much more detail in Level 13. First however you have to *identify* your triggers, via Table 3 below.

Table 3: Drinking Triggers A to Z

Trigger	Description, Related Triggers, Tips and Defenses
Anger	There are 2 types of Anger in the context of drinking: 1) How getting Angry makes you <u>want</u> to drink, or 2) How drinking makes you more prone to <u>becoming</u> angry. This is a major trigger either happens on regular basis. *Key Related Trigger(s) (RTs): Frustration, Yelling. Key Tips: Find safe space (to scream, throw things, etc.); Helpful Link:* http://alcoholrehab.com/alcoholism/anger-and-alcohol-rehab/. *Key Defenses: Engage Friends and Family (vent in safe environment), Therapy (analyze deep-seated and/or long-term Anger issues).*
Anxiety	*Definition of Anxiety: A displeasing feeling of fear and concern; or, a state of uneasiness and apprehension, particularly about the future.*[2] Anxiety can cause either a desire to drink, or drinking causes/ increases Anxiety-Levels. *Key Related Triggers (RTs):* Change, Depression. *Key Tips: Distract yourself, Pets; Helpful Link:* https://themighty.com/2016/04/self-care-ideas-for-a-bad-day/. *Key Defenses: Therapy (w/ drugs), Consider Spirituality.*
Boredom	There are several types of drinking Boredom: Drinking while alone; Binging while Bored; Habitually when little to do; Along with related triggers Loneliness or Escape; Drinking as 1st resort when Bored and nothing else going on. *Key RTs: Depression, Escape, Fun, Loneliness. Key Tip: Do something both mentally and physically draining; Helpful Link:* http://alcoholrehab.com/drug-addiction/boredom-and-substance-abuse/. *Key Defense: Develop New Hobbies.*

Trigger	Description, Related Triggers, Tips and Defenses
Change	Any change in routine in your life causes cravings to drink, particularly major everyday life disruptions such as moving, illness, or death. *Related triggers include: Anxiety (worry), Depression, Extreme Emotions, Guilt, Insomnia, and Powerlessness. Key Tips: Do some-thing routine or very familiar (that hasn't been impacted by the Change); Helpful Link:* http://www.wikihow.com/Deal-with-Change. *Key Defense: Engage Friends and Family (talk about the change).*
Depression	*Definition: Severe despondency and dejection, accompanied by feelings of hopelessness and inadequacy.* Severe and/or frequent depression should be medically treated. Two-edged trigger: depression causing a desire to drink, and/or drinking causing/increasing the degree of depression since it is chemically a depressant. *RTs: Many, part. Anxiety, Loneliness. Key Tips: Exercise, Pets; Helpful Link:* https://themighty.com/2016/04/self-care-ideas-for-a-bad-day/. *Key Defenses: Therapy, Consider Spirituality.*
Disorder	Disruptions in one's physical and/or mental environment, including unclean living arrangements or chaotic work/personal schedules. Very underestimated as trigger. *RTs: Change, Kids (Children), Mid-Life Crisis. Key Tips: Clean (keep one room clean at all times as "safe space"; organize schedule. Key Defenses: Develop New Hobbies (ones that emphasize simplicity, organization, and/or cleanliness.*
Escape	Defined as the desire to withdrawal from the world, or be in a completely different one (e.g. relaxing, fantasy, etc.). To "escape" one's problems is the goal and cause for drinking. Common reason to seek the "buzz-rush" of alcohol (See Level 11). *RTs: Many, but espec. "Fun". Key Tips: Physically escape (travel, outdoor activities), exercise; Helpful Link:* https://www.addiction.com/3276/25-ways-relax-without-using-drugs-alcohol/. *Key Defenses: Develop New Hobbies, Make Yourself Sick of Alcohol.*
Envy (includes Jealousy)	Being envious of people who <u>can</u> drink without problems, causing an intense desire/wish to drink. Is trigger when this happens regularly. *RTs: Fun, Peer Pressure, Social Situations, and Overconfidence.* *Key Tips: Get away from source of Envy; Helpful Link:* http://www.becomingminimalist.com/ungreen-with-envy/. *Key Defense: Join a Community (e.g. nobody drinks).*
Extreme Emotions	Extreme sadness, hatred, grief—any strong or overwhelming emotion can trigger a relapse in even the strongest individual. Identify your most likely extreme emotion scenarios and be ready for them—without alcohol. *RTs: Depression, Guilt, Loneliness, eX. Key Tips: Exercise (violently), meditate, volunteer, find ways to turn Lemons into Lemonade (negative to positive). Helpful Link:* https://www.wsj.com/articles/facebooks-surprising-role-in-bereavement-1499957730. *Key Defenses: Engage Friends and Family (talk about your feelings), Develop New Hobbies (e.g. that address or help source of emotion in some material way).*
Frustration	Frustration is a trigger that likely needs more detailed examination, as there can be many underlying causes of it. At its core it may even be a distinctly different trigger, such as Job or Relationship Frustration. Its *key related trigger* is Anger, with the Anger-Frustration combo being extensively studied in the medical field. *Key Tips: Exercise, find a physical outlet (e.g. hit a pillow); Helpful Link:* http://www.wikihow.com/Cope-With-Frustration; *Key Defense: Engage Friends/Family (talk out the roots of the Frustration).*

Trigger	Description, Related Triggers, Tips and Defenses
"Fun"	Drinking while having "fun" is the starting trigger for many alcoholics. Soon they can't have fun *unless* they are drinking—the association having been so tightly established. *RTs: Escape, Holidays/Special Occasions, Social Situations, UnFun/Uninteresting.* **Key Tips:** *Get new friends, laugh; Helpful Link:* http://www.sunnysanguinity.com/2014/06/fun-things-to-do-not-drinking/. **Key Defense:** *Develop New Hobbies.*
Guilt	Guilt is a close cousin of Extreme Emotions, but distinct in that it has several subtler variations like Embarrassment and Remorse. Is self-reinforcing in alcoholism because of the great damage done. *RTs: Many, including Depression, eX, Reminders, Victim-Mentality.* **Key Tips:** *IGNORE GUILT, volunteer (to help cause of Guilt); Helpful Link:* http://www.wikihow.com/Deal-with-Guilt. **Key Defenses:** *Engage Friends & Family, Therapy (deep-rooted Guilt).*
Health	Particularly Pain. This trigger is specifically limited to health problems that cause you to drink, particularly those related to pain and self-medicating relief from it. Consult your doctor if this is a trigger. *RTs: Anxiety, Depression, Escape, (Physical) Stress.* **Key Tips:** *SEE YOUR DOCTOR, Exercise, Meditate, Pets.* **Key Defenses:** *Listen to Your Body (assume the worst and act fast on symptoms), Develop New Hobbies.*
Holidays (includes Special Occasions)	Includes Special Occasions. New Year's Eve. Christmas. Birthdays. Whenever and Wherever people gather to "celebrate," alcohol is not far behind, creating an intense temptation to drink. *RTs: Fun, Peer Pressure, Relatives, Social Situations.* **Key Tips:** *Don't celebrate them; Helpful Link:* http://therecoverybook.com/sober-holidays-2014-1/. **Key Defense:** *Join A Community (e.g. go to a meeting)*
Hungry	Includes Eating Disorders. Multiple interpretations as a drinking trigger, but in general it is food, or lack-thereof, that initiates a craving for alcohol. *RTs: Proximity (to alcohol or food), Smell and Taste (to alcohol or food), Times of Day.* **Key Tip:** *See doctor if you suspect bulimia/anorexia.* **Key Defense:** *Listen to Your Body (pay particular attention to nutrition, vitamins, exercise).*
Insomnia	Alcohol intake can alter body chemistry so much that its absence causes problems, including Insomnia. Also, since Alcohol can serve as a short-term stimulant, even more alcohol may be "needed" to relax, increasing drinking volume. *RTs: (Physical) Stress, Tired.* **Key Tips:** *Exercise (to drain excess energy), Keep Regular Hours, Do not take naps, (post-sobriety) completely change out your bed, linens, pillows, etc. (due to smell, stains, and other drinking-related residue). Helpful Link:* http://alcoholmastery.com/quit-alcohol-sleep-5-tips-how-to-sleep-when-you-stop-alcohol-sda33/. **Key Defenses:** *Listen to Your Body, Develop New (strenuous) Hobbies.*
Job	Dissatisfaction with your Job is a very common trigger. Root causes can vary greatly however, e.g. is it the boss, the hours, lack of career, pay levels, co-workers, etc.? *RTs: Anger, Boredom, Change, Frustration, Money, and (physical) Stress.* **Key Tips:** *Identify specific Job issue, Change jobs/bosses (if possible); Helpful Link:* https://www.linkedin.com/pulse/20130709152707-5799319-the-top-10-reasons-people-hate-their-job. **Key Defenses:** *Know Your (specific) Triggers, Engage Friends/Family (vent, discuss options).*
Kids	Love 'em, but they are great stress (of all kinds) inducers, particularly for primary care-giver. Most common in parents of younger children and those not ready for children. ***Many Related Triggers***, including: *Disorder, eX, Guilt, Noise,*

Trigger	Description, Related Triggers, Tips and Defenses
	Relationships, Relatives, and Physical Stress. **Key Tips:** *Exercise, Meditate, Stretch, Massage; Helpful Link:* http://www.huffingtonpost.com/2012/04/04/nine-steps-to-stress-free-parenting_n_1403209.html. **Key Defense:** *Join A Community (Women's-only), Develop New Hobbies (ones without kids).*
Loneliness	Though a very common major trigger, it nonetheless can mean <u>very</u> different things to different people, from "natural" loners to ones who supposedly have many strong relationships. **RTs:** *Boredom. Depression, Victim.* **Key Tips:** *Pets, Volunteering; Helpful Link:* https://www.mind.org.uk/information-support/tips-for-everyday-living/loneliness/#.WQqRvYjyvb0. **Key Defense:** *Join a Community.*
Media	The influence of TV, Radio, and the Internet is immense, but very underestimated as a drinking trigger. Advertisements or content glorifying drinking in particular can cause great cravings. Social media in particular can cause great problems, and in general constantly being online can generate many kinds of ill-defined stress that are difficult to categorize or narrow down. **RTs:** *Envy, Fun, Music, Peer Pressure/Social Situations (via social media), Reminders.* **Key Tips:** *Quit using social media, Filter content and "friends"; Helpful Link:* https://www.realsimple.com/work-life/technology/social-media-addiction. **Key Defenses:** *Break Bad Habits (constantly checking online, "bad" apps), Develop New Hobbies (low-tech ones).*
Mid-Life Crisis	Generally this is a time of life when adults come to realize their own mortality and they realize that life may be more than halfway over, triggering a desire to drink. Typically happens between the ages of 40 and 60. Variation occurs in seniors at retirement. **RTs:** *Many, incl. Anxiety, Change, Depression, Escape, Sex.* **Key Tips:** *Don't do or buy stupid stuff!* <u>Schadenfreude</u> *(occasionally), Volunteer (leverage and pass on your wisdom and learnings); Helpful Link:* https://www.theguardian.com/society/2010/sep/29/10-point-guide-to-beating-that-midlife-crisis. **Key Defenses:** *Break Bad Habits (e.g. reboot your new life), Develop New (middle aged) Hobbies.*
Money	Money problems are one of the biggest causes of (general) stress, particularly lack of money. But root cause(s) of money-related cravings need to be identified, e.g. when rent is due, children's education, legal/tax bills, etc. **RTs:** *Anxiety, Depression, Health, Job, Kids, Relationships, eX.* **Key Tips:** *Get to root of money issues, Learn how to manage money, don't drink (& save a lot of money); Helpful Link:* https://pathwaysreallife.com/money-management-recovering-addicts/. **Key Defenses:** *Break Bad Habits (poor money mgmt).*
Music	An uncommon major trigger, but certain songs can initiate a cascade of related triggers, particularly Reminders. *Other* **RTs:** *eX (e.g. songs that remind of fun times with eX), Fun, Media, Noise.* **Key Tips:** *Change the station! Use* <u>Sirius XM</u>, <u>Spotify</u>, <u>Pandora</u>. **Key Defenses:** *Break Bad Habits (breaking association of certain songs with "good" drinking times). Develop New Hobbies (not involving music).*
Noise	Noise—either high volumes or certain pitches—can generate irritability, general stress, and/or general desire to drink. **RTs:** *Anger, Escape, Frustration, Kids, Music, Yelling.* **Key Tips:** *Have quiet time, Create quiet room, Use White Noise apps, Get hearing checked; Helpful Link:* http://lifeandhealth.org/lifestyle/reducing-noise-pollution/1736.html; **Key Defenses:** *Develop New (quiet) Hobbies.*

Trigger	Description, Related Triggers, Tips and Defenses
Over-confidence	Anyone who has made even a half-assed attempt at sobriety has probably felt at some point "Hey, I can do this! I can drink like normal people!" Typically happens early in sobriety. *RTs: Envy, Fun.* **Key Tips:** *Mindfulness Meditation, Volunteering (at rehab centers); Helpful Link:* https://www.psychologytoday.com/blog/enlightened-living/201205/addiction-s-blind-spot. **Key Defenses:** *Make Yourself Sick of Alcohol, Consider Spirituality (make yourself humble).*
Peer Pressure	Peer Pressure is a form of social pressure for one to take action in order to be accepted. As a major drinking trigger it generally comes in two time ranges: first, during our youth years (e.g. high school); and later when alone with alcohol-intensive "friends". *RTs: Fun, Social Situations, Unfun/Uninteresting, Zeal (Excitement).* **Key Tips:** *Drop old "friends" and make new ones; Helpful Link:* http://www.yourlifecounts.org/blog/20-ways-avoid-peer-pressure. **Key Defenses:** *Engage (new) Friends and Family, Develop New Hobbies (with or meet new friends).*
Power	Think politicians and celebrities, but also those in control—being the boss, etc. It can create a "high" that wants to be supplemented and enhanced (or even dampened) with alcohol. *RTs: Envy, Job, Overconfidence, Powerlessness, Social Situations, Zeal (Excitement).* **Key Tips:** *Read history, Volunteer; Helpful Link:* https://www.forbes.com/sites/alicegwalton/2013/08/06/why-the-brains-of-high-powered-people-may-be-more-prone-to-addiction/#149db7393736; **Key Defenses:** *Break Bad Habits (the intense desire to succeed), Consider Spirituality (e.g. humble yourself)*
Powerlessness	At its simplest form, refers to a lack of control over key dimensions of your life, such as your job, relationships, marriage, and getting older. Particularly acute in women. *RTs: Anxiety, Depression, Mid-Life Crisis. Victim.* **Key Tips:** *Stand up to bullies, just say no; Helpful Link:* http://www.the-alcoholism-guide.org/women-for-sobriety.html. **Key Defenses:** *Join a Community (e.g. women's-only, particularly Women for Sobriety), Develop New Hobbies (that are esteem-building).*
Proximity	For many alcoholics, the "nearness" of alcohol can set off a Pavlov's Dog-type craving for it. Unless you're a monk, there is no avoiding Proximity, but it can be made to work for you (See Level 11—Make Yourself Sick of Alcohol). *RTs: Smell, Social Situations, Taste.* **Key Tips:** *Associate sight/nearness with pain/bad things, Avoid alcohol (including Smell); Key Defense: Make Yourself Sick of Alcohol.*
Quitting (Fear of)	Almost every alcoholic encounters this trigger, though it often masks other underlying ones. At its core is fear of the unknown. What will life be like sober? Will I be bored? How will I relax/sleep? What will my personal life be like? Will I hate my Partner (or they hate me)? What about any Guilt? *RTs: Many, particularly Change, Escape, Fun, Guilt, Insomnia, and Relationships.* **Key Tips:** *Understand exactly your fears, Plan for a sober life; Read chapter; Key Link:* http://www.hipsobriety.com/home/sober-fears. **Key Defenses:** *Know Your Triggers.*
Relation-ships	Difficulties in a Relationship is a favorite "reason" to drink. The worse off the Relationship, the more excuses to drink, which of course worsens the Relationship...and so it spirals. Also, a partner that drinks is a great enabler. *RTs: eX, Frustration, Kids, Loneliness, Sex.* **Key Tips:** *Get sober for yourself, then*

Trigger	Description, Related Triggers, Tips and Defenses
	address Relationship issues; Helpful Link: https://www.addiction.com/in-recovery/relationships/partner-spouse/. **Key Defenses:** *Therapy (couples therapy), Develop New (joint) Hobbies.*
Relatives	The intensity of this trigger is a function of how close your relatives are, both physically and mentally. Family gatherings are particularly problematic. *RTs: Guilt, Holidays, Proximity, Relationships, Reminders.* **Key Tips:** *Avoid drinking/obnoxious relatives, Bring sober buddy; Helpful Link:* http://coachingthroughchaos.com/the-dysfunctional-family-holiday-survival-guide/. **Key Defenses:** *Break Bad Habits (includes rebooting relationships w/ relatives), Join a Community (to vent, and avoid them particularly during Holidays).*
Reminders	This tends to be either a minor trigger or a *huge* one, depending on the person and their history. If huge, practically anything can set it off. Guilt is a particularly severe related trigger. *RTs: eX, Guilt, Holidays, Music, Relatives.* **Key Tips:** *Get to "root" reminder, avoid them; Helpful Link:* http://www.wikihow.com/Stop-Thinking-of-Something-or-Someone. **Key Defense:** *Break Bad Habits (breaking associations between Reminders and alcohol).*
Respons-ibilities	People who are responsible for many people or the livelihoods/ happiness of others are particularly susceptible to this trigger. The pressure to perform, or fear of not performing, can become overwhelming. *RTs: Escape, Job, Kids, Power.* **Key Tips:** *Play (either simple/mindless, OR complex/intense); Helpful Link:* http://www.coping-with-stress.org/responsibility.html. **Key Defenses:** *Engage Friends & Family (e.g. stay connected with people who really know the real (pre-alcohol) you), Consider Spirituality.*
Sex	A multi-faceted trigger. Particularly intermingled with body image, sexual discovery/identity, and in general how and to what degree sex became associated with alcohol. *RTs: Anxiety, Fun (or UnFun), Mid-life Crisis, (Fear of) Quitting, Relationships, Victim-Mentality.* **Key Tips:** *Get to root cause(s), See a professional; Helpful Link:* http://alcoholrehab.com/alcoholism/alcoholism-and-sexual-dysfunction/. **Key Defense:** *Therapy (sexual issues associated with addiction can be very deep-rooted, including based on childhood issues/abuse— requires professional help).*
Smell	Like the sight of alcohol in Proximity, its Smell can set off an intense craving to drink in some people. The good news is that its Smell can be made to work for you, and against alcohol (See Level 11—Make Yourself Sick of Alcohol). *RTs: Proximity, Social Situations, Taste.* **Key Tips:** *Avoid being in the same room, Associate smell of alcoholic with nausea; Helpful Link:* http://www.recovery.org/pro/articles/the-gift-of-aversion-therapy-how-i-purged-my-way-to-sobriety/. **Key Defense:** *Make Yourself Sick of Alcohol.*
Social Situations	Parties, large gatherings, or even small gatherings of known or unknown people can cause the desire to drink. For some, it can be almost impossible to "go out" without some sort of bracer. *RTs: Anxiety, Envy, Fun, Peer Pressure, Unfun/Uninteresting.* **Key Tips:** *Avoid parties (short-term fix); Helpful Link:* https://sobernation.com/8-ways-to-just-say-no-to-alcohol-in-social-situations/. **Key Defenses**: *Join a Community (and participate!), Develop New Hobbies (clubs, Toastmasters, and other large entities).*
Stress (physical)	The term "Stress" is overused as a catch-all for a variety of triggers. This trigger focuses on physical Stress—the physical feeling of being worn-out, feeling achy, muscles tight and knotted, or headaches, and "needing" alcohol to relieve it.

Trigger	Description, Related Triggers, Tips and Defenses
	*RTs: Health, Insomnia, Tired. **Key Tips:** Exercise, Massage, Pets, Stretching; Helpful Link:* http://www.huffingtonpost.com/2013/03/17/reduce-stress-research_n_2884876.html. ***Key Defenses:** Listen to Your Body (see your doctor regularly and for any unusual ailments), Develop New (relaxing or strenuous, as recommended by doctor) Hobbies.*
Taste	A close cousin of Proximity to and Smell of alcohol, some beverages (and foods) can cause a desire for alcohol, particularly certain pairings, such as pizza and beer. *RTs: Proximity, Reminders, Smell. **Key Tips:** Avoid combos, Do <u>not</u> drink alcohol-tasting drinks (until you sure of your defenses). **Key Defense:** Make Yourself Sick of Alcohol.*
Times of Day	Refers to time period (and/or days of the week) when the desire to drink is particularly strong, such as "happy hour" or 5:30pm to 7pm period, or Friday and Saturday nights. *RTs: Escape, Insomnia, Tired. **Key Tips:** Exercise (at vulnerable periods), Break your patterns/ rituals. **Key Defenses:** Break Bad Habits (re-associate vulnerable times o day with new activities), Develop New Hobbies (at key times).*
Tired	Being physically and/or mentally tired can cause the desire to drink in some people. Last part of the trigger acronym H.A.L.T: Hungry, Angry, Lonely, Tired. *RTs: Insomnia, Job, Kids, Stress, Times of Day. **Key Tips:** Exercise, Eat right, Go to doctor (alcoholics can be very low on critical vitamins). **Key Defense:** Break Bad Habits (particularly if you have irregular routine that screws up sleep patterns).*
Unfun/Un-Interesting	Some people think they have a more "fun" personality when they drink. Conversely, they feel they are viewed as dull and boring when sober. Either can generate a perceived "need" to drink. *RTs: Fun, Holidays, Peer Pressure, Social Situations. **Key Tips:** Find new (real and sober) friends, Realize you are NOT more fun when drinking; Helpful Link:* http://elitedaily.com/life/things-you-learn-party-sober/1231236/. ***Key Defense:** Develop New (interesting) Hobbies.*
Victim-Mentality (Abuse, Low Self-Esteem)	Being the victim of child, domestic, and/or sexual abuse is horrific to begin with. Unfortunately, many such victims turn to alcohol and/or drugs to relieve the pain and anguish, making things worse. This trigger also covers drinking because of low self-esteem. *RTs: Anger, Guilt, Powerlessness, Sex. **Key Tips:** Explore online support groups; Helpful Link:* http://onlinelibrary.wiley.com/doi/10.1111/j.1530-0277.2011.01695.x/full. ***Key Defenses:** Therapy, Develop New Hobbies (to build self-esteem).*
Weather (Seasons)	Different types of weather (and/or the change of seasons) can be a significant trigger for some (particularly a very strong related trigger). Blizzards or storms can generate great distress (especially for persons with traumatic childhood experiences), while long, cold, dark winters are well-known to contribute to higher rates of alcoholism. *RTs: Anxiety, Boredom, Change, Depression, Escape, Reminders. **Key Tips:** Exercise, Travel (at vulnerable periods); Helpful Link:* http://gawker.com/winter-is-a-black-hole-how-i-deal-with-seasonal-depres-1652408745. ***Key Defenses:** Develop New Hobbies (change venues and activity, esp. outdoors).*
(e)X Wife/Partner/etc.	This can be a huge trigger for many, even years after a breakup. There are often many related triggers due to the high risk of conflict and disagreement when interacting. *RTs: Anger, Frustration, Guilt, Kids, Money, Powerlessness, Relationships, Reminders, Yelling. **Key Tips:** Kill with him/her with kindness, Avoid social media linkages with your eX, Not your job to make him/her happy anymore, ; Helpful Link:* https://www.psychologytoday.com/blog/emotional-

Trigger	Description, Related Triggers, Tips and Defenses
	fitness/201109/10-tips-help-you-deal-your-exDefenses. **Key Defenses:** *Engage Friends and Family, Therapy (to vent), Develop New Hobbies (to avoid Reminders, find new activities/new partners).*
Yelling (Conflict)	Yelling is distinct from Anger, in that Yelling, arguments, or even confrontations do not necessarily have a hostile, potentially violent aspect to them. But lesser conflicts, "only" with raised voices, can still be a major trigger. *RTs: Anger, Escape, eX, Frustration, Noise, Powerlessness, Victim (self-esteem). Key Tips: Improve communications skills, avoid politics, pick your battles; Helpful Link:* https://www.thebalance.com/overcome-your-fear-of-confrontation-and-conflict-1917869. **Key Defenses:** *Engage Friends and Family, Join A Community (both for building your support network).*
Zeal/Zest (Excite-ment)	*Def: Great energy or enthusiasm in pursuit of a cause or an objective. Synonyms: passion, ardor, love, fervor, fire, avidity, **excitement**, keenness, relish, gusto, vigor, **energy**, intensity.* Can be based on "positive" feelings, unlike many others. Excitement and corresponding desire to drink at sports events is one example. Similar to gambling addiction in many ways (see link). *RTs: Boredom, Escape, Fun, Holidays, Music, Sex. Key Tips: Control/avoid sports events, no caffeine, Exercise, Meditate/breathing techniques; Helpful Link:* http://www.counselling-directory.org.uk/counsellor-articles/the-10-most-successful-ways-of-overcoming-gambling-urges. **Key Defenses:** *Go to doctor (blood pressure), Develop New (calmer) Hobbies.*

This trigger list is not exhaustive, nor are the triggers mutually exclusive (e.g., there is some overlap in their definitions and impact). Some triggers are very common, while others impact only small portions of alcoholics. Frustration, for example, is arguably a trigger for many people in some form (either directly or as a related trigger), but Times of Day may only affect a small percentage of alcoholics. Nearly every alcoholic has more than one trigger, and probably several if they have been drinking or years. Determining your specific triggers is the purpose of this Level. I'd encourage you to spend a considerable amount of time reading and re-reading Table 3.

The success of The Conquer Program hinges on you accurately and comprehensively identifying your triggers.

Proximity, Smell, and Taste—The Axis of Evil

As introduced earlier, one of the most difficult aspects of drinking triggers is that they often occur in combination. Job problems seem to pile on top of Relationship difficulties at home; Money and Health concerns seem to happen more often together than not. *These concurrent triggers will require simultaneous (and often different) defenses.* What's more, they don't include the *related triggers* caused or activated by these major triggers, resulting in a kind of trigger explosion that can overwhelm the unprepared alcoholic.

A particularly insidious simultaneous occurrence of triggers is that of Proximity, Smell, and Taste—the "Axis of Evil." The combined impact of these three physical triggers can be *extremely* intimidating, particularly to those in early sobriety. For that reason, the first defense recommended for the "axis of evil" (as seen in Table 4) is to *avoid* alcohol in every possible way—sight, smell, and taste—particularly early in sobriety as you are building and tuning your defenses and are susceptible to temptations.

Table 4: Proximity, Smell, and Taste Defenses

Proximity Defenses	Smell Defenses	Taste Defense
Avoid Alcohol, including signs where it is sold or anything with an alcohol brand name.	Avoid the radius of Smell of alcohol (it generally will fill any sized room, or 50 feet away).	Avoid Proximity and Smell of alcohol—either is enough to activate the Taste trigger, e.g. a Pavlovian response.
Plan Ahead (particularly Holidays, special occasions, and social encounters).	Proactively identify and avoid the particular Smell that bothers you (e.g. Beer). Planning is needed to avoid situations likely to have that smell (e.g. sports).	Watch out for Smell – Smell and Taste are tightly intertwined. The beer smell at events can create an intense desire to taste beer, just for the taste.
Get alcohol out of your house.	"Distract"/overpower alcohol smells with other ones (e.g. onions, air fresheners, etc.).	Make sure any glasses that contained alcohol are thoroughly clean—even throw them away.
Don't let your guard down—alcohol or its signs can show up anywhere, anytime.	"Retune" your senses to find other smells pleasant (e.g. via Aromatherapy, certain air fresheners).	The memory of Taste does not last as long as the memory of Smell. Time will diminish this trigger.

Proximity Defenses	Smell Defenses	Taste Defense
Watch out for Smell and Taste triggers.	Watch out for Related Triggers (particularly Holidays, Peer Pressure and Social situations).	Avoid close resemblance or "cousin" tastes, such as non-alcoholic beer or wine, virgin cocktails, etc.
Mentally (& often) practice "replacing" any sign of alcohol with something unpleasant looking, e.g. feces, roadkill, etc.	In extreme situations put other substances on or by your nose, e.g. Vicks Vapor Rub.	In extreme situations put other very unpleasant tasting substances on your tongue (akin to when you sucked your thumb as a kid).
Make the sight of alcohol very unpleasant (e.g. Level 11).	Retrain yourself to make alcohol smell unpleasant (e.g. via Level 11).	Make the Taste of alcohol very unpleasant (e.g. Level 11).

Of course, long-term it can be nearly impossible to avoid stumbling into such alcohol situations: an after-work get-together, unavoidable social engagements, boozy relatives, even wine tastings at your grocery store! If these "normal" defenses do not work, or work well, and you think one or more are *major* triggers, something more radical may be needed. More radical approaches are discussed later in Level 11.

The Fear of Quitting—The Universal Alcoholic Trigger

While a part of the Table 3 trigger checklist, the brief description of the Fear of Quitting trigger does not do justice to how it can delay attempts at sobriety, or its universality among alcoholics. Just as every alcoholic goes through some type of denial, *every* alcoholic has at some point a fear of *not* drinking.[3] This fear usually appears when he or she is about to make their first serious attempt at quitting, and starts thinking about life *after* drinking. What will my life be like without alcohol? How will I deal with the pressures of life sober? What will I do *instead* of drinking?

Consider: life for the alcoholic has revolved heavily around alcohol for years, even decades, and has become as much a part of him or her as an arm or leg, eating or sleeping. Maybe that seems melodramatic, but it's the truth. Many alcoholics can't imagine or even *remember* a life without alcohol, and to the extent they can it scares them to death. They know a life with alcohol (as bad as it is); they *don't know* life without it. The unknown creates fear— *Big Time*. Testimonials abound:

My fears about quitting drinking were so numerous that they kept me from quitting drinking for over 22 years when I knew I was an alcoholic. I couldn't think of what I would do with myself without drinking. When I tried to cut back or stop on my own, I was fearful about everything and had panic attacks.

* * *

I was fearful of being alone without drinking and facing my feelings, since I always drank when I was alone. I thought I might go crazy. And I was scared to death of trying to quit drinking and failing, because that would mean I was really hopeless.

* * *

My main fear was how I was going to live without it. It was all I knew since I began in my teens. I had no clue as to what life would look like without booze. I was terrified of the idea of trying to live without having a drink. What would I do? How could I function without it? I realized I had no concept of normalcy that other people had.

The good news is you will find that this fear diminishes as you <u>really</u> start to understand your other triggers for drinking. Take Boredom:

My fears about quitting, hmmm?... I guess I don't want to be bored. As lame as that sounds it's true. I actually <u>fear</u> boredom.

A large part of this fear of Boredom in this context is related to the Change trigger. If you have been drinking for many years, alcohol has likely embedded itself into almost every aspect of your personal and professional life. Not drinking is going to require *many* big adjustments in so many areas that it induces fear to the point of terror! Nothing breeds fear like the unknown!

I believe it is the enormity of what lies ahead for most people that scares them. It is <u>far</u> easier to return to drinking than face the reality of what may need to change in your life. This may include what you do, where you go, who you socialize with even excluding certain people from your life if necessary.[4]

Triggers Change Over Time

Finally, <u>your triggers can change over time, both while you are drinking and after you get sober.</u> The triggers themselves may change; their number may increase or decrease, and/or their relative intensity, frequency, and/or impact (called "priorities") may change. My personal fluctuation and change in trigger priorities is depicted in Figure 11 on the next page.

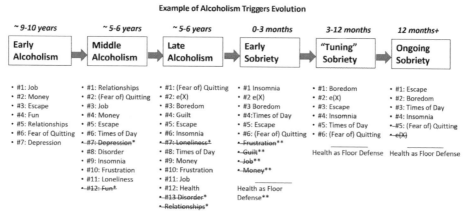

Figure 11: The Author's Trigger Evolution

As seen above, the *number* of my triggers increased the longer I drank, as anticipated by The Alcoholism Process discussed in Level 1. The good news is that once I got sober, the number of triggers decreased *and* become less severe. In other words, it is possible to *unwind* The Alcoholism Process!

It is worth spending <u>a lot</u> of time thinking about your triggers: what they are now, which are major vs. minor, what are their related triggers, their relative priority, and how they've changed over time. Once you've done that and have defined and refined your major triggers, you are ready to ready to start building your new defenses for them.

* * *

In the broader *How to Conquer Your Alcoholism* book, each trigger has a comprehensive set of tips to use as a practical, specific alcohol-free defense against each kind of alcohol attack. In addition, it provides a complete list of related triggers, and discusses how certain Levels of Defense are more important than others. An excerpt for the Boredom trigger is provided in Appendix A. Some of this information can also be found at www.ConquerYourAlcoholism.com.

* * * * *

Before we get into the specifics of how to build those new defenses, however, it is worth spending a little time in Level 3—Listen To Your Body, next, to understand how alcohol impacts your body and brain. Besides providing additional reinforcement about the need to get sober, it may help in identifying and refining defenses for your particular circumstances, particularly medical-related triggers.

LEVEL 3—LISTEN TO YOUR BODY!

This Level has two goals: First, to eliminate *any* remaining doubts that you are an alcoholic and that you need to change; and second, to help you refine and complete identification of your key drinking triggers, those that are either medical in nature, or that need medical attention incorporated into new defenses. But first, some background is needed.

While Level 1, particularly The Conquer Quiz, should have been convincing if you "scored" enough points, alcoholics are masters at persuading themselves that they don't have a problem. This is where Level 3 can help, by identifying how alcohol has already started to wreak havoc on your body. While most of the possibilities of damage are internal, there can be no question that alcoholism wreaks havoc on your outwards appearance, as evidenced before (on the right cir. 2011)-and-after (on left, 3 years later and 65 pounds lighter) pictures of the Author:

★ ★

The Author and Drinking-Related Health

By the time I finally got sober via this program in 2012, I had been an alcoholic by my estimate for over 20 years.[1] From a fairly steady 170 pounds, I had ballooned to at least 235. My skin was a complete wreck, with broken capillaries all over my face, and open sores covering my shoulders and legs; sores that would only start healing if I didn't drink for a few days (then immediately flare up again). My hair became limp, thinner, lifeless, and even strangely colored. I also had intestinal issues that had bedeviled me for decades (and made worse by drinking), and nearly killed me more than once before I got sober.

Also towards the end of my drinking days I tried to date via online dating services. On several occasions, I could see the disgust on the woman's face when I first met them. At the time, I couldn't understand why; now seeing some of the pictures from that time (such as the one on the right above) this reaction now makes total sense...

★ ★

Let there be *NO* question, alcoholism can be <u>very</u> detrimental to your health. It can impact many dimensions of your body and mind, including very negative impacts to your liver, nervous system, heart, skin, stomach/intestines, and of course your brain. But this is not all, not by a long shot.

Alcohol abuse and addiction also produce other medical side effects. Alcoholics frequently attribute these complications to other health conditions, as they attempt to avoid ownership of the consequences of their drinking. Common medical side effects include high blood pressure, sexual problems, stomach problems, osteoporosis in women, even cancer. There are also many types of non-lethal aliments, particularly skin disorders with pleasant sounding names such as <u>porphyria cutanea tarda</u>, <u>cutaneous stigmata of cirrhosis</u>, and <u>pruritus</u> (itching). Look these up—they are *not* pretty or fun.

Alcohol-Related Diseases from A To Z

Not enough for you? Even as I personally dealt with skin aliments[2] and several other alcohol-related health issues over the years (whether I acknowledged them or not at the time) I had no idea how many dimensions of health alcohol can affect until researching this book.

A good quick reference on the effects of alcoholism on health comes from _http://alcoholrehab.com/alcohol-rehab_, where it has succinct overviews of the health issues alcohol can cause or impact, many listed below.

Table 5: How Alcohol Can Destroy Your Health from A to Z

Anxiety	Gum Disease	Metabolic Syndrome
Bad Breath	Heart Problems	Obesity
Breast Cancer	Heartburn	Oral Cancer
Cancer(Other)	Hemorrhoids	Pancreatitis
Cardiomyopathy	Hepatitis	Panic Attacks
Chronic Fatigue Syndrome	Hormonal Imbalance	Post-Traumatic Stress Disorder
Crohn's Disease	Hypertension	Restless Leg Syndrome
DEATH	Jaundice	Schizophrenia
Dementia	Irritable Bowel Syndrome	Sexual Dysfunction
Depression	Kidney Stones	Skin Problems
Digestive Problems	Leaky Gut Syndrome	SUICIDE
Fetal Alcohol Syndrome	Liver Disease	Tinnitus
Fibromyalgia	Lung Disease	Ulcerative Colitis
Gallstones	Memory Problems	Ulcers
Gastritis	Menopause Problems	Wet Brain

For women, the news is even worse. Numerous studies show that women develop long-term health complications of alcohol dependence more rapidly than do men, with just one example being women's' increased the risk of breast cancer. And over time it has been found to have a negative effect on reproductive functioning in women, resulting in anovulation, decreased ovarian mass, problems or irregularity of the menstrual cycle and early menopause. The final indignity: _women have a higher mortality rate from alcoholism than men._

The list above highlights over two dozen illnesses that can be directly caused by or greatly aggravated by alcohol abuse. **I would <u>strongly</u> <u>encourage</u> you to see your doctor to see if you have any of these problems.** What is discussed here (and this Level overall) is for informational purposes only. Again, <u>the author is not a medical doctor</u>.

Liver Disease—One Horror of Many

There is no "better" alcohol-related ailment to illustrate the horror that alcoholism can inflict on your body than Liver Disease:

> *My husband has alcoholic liver disease. He has been told he has maximum of 5 years to live. He won't quit. He has yellow eyes, recently developed a swollen stomach, and sleeps every two hours for 2-4 hours at a time. He is on lactulose, is very angry and nasty towards our children, then nice as pie. No one will tell me how long this will go on, why this is going on or how bad this will get, what to expect? Can anyone help?[3]*

Part of the problem with health issues is that most are internal—out of sight, if not mind. But that doesn't mean the damage is not occurring, as Figure 12 below illustrates:

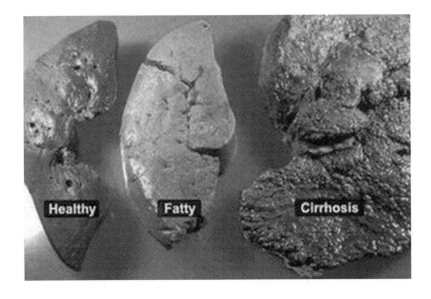

Figure 12: A Healthy vs. Diseased Liver[4]

The danger of from just this one disease can illustrate how alcohol can destroy you. Alcohol remains one of the most common causes of liver disease in the U.S., causing up to 50% of cases of end-stage liver disease according to the Center for Disease Control. It is also the third leading preventable cause of death. The mortality from alcoholic cirrhosis is higher than that of nonalcoholic cirrhosis, with a survival rate at 5 and 10 years of only 23% and 7%, respectively. Given these grim statistics, the mortality from liver disease is more than that of many major forms of cancer, such as breast, colon and prostate.

Like most alcohol-related diseases, the best "treatment" for liver disease is *not* drinking, which is both simple and very difficult. *Once alcoholic liver disease is established in the body, abstinence from alcohol use is the only accepted treatment outside of a liver transplant, which many facilities are reluctant to perform for active or high relapse risk alcoholics.*[5]

How does alcohol use cause liver disease? To start, alcohol is toxic to liver cells (known as hepatocytes) and causes inflammation. The effect of drinking on hepatocytes is immediate, but in most healthy non-alcoholics the body repairs itself. Unsurprisingly, it is the *repeated* levels of exposure to alcohol that causes chronic and continuing inflammation to the liver, resulting in scarring of the liver. This scarring is the beginning of alcoholic liver disease.

I am too an alcoholic. I'm a 38-year-old female, starting to consume many bruises on my body due to drinking, I can no longer go out.[6]

To add to the horror, there is even a genetic component. For some, it is believed that when you drink certain genes trigger an immune reaction that causes liver damage. For those people, your body will begin to attack itself and cause serious and even life-threatening damage to the liver including cirrhosis. *Once you have cirrhosis, you have a 50 percent chance of being dead in two years or less.*

There are three main stages of liver disease:

Table 6: The 3 States of Liver Disease

Stage 1: *Fatty Liver Disease*	**Stage 2:** *Alcoholic Hepatitis*	**Stage 3:** *Cirrhosis*
Precursor to alcoholic liver disease, and <u>will not progress further if you stop drinking, and is even reversible</u>. It causes the body to accumulate fat instead of healthy liver tissue, resulting in an enlarged and inflamed liver.	Caused by untreated Fatty Liver Disease (e.g., you did not stop drinking). Serious, progressively incurable. Hepatitis causes many problems including cholesterol and protein metabolizing, processing of fats and sugars, hormone regulating, and impaired immune functions. Up to 35 percent of heavy drinkers develop alcoholic hepatitis. Mild cases can be reversible w/ abstinence.	The liver becomes so scarred that it is no longer able to repair itself. Major contributor to the development of liver cancer and death. **Death for 50 percent within two years**. <u>The only "treatment" for cirrhosis is an organ replacement, and even if possible, it is no guarantee of success, even if you are no longer drinking.</u>[7] Between 10 and 20% of heavy drinkers develop cirrhosis.[8]
Symptoms: Fatigue, nausea and vomiting, weakness, confusion, abdominal discomfort (right upper abdomen), weight loss, and jaundice.	**Symptoms:** Loss of appetite, nausea, vomiting, abdominal pain, fever and jaundice.	**Symptoms:** Similar to those of severe alcoholic hepatitis.

The agony these stages (particularly 2 and 3) inflict is incredible:

I know how difficult it is to deal with a bullheaded husband. Mine ignored his hepatitis C for years. He ignored the diagnosis of fatty liver for about 4 years and then he found himself in the hospital this past February with Hepatic Encephalopathy. Very nasty symptom of liver failure. The man truly thought he could dodge this bullet (HepC and fatty liver) but he was sadly mistaken…

Obtaining a liver transplant is very difficult for non-alcoholics; for alcoholics it becomes even more difficult, and complicated.

*…I'm afraid he has damaged it to the point that the only thing that will help him is a liver transplant **and he can't get that until he has achieved one year of sobriety***

and is determined to be sick enough to be placed on the list. He has type O blood so he can only get a transplant from another person who is Type O. Our doctor says that could take quite some time. He may very likely die while waiting. One day doing fine and the next almost in coma.[9]

I have bolded a key part of the above testimonial, which is often overlooked until too late. You will NOT be eligible for a liver transplant until you are sober, and have been sober for at least 6 months to a year. In other words, *if you are still drinking and need a transplant, the odds are very "good" that you will be <u>dead</u> before you become eligible for a transplant.* Six months does <u>not</u> include the waiting for an eligible organ.[10]

If and when the liver is severely damaged by alcoholic hepatitis, these immune functions deteriorate to the point that the liver is unable to function.

I lost everything, career and family. This only gave me more reason to continue. At 45 years old, I was told I needed a transplant or I would die. I've been through it all, throwing up blood (five times) that required transfusions and ascites. The symptoms of cirrhosis are horrific. I had a transplant two years ago and was doing well until I began to reject recently. I just got out of the hospital after a 23 day stay and was told things could go either way.[11]

Liver disease is not the only fatal disease associated with alcohol. With a few exceptions (e.g. heartburn, gum disease), nearly all aliments listed above are fatal or at least extremely painful. **Dying peacefully and pain-free in your sleep is <u>not</u> the likely end for an alcoholic.**

My father is in the hospital [again]. He has the yellowing, liver is dead, kidneys are failing to work they have him on meds but we won't know if they are working till tomorrow. He is really bad we don't know what to do anymore I guess just wait and be prepared for the worst. My dad has been in AA for 10 years and he just had a relapse just 2 months ago and this is when he started to get sick now it's too late. To all that have a family member or friend [who drink] please help them.[12]

What's the Buzz—What It Is and Why We Want It

Closely coupled with these "evil" triggers is recognition of the <u>extreme</u> importance of the *effect* of alcohol to many if not most alcoholics. Whether it is the initial *"rush"* that comes with the first drink, to the *"buzz"* after a few, to being "comfortably *numb"* after several, to the complete *"checking out* from the world" that comes after many (I call this rush/buzz/numb/checkout continuum, "buzz-rush" for short),[13] the desire for these effects are intertwined with many triggers that underlie our desire to drink. Arguably the desire for "buzz-rush" is the single biggest cause of alcoholic relapses.

★ ★

What Happens if I Relapse?

The good news is that unlike many programs, the Conquer Program does <u>not</u> consider you a "failure" if you have a relapse, nor that you need to restart your attempt at sobriety as if you had never tried before. In other words, you are not thrown back to 1st Grade, you Don't Pass "Go" without collecting $200,[14] or go back to Step 1 in AA, etc.

What is *does* mean, however, is that you did not do well enough earlier at a) identifying your major drinking triggers (and their related ones), and/or b) identifying an effective set of defenses against the trigger(s) that caused your relapse. So you may well need to go back to Level 2 and reread those sections to help yourself fully understand the reasons for your relapse. Also, you might "reconfigure" or redesign your defense progressions (discussed in Level 13—Develop Your Defense Progressions).

★ ★

Even if you don't relapse, and even if the "evil" triggers individually or in combination don't greatly affect you, or you believe you have the right defenses, you still may have the intense desire to get back into the buzz-rush continuum (perhaps due to *other* triggers[15]). This is a version of "white-knuckle" sobriety[16], where you are sober but not happy about it. Something more radical may be needed.

Buzz-Rush and Blood Alcohol Content (BAC)

The science behind what I call "Buzz-Rush" is helpful to know the closer we get to actually describing how to "get sick" of alcohol. The *Office of Drug and Alcohol Education* at the University Of Notre Dame[17] lays out a table of what to expect mentally and physically as you progress through different blood alcohol content levels, which tracks closely to what is felt in Buzz-Rush.

Blood Alcohol Content (BAC) is the amount of alcohol in one's system based on weight, number of drinks, and the period during which alcohol is consumed. Notre Dame makes a very specific point that BAC it <u>totally unrelated</u> to your *tolerance* of alcohol.[18] Thus the same BAC in two people could result in <u>far</u> different effects in their behavior and mental and body reactions, regardless of how similar they are in weight, gender, age, etc.

Notre Dame also frequently uses the term *"Euphoria"* in its BAC analysis. While it doesn't define the term, a reasonable definition based on their use is: *A mental and emotional condition in which a person experiences intense feelings of well-being, elation, happiness, excitement, and joy.* (Dysphoria is essentially the opposite).[19] This definition of Euphoria very much describes the "rush" and "buzz" portions of the rush-buzz-numb-checkout continuum.

Table 7 next summarizes Notre Dame's assessment of Blood Alcohol Content (BAC) levels:

Table 7: Blood Alcohol Content Level Generalized Dose Specific Effects

BAC Level	Effect of Alcohol
BAC = 0.02 to 0.03%	No loss of coordination, **slight euphoria** and loss of shyness. Depressant effects are not apparent.
BAC = 0.04 to 0.06%	Feeling of well-being, relaxation, lower inhibitions, and sensation of warmth. **Euphoria.** Some minor impairment of reasoning and memory, lowering of caution.
BAC = 0.07 to 0.09%	Slight impairment of balance, speech, vision, reaction time, and hearing. **Euphoria.** Reduced judgment and self-control. Impaired reasoning, memory, and sense of cautiousness.
BAC = 0.10-0.125%	Significant impairment of motor coordination and loss of good judgment. Speech may be slurred; balance, vision, reaction time, and hearing will be impaired.
BAC = 0.13-0.15%	Gross motor impairment and lack of physical control. Blurred vision and major loss of balance. **Euphoria is reducing** and **dysphoria[20] is beginning to appear.**
BAC = 0.16-0.20%	**Dysphoria** predominates, nausea may appear. The drinker has the appearance of a "sloppy drunk." May vomit.
BAC = 0.25%	**Needs assistance in walking; total mental confusion.** _**Dysphoria**_ **with nausea and some vomiting. Considered a medical emergency; Death has occurred at this level.**
BAC = 0.30%	**Loss of consciousness.**
BAC = 0.40% +	**Onset of coma,_ possible death due to respiratory arrest._**

What is needed is a way of turning the "Euphoria" into "Dysphoria" at a much earlier Blood Alcohol Content level. Or put another way, causing Dysphoria at *any* BAC level. There are no "conventional" methods that do this—something radical may be needed.

Medical Problems in Trigger Identification and Defense

You are now (hopefully) scared to death about how alcohol traumatizes your body, and fully committed to the need for change. You also have identified at least an initial list of triggers. This Level can potentially refine that list, as well as identify or exclude possible defenses. Specifically, do the following steps:

- *Consult your doctor.* Make sure he/she **_knows_** you are an alcoholic, are trying to stop, and ask if there he/she has any particular concerns.[21]

For example, if you have high blood pressure, your doctor may fear that it may spike dramatically while you detox, and may want to adjust your medication.[22]

- _It is critical that you tell the truth about your alcohol intake_. This is not just to make you feel good; your doctor may want you to take tests that he/she would otherwise not think of doing, such as a Liver-Function test or certain types of cancer screening. Ask for a complete physical so you can measure the impact of your coming sobriety against key health readings.

- _Revisit your trigger list (with your doctor if possible)_. Make sure that you have carefully considered and appropriately prioritized all medically-related triggers. These include: Anxiety, Depression, Health problems (particularly Pain), Hungry (specifically eating disorders), Insomnia, Sex (particularly performance issues), (physical) Stress, and being continually Tired. It may be that medical concerns could push certain triggers from being "minor" to be "major", or vice versa.

- _Include/Exclude key defense activities_. Also in consultation with your doctor (if possible), identify key "defensive" activities that you should exclude or include. For example, many triggers advocate specific kinds of exercise as a defense mechanism. However, your doctor may not want you to run (say because of knees or blood pressure), and instead mandate a slowly-increasing walking schedule. If you have a tendency towards lower-back pain; he or she may discourage certain hobbies such as cycling, weight-training, or even bowling, in favor of other activities such as Yoga or Wii-U Bowling (e.g. virtual bowling).

One thing positive that can be learned from all of the above is to turn health concerns into a kind of _defense_ against drinking, or more generally the fear of health problems as a kind of last-resort safety net defense. This is called a "floor defense", one that is applicable to most if not all triggers and will likely work when all other defenses fail. Floor defenses will be discussed in more detail in Level 13.

* * * * *

This completes Phase 1—Lay the Foundation for Sobriety. You now are (hopefully) fully aware about the extent of your alcohol problem. If you now 1) truly accept that you are an alcoholic, and 2) know the detailed reasons why you drink (your triggers) you are ready to start Phase 2—building your new defenses against alcohol.

LEVEL 4—ENGAGE FRIENDS AND FAMILY

We now begin Phase 2 of The Conquer Program. In Phase 1 we laid the foundation for sobriety by getting you to admit your problem, and identified the root causes—your triggers—of your drinking. Level 4 is the first of five Levels that look to use the best of conventional methods to build a new set of defenses for those triggers.

PHASE 2—Build New Defenses

LEVEL 9	DEVELOP NEW HOBBIES	*Fill Your Newfound Time*
LEVEL 8	BREAK BAD HABITS	*Clean Out The Garbage*
LEVEL 7	JOIN A COMMUNITY	*Expand Your Support Network*
LEVEL 6	REHAB AND THERAPY	*Learn Techniques, Tips, and Yourself*
LEVEL 5	DETOX	*Understand Detoxification*
LEVEL 4	ENGAGE FRIENDS AND FAMILY	*Start Building Your Support Network*

Figure 13: Phase 2—Build Your New Defenses

The key to Level 4 is:

You Can't Do It Alone.

If there is one simple truth in trying to conquer alcoholism, it is that while you have to get sober <u>for yourself</u>, you <u>can't do it alone</u>.[1] Engaging friends and family early in the process of any program is a must, including this one. While it seems simple, it is *not*. Pride and shame are the main obstacles.

If you are like me, you tried to hide your drinking for as long as you could, even after admitting it to yourself. Who wants to seem "weak", "deficient", "powerless", etc., even if none of those words are true? This is a frigging disease, but even after many years of becoming "mainstream" many people still have outdated (and very unpleasant) perceptions of alcoholics. Many of us (particularly older ones, say over the age of 35), still consider it a particularly shameful condition whether we admit it or not.

Of course, your friends and family are likely to have seen your addiction long before you eventually admitted it. Indeed, <u>many of them probably did their best to make your life a living hell, under the totally misguided notion that they could "guilt" you into stopping drinking.</u> I emphasize this point for you non-alcoholics reading this book. <u>*"Guilting" does not help the vast majority of alcoholics, and may well make things much worse.*</u> My guess is that "Guilting" added at least two years of drinking to my life, maybe more.

Even once you admit you are an alcoholic and resign yourself to having your friends and family know, it is still a far cry from asking them to help you out. Frankly, it is far easier to engage a stranger with the same problem than to ask someone you know (without the problem) for help. <u>But you need to do it</u>.

Who and How to Ask for Help

When we say you can't do it alone, it does <u>not</u> mean that *everyone* has to help. On the contrary, for numerous obvious and more subtle reasons you only want a handful of people to be involved (at least initially). Once you are firmly in command of your sobriety, it is then ok to loosen up and let people know about your alcoholism (once it is no longer an issue). Initially the best idea is to keep it to a select few.

First however you've got to identify and select a handful of people (as few as a single person) to help you get sober and in the early days thereafter. Selecting the *wrong* person can be devastating in numerous ways, from sapping your motivation to not being there for you during the most vulnerable times of your journey.

To pick the *right* person(s), identify those around you who best meet the following criteria:

- Are not judgmental, and even better can be objective
- Have a basic understanding of alcoholism as a disease
- Are fairly patient
- Are not gossips
- Are decent listeners
- Are willing to dedicate a reasonable amount of free time for you over a period of several weeks
- Will be there in an emergency
- Can deal with pressure and responsibility.

Hopefully, your first reaction is not: "Right! Like that is going to happen in my family!" It will probably be tougher to find family members who meet these criteria than it will be friends, but it is important to find at least one family member, as they are more likely to be willing to see you through the toughest times than friends who have their own family obligations. It is also important, if possible, to have more than one person on your list, in case the first declines or has limited time, requiring a kind of "tag-team" support.

For some (not all) people, the best single person (in theory) can be your spouse/partner (if applicable).

> *[Responding to a post by an alcoholic] You are already on the right track. You know your drinking is a problem and it sounds like you are fed up with it. You have a support system behind you in your husband, who knows you have a problem but hasn't pushed you to confront it until you're ready.*[2]

Unfortunately, your spouse or partner may not fit all the criteria listed above, particularly if you are going through tough times (which is very common with alcoholics, *but it is unlikely you can embark on this journey without his or her becoming aware of it.*

For one thing, it is highly likely that your behavior during and immediately after detox will be erratic, even unpleasant. If one of your triggers is Relationships or Yelling (Conflict), then this behavior and his or her reaction stands a good chance of activating that trigger, which in turn could derail your sobriety before you barely get started!

Even if they are not the right person to help you day-to-day, some degree of support (even just pats on the back and not drinking in front of you) from them will be essential. In addition, your partner being aware of the process you are going through will help them begin _their_ healing, no small matter for improving the odds of your relationship being successful in the long-term even with your being sober.[3]

The person(s) you select (and agrees to help you) will be particularly important as you go through some of the tasks associated with parts of the program such as Detox (Levels 5 and if needed Level 12) and Level 11— Make Yourself Sick of Alcohol. Indeed, you may have to live with one of them for part of the time. They will also continue to be very important once you have achieved sobriety, as a key Level of Defense in the circumstances where familiar, friendly, intimate faces are your best option for defense in certain types of vulnerable situations.

It is the *moral* support that family and friends can provide that is the most important reason for engaging them. While fellow alcoholics can provide a unique degree of support that (nonalcoholic) friends and family cannot, at the end of the day they are strangers who can only provide certain degrees and types of support, and can't be counted on to help you when things get really ugly, which they are likely to do at some point.

★ ★

Can Strangers Help?

One exception to not being able to depend on strangers for support is if you attend Alcoholics Anonymous, Women for Sobriety, or similar meetings and you get a "sponsor" as part of that program (both are discussed in Level 7—Join a Community).

A sponsor is someone you ask to help guide you through that particular program. A sponsor can be a great type of person to have in your court when you are struggling for sobriety, including being there for late night calls and similar unexpected situations. The particulars of some programs are not for everyone, and some sponsors can be very intense in their approach and adverse to anything not "their" way (particularly AA). In addition, sharing your deepest feelings and problems with a complete stranger (at first) makes many people very uncomfortable, another reason a sponsor may not work for you.

★ ★

So, the bottom line here is: swallow your pride, put aside any "shame" you might feel, and ask for the support of (a few) of your friends and family. *Besides being an essential Level in this program, you will find that just asking for* _support (and in the process maybe admitting your alcoholism to them for the first time) will be very cathartic by itself._[4]

Ways to Get Started

Even when you've found the right person(s) to ask, actually _asking_ may be difficult. How do you bring up the topic and ask for help in the first place?

Obviously how you do this will depend very significantly on whether that person knows about your excessive drinking or not. This is more likely a to-what-degree question; if they are close to you in any way they are very likely to perceive you are a heavy drinker. Even so, that is not the same thing as _knowing_ you are an alcoholic.

The challenge might be compounded if you tried to stop before and failed. In this case, you will need to introduce them to The Conquer Program (a good idea in any case). Get their opinions on how you scored on The Conquer Quiz and your initial take on what your major drinking triggers are. Not only will that help convince them that you are really serious, you will undoubtedly get great feedback, such as highlighting a trigger that you missed, or helping you figure out which are the highest priority for you.

If the person does not realize you are an alcoholic or that you even have a serious drinking problem (meaning you were great at hiding it), then you may need to open up a conversation something like this:

> _"Hey [insert name here], you may have noticed that I seem to be drinking a lot lately. Well, I've been doing that a long time, a lot more than you many realize, and I think I have a big problem. I am going to try a program that I think will help. Part of the program strongly suggests having a close (friend, family member) involved in various parts of the program. Since I consider you a very close (friend, family member), I was wondering if you would be up to being involved in it."_

If they say yes, one of the first things they will ask is what is involved on their end. Besides suggesting they skim through this book, you might also say something like:

"It depends on where I am in the Program. It has 13 levels, most of which will not require much if any effort on your part."

At this point, what else you say will depend on where you think they can really help. If you have it mapped out, fine, but odds are you haven't fully thought through it at this point in the program. You can say something like:

"I'm not 100% sure. I would like someone to call while I am in Detox. You might also go through the trigger list with me to see if I've left any off, or you think I should prioritize some higher than others. And for some of those triggers you may be very high on how I cope with them without drinking. It might be a few hours a week."

Odds are they will be flattered and honored at your request, particularly as they learn more about it. You might ask them to go through The Conquer Quiz with you, both to confirm your initial answers (or add more points to it), as well as using it as a basis of discussion and opening up about your problem, which can only help both of you to start interacting (and even bonding) about the experience. You could also ask them for help in identifying your bad habits (discussed in Level 8—Break Bad Habits), which are often very hard for someone to see for themselves. They likely will find great fun in pointing them out! If so you should not take it personally; instead, view it as a kind of a partial "makeover" of your personality that will only result in good things.

The above should be a reasonable list of activities and expectations for a close friend or family member to accept. Make sure though that you have gone through the vetting process described above to make certain they are a good fit against the criteria. Once you ask it may be difficult to "un-ask."

You might prepare for a rejection, as some people may not have the time or even freak out about the whole thing. If so don't take it personally, just say you understand and ask them to keep it to themselves. For these reasons, it is good to have a "backup" person.

★ ★

What if I Self-Detox?

DON'T. As will be discussed in Level 5—Detox, detoxing under medical supervision is _very strongly_ recommended. Self-Detoxing can be deadly. Shortly before the publishing of this book, True Blood actor Nelsan Ellis died from complications arising from self-detox of alcohol.[5]

However, there are situations (usually involving time and money) where you may feel you can't go the medically supervised route and that you can detox "on your own". But on your own should _not_ mean by yourself. You need someone near you as much as possible to help you deal with possible problems, particularly any emergency situations that may arise, such as DTs (also discussed in Level 5—Detox).

★ ★

You will need to make that someone understand that it is a serious commitment you are asking, one that requires them to be checking up on you pretty frequently and possibly even living with you part of the time or vice versa. They may even need to be ready to take you to the ER if the detox becomes particularly worrisome. This kind of commitment is a game changer in terms of commitment, and they should understand that an emergency is possible, if unlikely.

Once you are sober, the "use" of friends and family doesn't end, it changes to "defense mode." Indeed, some of the most important defenses against alcohol are judicious use of those closest to you, to help you vent about your triggers and help you get alcohol off your mind, discussed next.

Using Friends and Family as a Defense Against Alcohol

You will find that you will use this Level very often for triggers that require some degree of relaxation or activity in a social interaction, such as Anger, Kids, Loneliness, and Social Situations among many others. You will also particularly need them in circumstances where their awareness of what you are trying to do and intimate knowledge of your history will be of particular value, such as Change, Mid-Life Crisis, Relationships and Relatives issues.

While fairly intense face-to-face interactions with friends and family are the ideal defense for many situations, talking on the phone will often do the job, depending on the trigger(s) and the particular circumstances you are facing that day. Have the interactions in environments that exclude other possible triggers to the extent possible. This means no bars (for the Proximity and Smell triggers), and not at their house if they have children (if Kids or Noise are triggers), etc. Also do them when you both have enough time to deal with the circumstance you are dealing with. If a brief phone conversation will do it, great. If more time is required, make sure you find a way to do it so your conversation is not cut short; that leads to Frustration.

In today's world, of course, there are many other ways of getting together with friends and family other than face-to-face or a phone call. Email is one, though the time lag can defeat the purpose. Texting is better but is inherently limited on how much you can say. But it can work well in many situations. Both email and texting, and of course phone calls and in person conversations have the added advantage of being private, which can be extremely important when you are talking about alcoholism and alcoholism treatment.

★ ★

Is Online Social Media Your "Friend"?

Social media (Facebook in particular) is great for venting and in general connecting with people you might otherwise rarely do so via phone or person. <u>However</u>, be *very* aware that these online forums, and in particular those where you can<u>not</u> be anonymous, are NOT private—not anywhere close to it. <u>Everything</u> you post on Facebook and Twitter is monitored by people other than your "Friends"—total strangers looking for objectionable content, by legions of advertisers, and often by total strangers just looking to snoop.[6]

The social medial rule of thumb is "*if you don't want the world to see it, don't post it on the Internet.*" This "rule" is becoming a near certainty as everyone tries to make money off of what everybody else on the Internet is saying. **SO, if you do not want the world to know you are an alcoholic, do NOT post anything related to your problems with alcohol on Facebook or any forum that can be personally linked with your identity.**

But if sharing alcohol-related feelings is what you need to do at the moment—and online is the only option—there are safe options to do so. Alcohol-specific sites such as www.alcoholism.about.com and www.cryingoutnow.com, as well as other community sites sponsored by programs such as WFS (http://www.womenforsobrietyonline.com/) provide relatively safe, anonymous outlets for your issues with alcoholism. Other sites such as www.socialanxietysupport.com provide trigger-specific outlets and sharing forums.

★ ★

Additional Ideas and Concerns

Asking for the kind of help discussed above can put a lot of pressure on a person, so be *sure* in your vetting process that your candidates are both willing and able to take it. Not everyone can, even a close family member.

Additional pressure will be felt on all sides if this is not the first time you have tried to get sober. *Your friends and family may be extremely skeptical.* In those cases, strongly urge them to read this book in its entirety to have them fully understand how the program is different.[7] Sitting down with them to discuss each of the Levels will help both of you greatly even if they are reluctant to read the book.

* * *

Now that you have at least one friend and/or family member ready to assist you, let's turn to what many alcoholics fear the most: detoxification.

LEVEL 5—DETOX

Detoxification is not exactly about *building* defenses (unlike the other Levels in this Phase of the program) as it is *clearing the debris* from your mind and body from its past battles with alcohol. To continue the war analogy, this will allow you to continue building your broader defenses on a clear(er) field, instead of trying to do so upon the rubble of your previous active drinking. If you haven't stopped drinking by the time you reach this Level, well, <u>now</u> is the time. Dependence on alcohol gets worse with time in every way—mentally, emotionally, and physically—and hoping it will go away on its own over time is *not* going to happen. Detox follows a similar path; the more and longer you drink, the more difficult the detoxification process. If you take one message away from this Level, it is this: <u>*Do NOT Detox without medical supervision, particularly if it is your first time*</u> (and just not drinking for 1 or 2 days does <u>*not*</u> count). Why will become clear shortly.

What is Detoxification?

Type in "what is detoxification" in Google, and you get:

- *The process of removing toxic substances or qualities.*

- *Medical treatment of an alcoholic or drug addict involving abstention from drink or drugs until the bloodstream is free of toxins.*[1]

Detox's overall goal is to <u>remove</u> the physical dependence your body and mind has on alcohol, a dependence that has developed due to the drinking of large amounts over an extended period of time. In the context of The Alcoholism Process, shown in Figure 14 next, the intent is to *break* the Physical Dependency part of the process, and make the body and brain chemistry revert (at least part of the way) back to normal.

The Alcoholism Process
Detox—Breaking the Physical Dependency

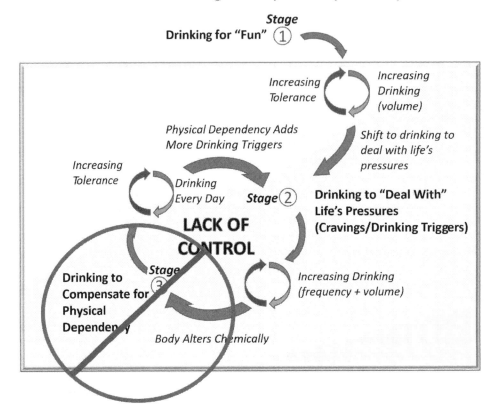

Figure 14: The Alcoholism Process—Post-Detox

★ ★

What is Physical Dependence on Alcohol?

Dependence on alcohol has two main components. One is mental, where you have come to <u>associate</u> alcohol as a way to "deal with" various issues such as Boredom or Guilt.

The second is <u>physical</u> dependence, where your mind and body have become so chemically acclimated to the presence of alcohol in your system that its absence starts to have a material, visible effect on you. In other words, you experience physical <u>withdrawal</u> from alcohol when it is out of your system for too long. Signs include:

- Getting sweaty
- Tremors or shakes
- Feeling sick or vomiting, and/or
- Feeling panicky, anxious and agitated.[2]

All of these symptoms or behaviors will get progressively worse, at least for a day or two, before they start to subside. Not fun.

★ ★

While a great deal of research has been done on Detox,[3] from an alcoholic perspective it is quite simple: How do I survive multiple days of hell?

This is partly what this Detox Level is about: helping you navigate the hell involved with undoing your chemical dependence, doing so safely and effectively, and with as little discomfort/agony as reasonably possible. *However, its main goal is to fully prepare you for the detox experience—<u>so you never have to go through it again</u>!*

What happens in Detox?

This section is not to scare the bejezzus out of you, but to make you aware of the *possible* serious side effects of the process. While these effects are statistically unlikely, in my opinion the more you know of the possibilities (and probabilities), the more relaxed you will be throughout the process.

The first time you go through a <u>serious</u>[4] effort to stop drinking is universally a scary one. You don't know what to expect; you've heard a ton of horror stories, and bottom line you are probably scared shitless about facing the world without alcohol. But the key idea is to think positive; you will be FAR better off at the end of the detox than you are entering it! <u>Keep refreshing your mind about why you are here—to get your life back on track again.</u> Repeating that will give you the strength to get through detox. And detox *does* require strength; there is no way around it.[5]

The first three days were living hell. I slept a total of five hours in three days. Went through withdrawals, tremors, etc. Blood pressure went through the roof. I truly believed I thought I was going to have a heart attack. Anxiety set in bad. Now it's been five days and I feel much better. I still feel a little funky, but much better.[6]

The first and most important rule about Detox, particularly your first time, is:

<u>DO NOT DETOX ALONE, (PARTICULARLY YOUR FIRST MAJOR DETOX), AND IF AT ALL POSSIBLE DO IT UNDER TRAINED MEDICAL SUPERVISION</u>.

Detoxification can be *extremely* dangerous as the body reacts to the absence of the substance it has become accustomed to, often over a period of years if not decades. **If it is your first time going through major detox (and previously going 1 or 2 days without drinking does *not* count as major detox if you went right back to drinking, as many major symptoms happen after this time period), it is particularly important to do it under medical supervision, as you have _no_ idea how your body (and mind) is going to react.**

Within 24-48 hours of the last drink, the following can happen:

Major Symptoms of Alcohol Detoxification

Mental and Neurological	*Sudden Acute Conditions* *(Heart Attack, Stroke, Death)*
Visual, auditory, or olfactory hallucinations may occur in which the heightened effect of images, sounds, or even smells in any type of environmental situation may induce extreme flight or fight responses. Seizures are often brought on by delirium tremens (DTs), and may range in severity from mild to grand mal. Other withdrawal reactions include confusion, disorientation, difficulty talking, and temporary loss of short-term memory.	*Seizures and DT's often create irregular cardiac activity such as palpitations, heart arrhythmias, tachycardia, and abnormal spikes in blood pressure that increase the potential risk of succumbing to cardiovascular injury or death.*[7]

Clearly this is NOT something to mess around with. DTs in particular are something to be worried about. Though I never experienced them personally, in rehab (my first detox) I temporarily "roomed" with someone who had the DTs, and he was not a happy camper.[8] They were coming to check on him every 10 minutes. They apparently were waiting on a free room in their dedicated DT area or equivalent, as he was moved in a few hours. It was NOT a fun few hours, with his constant moaning and groaning punctuated by occasional yells and vomiting or dry heaves.

★ ★

More on Delirium Tremens

Latin for "shaking frenzy," —also referred to as The DTs, "the horrors," or "the shakes."— Delirium Tremens is an acute episode of delirium (severe confusion) that is, usually, caused by withdrawal from alcohol and other substances. The withdrawal reactions as a result of physical dependence on alcohol are considered the most dangerous and <u>can be fatal</u>. Its effects are very physical: shivering, palpitations, sweating, even convulsions, if not treated.

The main symptoms of DTs are nightmares, agitation, global confusion, disorientation, visual and auditory hallucinations, fevers, hypertension, diaphoresis, and other signs of autonomic hyperactivity (tachycardia and hypertension). These symptoms may appear suddenly but can develop 2–3 days after cessation of drinking heavily with its highest intensity on the fourth or fifth day. Generally, these symptoms are worse at night.

In general, <u>DTs are considered as the most severe manifestation of alcohol withdrawal, which occurs *3-10* days following the last drink</u>. Other symptoms include intense perceptual disturbance such as visions of insects, snakes, etc. These may be hallucinations or environmental illusions, e.g., patterns on the wallpaper or in the peripheral vision that the patient falsely perceives as a resemblance to an insect, and are also associated with tactile hallucinations such as sensations of something crawling on the subject. DTs usually include intense feelings of "impending doom," as well as severe anxiety.

DTs should be distinguished from alcoholic hallucinosis, which develops about 12 to 24 hours after drinking stops and involves auditory and visual hallucinations, most commonly accusatory or threatening voices. This condition is distinct from DTs since it develops and resolves rapidly, involves a limited set of hallucinations and has no other physical symptoms. <u>Alcoholic hallucinosis occurs in approximately 20% of hospitalized alcoholics and does not carry a significant mortality</u>. In contrast, DT occurs in 5–10% of alcoholics and carries up to 15% mortality with treatment <u>and up to 35% mortality without treatment</u>.[9] *THESE POSSIBLE SEVERE WITHDRAWAL SIDE EFFECTS ARE WHY YOU DO NOT WANT TO SELF-DETOX IF YOU CAN POSSIBLY AVOID IT.*

★ ★

The possibility of DTs is a sad reality. The good news is that you have a relatively small statistical chance of enduring an acute detox such as described above, <u>but you won't know until you've done it</u>. **To Repeat: It is best to have your Detox done under clinical/medical supervision if you can possibly can.** If you can't, do it with someone else who is in a position to call 911 if things start to seem bad. This may require you living with them (or vice versa) for the entire detox period. You should also make your medical doctor aware of what you are doing and when.

Types of Detox Programs

The unabridged *How to Conquer Your Alcoholism* book goes into great detail on the types of Detox facilities available, summarized here. I would encourage you to do your own research on local (e.g. within your state) facilities and particularly those covered by your insurance.

There are five types of professional detoxification care available. They vary primarily by two dimensions: 1) if they are inpatient or outpatient, and 2) the amount and intensity of medical care provided. Note: these 5 types of Detox very closely mirror the 5 types of Rehabilitation, particularly in the level of medial supervision.

Figure 15 shows these 5 types, with the base/bottom of the pyramid representing the most basic outpatient detox/rehab services, and the top the most medically-intensive in-patient services.

Figure 15: Types of Detoxification/Rehab Care

If you are being detoxed under the care of doctor, he or she will likely direct you to which type of care you need. If you are essentially a "walk-in" without a doctor's order, you will need to undergo an assessment to determine what kind of care you need.

Many rehabilitation programs, particularly ones done in hospitals or hospital-like[10] facilities, offer medically-supervised detoxification periods and services as part of a much broader set of addiction services. These services are a natural extension of their broader Rehab programs, as all require you to be detoxed before entering the main body of their treatment. More details on rehabilitation services are in Level 6—Rehab and Therapy.

As indicated by the diagram, the "lowest" level of detoxification services is where you detox yourself. **This is not recommended**. While very understandable from a money and self-pride standpoint, **it can be very dangerous**. There is *no* telling what might happen.

The Inpatient Care Process—What to Expect

Each type of care has its own routine and process. For illustration purposes, below describes what can be expected in "Residential Services", the next to most-intensive inpatient detox. This is based primarily on the author's experience, supplemented by other research; each facility will be slightly different. First however you have to figure out which facility to go to, not necessarily a straight-forward task.

Selecting the Treatment Facility

The "easy" way to do this is to have your medical doctor or psychiatrist (whoever is treating your alcoholism, if anyone) select the facility for you (one more reason to tell your doctor about your alcoholism, so they can select the best facility for your specific needs). The selection will be based on your situation, their experience, and possibly relationships with various facilities (and of course your insurance). It may also greatly depend on your *commitment* for a full Rehabilitation stay beyond the initial Detox period.

Many facilities that offer Rehab services require you to be detoxed before arriving, thereby excluding those facilities (or in effect pressuring you into using their detox services). Some facilities only offer "packaged" detox/rehab services, while others (particularly traditional hospitals) offer Detox-only services that may be your best choice if Rehab is not in your plans. In other words, there are a lot of options. It also may be a simple matter of who and what your insurance covers.[11] In any event, *remember it takes 2-5 days to get alcohol completely out of your system*, depending on your drinking history, how recently you drank (and how much) and personal physical characteristics. Rehabilitation services can add weeks or even months, discussed in Level 6—Rehab and Therapy.

If you are selecting the facility yourself, with no professional guidance, choosing a facility can be difficult. The Website Resources section at the end of this book may help, as may general web searching using "Detox" or "Alcoholism Treatment" keywords. If possible obtain testimonials about particular programs directly from former patients.

One particular type of resource can be very helpful, depending on the state you live in (or want to Detox in). Most U.S. states have a state-run department specifically for substance abuse, such as the *New York State OASAS (Office of Alcoholism and Substance Abuse Services)*: https://www.oasas.ny.gov/accesshelp/index.cfm. A more comprehensive list of similar state-run organizations can be found at https://www.samhsa.gov/sites/default/files/ssadirectory.pdf. There are also a number of private websites that offer indexes of treatment centers, any one of which may (or may not) include detoxification services, such as www.theagapecenter.com/Treatment-Centers/index.htm. Be aware that many of these have commercial ties to various facilities and/or services, thus may be biased in the "suggestions" they provide.

Planning—Work and Child Care

A critical part of Detox planning (and even more so if a full Rehab stay is also included) is taking time off from work and child care. If you are employed, and your co-workers (and boss) don't realize you have a problem, taking time off to detox can be tricky. You need to carefully examine your options. A good resource explaining those options can be found at http://www.newbeginningsdrugrehab.org/the-guide-to-keeping-your-job-before-during-and-after-rehab/. The Family and Medical Leave Act (https://www.dol.gov/whd/fmla/) is a particularly important legal protection, as is the Americans with Disabilities Act. The tricky part is that you don't want your employer knowing about your addiction until *after* you are in treatment (and no longer drinking). If they find out *before* you enter treatment, you run the risk of being (legally) fired if they assert your job performance has been impacted by your drinking. A difficult balancing act.

Child care can be even trickier, particularly for a longer rehab-stay and if it is during the school year. Depending on their age, children may or may not be aware of what has been happening in the alcoholic household. A simple explanation that Daddy or Mommy has been sick and is going to get help is usually the best—simple and truthful. But who can you trust to take care of them while you are away (especially if you are a single parent)? Relatives are best, and having them stay in your house will minimize the disruption to the children's lives. Some treatment facilities do offer child care, but it has the challenges that come with a stranger taking care of your kids, combined with the unusual situation of all the other kids in the facility being there for the same reason: Mom or Dad is an alcoholic. Besides not being offered by many facilities, in-facility child care for inpatient alcoholics is not an area that has been studied for its impact on the children. It is possible that such an unusual arrangement may have a negative impact.

Making Your Arrangements

Once you've selected your facility, you will likely have to make a reservation, just like a hotel, though some facilities allow walk-ins. There may be a waiting list to get in (known as an "available bed"), so it might be as long as a couple weeks between making the call to the center and actually being admitted. This delay can obviously create problems about what to do in the meantime. Many people understandably get cold feet and back out if they cannot get in within a couple days of making the decision to detox.

The possibility of delay between deciding to Detox and actually entering a facility provides an example of the importance of Level 4—Engage Friends and Family, by having one of your key friends or family members step into the void. He or she can keep you committed to the detox process and make/handle the reservation process for you so you won't obsess about it—a kind of detox travel agent (and chauffeur to take you when a slot opens up).

While not drinking before your detox stay is probably too much to ask for, try if you can to gradually cut down. That will make your actual detox significantly easier. Do NOT go on a drinking tear the night before you check in—that *will* make detox worse. Also, try and get as much exercise in as you can during the wait before check-in. Being in good shape makes the physical aspects of detox much more bearable, and some studies have shown it to reduce the chances of DT's and other major detox complications.

On the day you start an inpatient stay, you won't want to take a car (even if you happen to be sober at time), so here is another instance of friend/family member support. You will probably not even be *allowed* to have a car on the premises in order to prevent you from going "off-campus" to get alcohol. This is particularly true if you are also doing broader rehabilitation, with its longer stay and possible temptations.[12]

Preparation - What to Bring (and Not Bring)

You should be very aware that <u>all</u> of the possessions you bring to any medically-supervised Detox may be examined, and possibly rejected or held for the duration of your stay. You should contact the facility about what you can bring with you. You may or may not be allowed to smoke on the grounds, but they may give you a nicotine patch if smoking is not allowed.

See if you are allowed to bring some books to read; you may have to leave your laptop/iPad, etc. at home. They want you focused on your Detox (and if applicable) your broader Rehab. You can bring your phone, but it may be held and you probably won't be able to use it often. It is even possible that you may have to use an old-fashioned pay phone, so plan accordingly, e.g., bring your contact numbers and even lots of quarters for the pay phone, or an old-fashioned phone calling card. People visiting you <u>cannot</u> bring you food or drink.

Check to see if the facility will provide cosmetics (e.g., shampoo); some of these can contain alcohol and as such bringing your own is often prohibited.[13] In general, the facility will be very paranoid about anything that can be used to hide booze or drugs, particularly if you or other patients are there any less than voluntarily.[14] You may be required to bring comfortable clothing that does not have any slogans on it, or have drawstrings, including sneakers with laces.[15]

You will be required to hand over all your medications upon admission, which they will dispense to you at the time and amount you need them, or they may prescribe and source the medications themselves. Depending on how you are handling detox (e.g., shakes, DTs), they may also prescribe medications to help during the worst of it (this is more common with drug withdrawal than alcohol withdrawal).

Table 8 next summarizes the pre-detox process.

Table 8: Pre-Detox Activities

Select Your Treatment Facility	Make Arrangements	Preparation
• Consult Your Doctor • Check Your Insurance • Determine Stay-Type (Detox-only, Rehab-only, Both) • Plan your work and child-care coverage while you are out. See http://www.newbeginnsdrugrehab.org/the-guide-to-keeping-your-job-before-during-and-after-rehab/	• Make a reservation, just like a hotel. • Plan for being away from work, children. • Be prepared for a delay in checking in; have a plan to wait it out (with minimal drinking if possible). • Exercise as much as you can. • Don't take your own car to the facility; Uber it or better yet have a friend or family member drive you and be there to make sure you don't back out at the last second.	• Obtain facility checklist, including dos & don'ts, and what to bring/not bring. • Do bring your list of medicines (including dosage) and doctors name and contact information. • Check on policy regarding medicines. If you bring your own medicines, be prepared for them to be confiscated for the stay. • Do bring allowed entertainment (e.g. books). Check if phones, iPods/iPads, etc. are allowed. Possibly bring phone card or even quarters. • Check to see if the facility will provide cosmetics (e.g., shampoo; bring if allowed. • Do bring comfortable (and unprovocative) clothing.

In some respects, pre-detox is the hardest part of the overall detoxification process, both in what you have to do in terms of planning and prep, and of course getting up the nerve and courage to go through with it. What's next?

Check-In

As mentioned before, do not drive yourself to the facility; it is highly unlikely they will allow it (to prevent going offsite to obtain alcohol). Upon arrival, you will need to answer numerous questions during check-in as a broader effort to compile a complete profile of your addiction. Most of these will be about your medical and drinking history (including past detoxes), as well as what/how much/when you have been drinking over the last several days and weeks. They may also ask about what your home life is like, such as if you are depressed, is there a lot of stress (and its sources), and other personal questions. Answer honestly. They will also want to know about your post-detox plans (if you have not already committed to their post-detox rehab). They may offer suggestions—consider doing them!

After Check-In

You will be assigned a room—either one or two-person, depending on the facility, availability, type of detox, and insurance. An exam is likely after check-in to take basic vitals. It will likely include urine or other tests to determine Blood Alcohol Content (BAC) levels, as well as blood pressure, weight, etc. More extensive tests may be done, particularly in acute cases.

Once you have settled into your room, you may be given a tour of the facilities, as well as a schedule of daily activities (discussed next). You may be allowed to wear your own clothes, or given a patient gown, depending on what kind of condition you are in. Meals will also depend on your condition, and are generally strictly scheduled and controlled. In general, by the time you are finally in your room that first evening you will be exhausted, not to mention the beginnings of your detoxification.

Days One-Two

Unless you have a severe withdrawal, you will not just be lying in a bed for 2-5 days. Generally 2-5 days is the normal time to get alcohol <u>completely</u> out of your system, depending on your drinking history, how recently you drank (and how much) and personal physical characteristics. But the first couple of days is the most important.

What happens in that first day or two? It very much depends on the individual and the severity of the withdrawal. A "normal" withdrawal will be one of the shakes and sweats, perhaps some nausea and headaches—nothing to freak out about, but still benefiting from periodic oversight by professional staff. How "periodic" will depend on your entry diagnosis, type of facility and detox services, day of detox, and time of day. For your first full day, at least, you will likely be confined to bed (and glad for it). You will be checked on as little as every couple of hours, continuously, or somewhere in between. Depending on the severity of your condition it is possible that you can leave your room for meals and obtain prescriptions, but in general you should assume staying in your room all day.

Day Two+

After the first day or two you will likely be up and around for meals, meetings, and even socializing. Odds are that you'll be in a unit where you are going to be around others who are detoxing from various substances (not just alcohol), and lots of different personalities, many whom may be *very* unpleasant in their current state. *It is not your job to make these people feel better.* In fact, you are best off avoiding them—some may try and take advantage of you.

* *

Other People You May Encounter

During your stay at a detox/rehab facility—particularly when in residential/"social"-type detox/rehab—try to keep to yourself, as you have enough to deal with without getting involved in other people's problems. There may be a few people who may go out of their way to befriend you, which may or may not be ok depending on the person. There are addicts (not just alcoholics) who may want to just be friendly so they're not going through the process alone (certainly a worthy motivation), but others may have more sinister purposes, such as making new contacts to assist in smuggling substances into the facility (particularly drugs)—another reason not to want a car onsite. A sad reality.

* *

The balance of your stay in Detox will be highly structured. A typical daily routine is described below in Table 9.[16]

Table 9: The Daily Routine (once ambulatory, Day 2+)

Time	Activity
7:00 am:	*Wake Up.* They may even wake you up earlier to take your blood pressure and/or do other tests. During the first day, these tests may be done every few hours, including the middle of the night).
7:30 am:	*Breakfast.* This may be brought to you at first, then later you may go to a cafeteria-type area). You may shower during this time as well. Possibly a little free time to clear your head so to speak; detox/rehabs are not done with a military mindset.
8:45 am:	*Take medications.* These will likely be controlled and doled out by an onsite pharmacy at regular times.
9:00–11 am:	*Morning Meetings/Counseling session(s).* Likely a combination of individual and group sessions. Snacks may be available.
11:00–11:45 am:	*Free time.* On campus only; possible access to library, phones, or exercise facilities.
11:45–12:30 pm:	*Lunch.* Done in a defined group setting, with rotating tables and/or time slots. Some types of cases (e.g. acute cases/ involuntary/juvenile) may have their own segregated tables.
1 pm – 2 pm	*Free time.* May or may not be "structured" (e.g. in exercise area).
2 pm–4 pm:	*Group and/or personal counseling sessions.*
4 pm–6 pm:	*Free time* (e.g. phone and computer access, exercise)[17]
6 pm–8 pm:	*Dinner and Free time.* Depending on date/day of the week friends/family members may be allowed.
8 pm–9 pm:	*Alcoholics Anonymous or similar group meeting.* This is usually a "speaker" meeting, describing their personal life story. Usually very entertaining. Each person in the group may be "required" to speak about a related experience.
9 pm+:	*Free time until bedtime.* Lights out may be dictated, such as 11 pm. Computer/ TV use may depend on facility, type of care, and where you are in your detox.

Throughout the day social workers, drug counselors, and others may pull you aside to talk to you. Nurses may periodically take your vitals, and possibly medicate you if one of your symptoms starts worsening.

You will also attend meetings. The number and types you will attend will depend on where you are in your detox process, the facility, and whether you will also be staying at the facility post-detox. Assuming you will be staying at the facility as part of a broader rehab, there will be progressively *more* meetings as the focus shifts from your immediate physical health to your longer-term mental health and sobriety. Even in short-term detox you will be expected to attend meetings/counseling sessions as soon as you are physically able to.

These meetings and other sessions may be boring to some, but it is better to go, and <u>participate</u>, even if you don't want to or still feel unwell. They can be very helpful, not just educationally but particularly in getting you out of your head and the misery you are going through. They are often mandatory, so you won't be able to vegetate in your room anyway if you are physically able to attend.[18]

Checkout and the Next Few Days

Once you complete your program, you will be checked out in a manner very similar to a regular hospital: returning your belongings, signing forms, completing surveys, etc. If you are continuing in a Rehab program at the same facility after your Detox, there should not be any discharge/readmission. In fact, not much will change except you will likely be transferred to a room in a non-detox housing unit, and you will attend more/different meetings and counseling sessions.

* * *

The above (including the example schedule) may be very similar to what you can experience in Rehab, discussed next. _I strongly urge you to combine Detox and Rehab (in a medically supervised facility) if you can_. At a minimum, it provides a protected and controlled environment post-detox. More importantly it provides an excellent baseline of alcoholism education, which by itself is a solid, if unglamorous Level of Defense (discussed next). If you can, it is very important to avoid any time gap between Detox and Rehab, as it breaks your "momentum" and adds to the risk of an early relapse.

If you do have to have a gap (for work considerations, scheduling issues, etc.), try to spend the first few days after release/check-out with a trusted family member or friend (again, the importance of Level 4 is demonstrated). They can help you deal with any lingering feelings of unease and doubt, and protect against any temptations, meaning triggers. I strongly urge you to read and re-read this book throughout the process if you can, and particularly during the time immediately after your release from Detox or Detox/Rehab, as it can be a very vulnerable time for many newly sober alcoholics.

LEVEL 6—REHAB AND THERAPY

Rehabilitation programs and types of therapy are grouped together in this Level since many alcoholics initially (or only) encounter them in combination. It should also be noted that it is possible that Level 5 (Detox), Level 6 (Rehab and Therapy), and Level 7 (Join a Community) do not have to occur in that specific order, and can even be interwoven with each other as a practical matter.[1]

Regardless of timing, rehab and therapy have a similar purpose: to get the alcoholic to understand more about him or herself, their disease of alcoholism, and the alternatives to a life of drinking. They can also help refine your trigger list, priorities, and defenses. Depending on the specific rehab and/or therapeutic approach (and, more importantly, the attitude of the person undergoing the treatment) the result can be very effective. Both are highly recommended for the newly confessed alcoholic.

That said, while rehab and/or therapy can be sufficient to help an alcoholic get sober, their benefits are <u>often not long lasting</u> once the rehab or therapy is over. This comment is not meant to be an indictment of those approaches. Rather, once an alcoholic is back out on his or her own without the professional handholding, the pressures and temptation to relapse is much greater. That is the reason this Level is just one of many Levels of

Defense in this program. You will likely need *all* of them to defend against alcohol attacks *all* of the time.

Rehab and therapy are best at helping you to better understand the bigger picture of the disease of alcoholism, as well as helping you identify and explore deep, or even hidden, reasons for drinking (e.g. triggers) that you may be unable to unearth without therapeutic help. The discussion here is a synopsis of a much more comprehensive analysis provided in the main *How to Conquer Your Alcoholism* book; however, the key practical and immediate dimensions are covered here, particularly:

- What to expect in Inpatient Rehab
- What to expect in Outpatient Rehab, and advantages/ disadvantages to Inpatient Rehab
- How to select a Facility/Program, and
- Types of Therapy.

What is primarily not covered here are that is covered in the main book are the key legal and regulatory frameworks, laws, and regulations covering alcoholism treatment. At the time of this publication (July 2017) it is very likely such dimensions will change significantly in the pending repeal and replacement of the Affordable Care Act (Obamacare).

REHABILITATION TREATMENT PROGRAMS

Overcoming a dependency as invasive in nature as alcoholism can be tough to manage without help and, in some people's view (including mine), almost impossible. This difficulty is why many people advocate some type of formal rehabilitation treatment program. However, before you go down that road, you might consider talking to your general practitioner. Besides being aware of the current condition of your body (and hopefully <u>aware of your alcoholism and the specifics of how much you drink</u>), he or she might be able to refer you to an alcohol-related program in your local hospital. Many hospitals have addiction programs/departments that can help, potentially at much lower cost than a dedicated rehabilitation clinic. These types of hospital programs often require a doctor's referral, and there may be a wait time of days or weeks, which, of course, may sap your motivation to go. If this is the case, do as many positive things as you can (including rereading this book), and talk often with the family member(s) and friend(s) selected in Level 4 to keep your spirits and motivation levels up.

★ ★

Is Rehab Even Effective? Well...

Every day it seems there is news about some celebrity going "back" into rehab. I find it odd that hardly ever is there any questioning of the effectiveness of rehab such that it requires return visits. The implicit assumption in the media is that rehab is supposed to wipe the record clean, and somehow make you a new person, never to relapse again. Yet these celebrities go back to rehab again and again, and the press never explores why it didn't work the first time. This does a disservice to all involved.

According to the Substance Abuse and Mental Health Services Administration, **<u>six people out of every ten admitted were going back for repeat treatments</u>** in 2010. In other words, they had been to treatment before but relapsed after they got out.[2] The percentage of relapses is likely far higher since it doesn't account for people who gave up on rehab after the initial stint.

I was a bit surprised on learning the number was that high, but not *that* surprised. Rehab is not a *bad* process; in fact, it can be quite excellent in terms of getting you <u>initially</u> sober and arming you with some basic facts about the disease you are facing. However, the positive effects cannot be reasonably expected to last forever; the disease is just too powerful, and there are too many ways one can succumb. The relapse rate just reinforces the importance of the multi-level approach of The Conquer Program.

★ ★

There are two types of rehab programs: *Inpatient*, where the addict checks into a hospital or hospital-like setting and goes through a set of programs in a controlled environment, and *Outpatient*, where the addict goes through a similar set of rehabilitation activities but without the degree of control and oversight present in inpatient programs—essentially doing it part-time a few hours a week.

There are many hundreds if not thousands of rehab treatment programs in the U.S. How to find the right one for you is discussed later in this Level.

Inpatient Rehab

Inpatient rehab programs are usually <u>highly</u> controlled, strictly dictating patient activities and their do's and don'ts, often with the underlying assumption that patients will attempt to evade significant portions of the treatment program and indulge in their abused substance if given the chance. At a minimum, inpatient programs are intended to fully consume a patient's time and attention, from the time they wake up until "lights out" time.

Specifically, going into an inpatient treatment program involves entering a structured and restricted form of living. The rules and expectations will differ from rehab to rehab but will, usually, include:

- Patients will need to remain <u>completely</u> abstinent of alcohol during your stay. They will very likely kick your ass out (no money refunded, the court notified, etc.) if they catch you drinking. I saw some very creative ways of people trying to get their fix (both alcohol and drugs) while I was in rehab. As far as I know <u>all</u> were caught. It's tough to be drunk or high and not be caught at a Rehab facility!

- Patients will be expected to take part in the prescribed/ scheduled activities. If you are medically able to, you <u>will</u> be expected to go to these things; there is no sitting around on your ass just because you want to or don't feel "good". Each day will usually be highly structured, and you will need to adapt to this, or many facilities will kick you out as uncooperative.

- There will be rules to ensure that individuals maintain a high level of civility to each other. Patients may experience a lot of anger, but this will need to be managed effectively without causing too much disruption. Physical violence will very likely get you kicked out.[3]

- There will be restrictions on where you can go. You will, usually, not be allowed to leave the treatment facility; they may prohibit you parking your car on campus to help avoid the temptation.

- Contact with the outside world is usually limited. It might only be permissible to contact family members at certain times, including visitation, done on select days of the week, often around dinner time.

- You will be expected to attend groups where you will be asked to share personal information about yourself. Some group meetings will be Alcoholics Anonymous-type meetings.[4]

- Therapists and other clients may challenge the behavior of the individual (meaning get in your face).

- There are expectations that you will be completely honest. I strongly encourage you to do so; not doing so will diminish the possibility of success, and everyone can see you lying anyway.

- If the rehab is not gender-specific, there will be rules discouraging any romantic/sexual encounters. I saw/was told of a significant amount of such encounters. New sobriety plus daily/hourly contact with someone you are attracted to and have a lot in common with often equals strong sexual attraction. For this reason, housing is usually not coed.

The advantages of an Inpatient treatment program include:

- *Safety*. Believe it or not, protecting you from yourself and others is a key benefit of inpatient rehab. It reduces temptation, addresses if not soothes stress, and most of all helps protect you from the stresses and strains that would normally provide an excuse to drink, meaning that triggers can be avoided or carefully controlled. Inpatient programs also have medical staff on hand at all times to deal with everything from emergencies to daily medication needs.

- *Focus.* The individual is expected to and driven to devote themselves fully to overcoming their addiction. For this reason, taking sick time or a leave of absence from work is best,[5] otherwise use vacation time or other personal time.

- *Knowledge and Resources.* This includes training and educating the addict on how to deal with their alcoholism, as well as providing advice for how to handle challenges that will arise when they return to normal living. To me this is the #1 benefit of rehab programs.

- *Planning for the future.* These types of programs provide you time and encouragement to reflect on your life up to now and make plans for the future. My experience is that this is a worthy goal, rarely accomplished, but definitely worth trying.

- *Support.* This not only comes from the professionals but also from other patients, 24/7.[6]

There are some disadvantages associated with rehab that need to be considered including:

- *Transition.* The transition from rehab back to home can be a treacherous time, with a high risk of relapse. It can come as a shock to move from such a protective and supportive environment back to the real world.

  I did 28 days in a treatment center, and that was good while I was in there. But when I left the center, I was back in my own environment. The center actually gave me a false sense of security. I was safe there, when I got out, I wasn't so safe.[7]

- Publicly-funded rehabs can be overcrowded and may not provide enough individualized attention for clients. There can also be a long wait to get into public inpatient treatment programs.

- Entering rehab means devoting much time to recovery. It can be difficult for people to walk away from their responsibilities for this length of time.

A lot of the above may seem scary, even onerous. But everything is relative. Treatment centers in the U.S. are generally very compassionate, whereas in Russia drug and alcohol abuse is seen as a personal failing and addicts are treated *very* harshly, with the health care system and law enforcement placing sole blame on the individual for not succeeding at kicking their habit.

> *The treatment center does not handcuff addicts to their beds anymore. But caged together on double-decker bunks with no way out, they have no choice but to endure the agonies of withdrawal, the first step in a harsh, coercive approach to drug treatment that has gained wide support in Russia.*
>
> *A thick silence fills [a] little room crammed with tall metal beds, obscuring the fact that there are 37 men lying shoulder to shoulder, each lost in a personal world of misery. Outside the chamber, known as the quarantine room, 60 men who have emerged — after as long as a month with only bread and water or gruel — work at menial jobs, lift weights or cook in a regimen of continued isolation from the world that staff members said usually takes a year.*[8]

Much, much more than scary. Comparing rehab (in the U.S.) to something like this (or death) is one very effective way of looking at rehab—there are *far* worse things out there.

Outpatient Treatment Programs

Having done both Inpatient and Outpatient Programs, my view is that Inpatient programs are more likely to get you sober and on the <u>initial</u> path for continuing sobriety. This is obvious in many respects: you are in a dedicated environment, strictly controlled, monitored, and kept away (forcibly) from indulging in your habit. Good, if in a big brother sort of way.

It is also obvious as to why many people don't "do" inpatient. Giving up near total control over one's life can be very disconcerting. And there is a practical side: the addict can't afford to be away from their job and other life responsibilities for 30 to 90 days or longer. Cost is another key concern; even with insurance there can still be a hefty out-of-pocket. Here outpatient help can be key:

> *I entered an 18-week outpatient program and committed myself to changing how I viewed myself and the world around me. This was key to my successful recovery to date. There was no "graduation" from the program. I was provided an invaluable education in what tools and resources are necessary and available to begin the second half of my life, sober.* [9]
>
> *The decision was made for me. Once it was made clear to me that I was an alcoholic, and the consequences of the path I was on were dire, I committed to change. I went into an outpatient rehab program. I was fortunate. I committed to change and gave up fighting, and submitted to my higher power. Find a good outpatient program, they are around. Health insurance may cover the cost. City / county assistance may be available. Stick to it.* [10]

There is also a concern regarding the perception as it is hard to hide a weeks-long absence from your coworkers and friends without them guessing at the reason. Outpatient programs have certain advantages in that regard, including:

- Ability for the patient to stay in school or continue with employment while attending outpatient rehab.

- Easier to deal with the transition from rehab to home. The patient continues to live at home!

- It is a lot easier to keep attendance at an outpatient program a secret.

- An outpatient program will, usually, be a lot cheaper than an inpatient program.

- The individual will still be able to go home every night while attending the program. Of course, this may not necessarily be an advantage if the home life is chaotic and home to many triggers.

- Much lower cost compared to inpatient, even with insurance.

Outpatient programs will vary greatly, but they tend to include the following:

- The expectation to remain completely abstinent from alcohol or recreational drugs.

- An agreement to attend a certain number of therapy sessions each week, as well as seminars and activities.

- Rules governing the behavior of the individual while they attend the rehab. Ejection is a possibility for rules violation.

- Ability to modify the treatment plan if it is ineffective.

- An expectation to divulge personal information in one-on-one sessions and in group with other patients.

Outpatient rehab is not for everyone. The disadvantages roughly are the opposite of inpatient advantages, and include:

- Many more opportunities for temptation than those staying in inpatient rehab and much greater potential for acting on it.

- Far less support for addicts versus inpatient programs. Those personnel leading outpatient programs tend to be less well trained than inpatient staff, and not as accessible. The latter is based on my experiences, but could be totally different depending on the specific program.

- Far more distractions. This is far from trivial, and it can be difficult for people to build a new life if they have too many distractions at this phase of recovery.

- Little avoidance of triggers, except during actual program attendance.

In short, both Inpatient and Outpatient programs can be very beneficial to the newly admitted or newly relapsed alcoholic. In my experience and opinion, Inpatient is much more effective for achieving *initial* sobriety (not surprising given the degree of control). Outpatient is better (particularly from a practical standpoint) for *"refreshing"* inpatient lessons and helping maintain already achieved sobriety. However, the "staying power" of this refresh in keeping you sober can have limited longevity.

The huge problem, of course, is that both cost money. Even if you have insurance, it will only cover certain types of treatments, restrict your facility choice, possibly cap the amount of coverage in terms of $ or days,[11] and still have a hefty co-pay/deductible. Those with no insurance, or more common today, unaffordable deductibles are much more limited in terms of options of course, but there are some public funded programs that may be available depending on the state you live in and your financial situation.

So even if formal treatment programs seem to work for you initially, they have a natural "expiration date" after which you are on your own. **This is one more example of why you have to have a "multiple layers of defense" strategy in building a sober life. Just going to rehab and expecting that to have miraculously "cured" you for all time no matter how successful it was is naïve at best and incredibly stupid at worst.**

* * *

The availability of both inpatient and outpatient rehabilitation services is of course highly dependent upon an alcoholic's insurance coverage. In addition, for employed alcoholics a major concern is how they practically obtain full-time or near full-time treatment without jeopardizing their job. Regulatory protections are in place to help address both of these concerns.

How Do I Select a Facility and Program?

As mentioned in the Detox section, the good news/bad news here is that *you* may not be able to select it, your insurance carrier will. While that will most likely be the case for inpatient treatment, you will likely have more flexibility for outpatient care.

If you do have a choice, there are several considerations beyond cost (if you have that luxury). There are several commercial online sources to help such as Recovery.org (http://www.recovery.org/topics/find-the-best-residential-inpatient-rehab-center/), The Gape Center (www.theagapecenter.com/Treatment-Centers/index.htm), and Rehabs.com (http://www.rehabs.com/about/alcohol-rehab/), which like all such sites have a profit motive and hence possibly bias. Non-profit sources include the Substance Abuse and Mental Health Services Administration's (SAMSHA) Substance Abuse Facility Locator at http://www.samhsa.gov/Treatment/, and various state-specific organizations that can be found at https://www.samhsa.gov/sites/default/files/ssadirectory.pdf.

If you do have options, there are several criteria you should look for besides inpatient versus outpatient, coverage, and overall cost (make sure you pay close attention to how your deductible works). These include:

- *Variety of programs.* Types of supervised programs are covered in Level 5, and should be primarily determined by your doctor and possibly the facility itself, depending on your condition at the time of entry.
- *Family Involvement.* Some (inpatient) centers allow frequent interaction with family members. This interaction may or may not be desirable; you will have to decide that for yourself. For some, it can be an integral part of engaging key family and friends (e.g. Level 4),

while others may not want any reminders of the outside world. There is no right or wrong decision here, just what is best for <u>you</u>.

- *Child Care.* As discussed in the Detox level, the need for child care can be a significant issue. In Rehab it is even worse, due to the longer stay involved. Some Rehab facilities do offer child care, but in the Author's opinion having the children stay at home with a relative is the better course of action.

- *Certifications and Licenses.* All quality facilities should have competent counselors certified in treating chemical dependency, such as <u>American Society of Addiction Medicine (ASAM) certification</u>.[12] Ask. Check to see if the facility is licensed as a hospital by the state (such requirements may vary greatly by state).

- *Transition help.* Is there a transitional program to help individuals move from inpatient or residential treatment back into community life? Or do they kind of show you the door and forget about you? This can include:

- *Follow-up and support services.* These could include Internet webcam consultations and follow-up by a physician. A relatively new twist in the treatment world that can be effective.

- *Experience.* I love it when counselors are former addicts. Conversely, I don't have a great deal of faith in people who do not have personal experience in addiction, either themselves or with a loved one. They are just ivory tower academics, no matter how many "studies" they have under their belt.[13]

- *12-Step programs.* Despite my criticisms of Alcoholics Anonymous (discussed briefly in Level 7, and more extensively in the main book) there is much good that can come from such programs, particularly in introducing you to the concept of an alcoholic community.

- *Attitude on withdrawal-related drugs.* This can be interesting, in that some facilities may support the use of various drugs to help with your treatment (more information on such drugs can be found at https://en.wikipedia.org/wiki/Alcohol_detoxification). I divide the use of drugs during detox/rehab into two categories: *medical need* and *patient comfort*. The ability to treat any acute medical need such as the treatment of DTs is an important safety net element of *any* inpatient treatment facility. However, some facilities (particularly outpatient) also use drugs to treat other aspects of alcoholism such as using Naltrexone to reduce cravings. Doing so comes with its own tradeoffs.

- *Convenience.* The need for treatment to be intertwined between personal and work commitments can be logistically difficult, awkward, or downright scary.[14]

This last item, convenience, is a tricky one, particularly as the best programs for you may well not be the closest to you. This is particularly true if you want the "best" (as in most well-known at least) such as Hazelden (http://www.hazelden.org/) with multiple locations skewed towards the west half of the country, or The Betty Ford Clinic (http://www.bettyfordcenter.org/index.php) in California. You will likely have to expect pretty large out-of-pocket costs regardless of insurance for these kinds of programs.

For outpatient programs, convenience leaps to the top of the list next to the cost. Since you are trying to live the rest of your life at the same time (e.g. work, school, kids), convenience may trump everything else, so you might expect some great variability in quality. In my experience though all seemed to cover the basics well.[15]

THERAPY AND THE CONQUER PROGRAM

There are *many* types of therapy, with over 100 listed on www.GoodTherapy.org alone.[16] The two key questions: 1) Is it worth the bother? And 2) How do I choose one?

During my time in therapy (off and on over three years not counting rehab-based therapy sessions) I was a (very) reluctant participant, pushed into it by my (now) ex-wife. Furthermore, I had no idea and less interest in the specialty of my therapists let alone the different types of therapy that were possible. This indifference naturally led to therapy having zero impact on my alcoholism.

Is Therapy Worth the Bother?

In hindsight, I now recognize the value therapy can provide in defending against alcoholism, *if* the patient is a willing participant in the therapy, *if* the therapy is part of a broader treatment effort, and *if* the type of therapy is synergetic with that program.

You will have to decide for yourself if you will be willing to go to therapy. If you are coerced into it or have problems talking to strangers, therapy may well not be for you. But if you are open to the concept, and can afford at least a few sessions, *I would strongly encourage you to try it.* While not a necessity for The Conquer Program, if done right Therapy can help you more quickly and accurately determine and refine your triggers and trigger defenses. Done incorrectly however, it will be a waste of time and money.

The key to doing Therapy "correctly" is finding the right therapist. While you may be constrained by your insurance in your choice of doctors, most insurers have some flexibility in the specific selection of therapists. For purposes of being <u>synergistic</u> with The Conquer Program, use the following explanations of different therapies as a starting point. Again, I am not a doctor, but when it comes to mental health therapy, particularly for a motivation-sensitive issue as alcoholism, I believe it is the *patient* that should drive the therapy, otherwise there will likely be little impact.

★ ★

What Triggers Can Particularly Benefit from Therapy?

Table 3 in Level 2 provides synopses of all the triggers analyzed within The Conquer Program. In particular, each trigger as a "Key Defense" section that lists at least one Level of the program that should form the core of its defense. Several list Therapy as a possible defense. These include:

- Anger (for deep-seated, long-term Anger issues)
- Anxiety and Depression (particularly psychiatric therapy w/ drug treatments)
- Guilt (deep-rooted, long-term guilt), and
- Sex and Victim (particularly for childhood abuse-related issues).

All of these can be very complex, and potentially very difficult to get to the root causes/issues behind their being major triggers for you without professional assistance. In finding the right therapist for you, make sure that if you have one or more of the above issues that that your therapist also specializes in (or at least has experience with) the treatment of those issues.

★ ★

Although there are many types of therapy, when it comes to synergies with The Conquer Program, the options become much clearer and simpler. It is those therapies that focus on the *motivations for* and *root causes of* your reasons for drinking that are the therapies best suited for this program; of which there are just a handful—most based on some form of behavioral analysis. Table 10 next summarizes (in alphabetical order) the types of therapy most likely to be synergistic with The Conquer Program. Additional information on each follow next in Table 10.

Table 10: Types of Psychotherapy Best Suited to The Conquer Program

Therapy	Description	Pros	Cons
Alcoholism Behavioral Couples Therapy (ABCT)	ABCT is based on two assumptions: Intimate partner behaviors and couple interactions can be triggers for drinking, and a positive intimate relationship is a key source of motivation to change drinking behavior. *Using cognitive-behavioral therapy* (discussed next), ABCT aims to identify and decrease the partner's behaviors that cue or reinforce the client's drinking; strengthen the partner's support of the client's efforts to change; increase positive couple interactions by improving interpersonal communication and problem-solving skills as a couple; and improve the client's coping skills and relapse prevention techniques to achieve and maintain abstinence.	• Outpatient; • Cognitive-Behavioral- based (CBT) (Trigger-focused)	• Different motivations or level of commitment can jeopardize chances of success; • Unlikely to address triggers not involving partners
Cognitive-Behavioral Therapy (CBT) **RECOM-MENDED**	Cognitive behavior therapy is based on the idea that feelings and behaviors are caused by a person's thoughts, not on outside stimuli like people, situations, and events. People may not be able to change their circumstances, but they can change how they think about them and therefore change how they feel and behave, according to cognitive-behavior therapists. In the treatment for alcohol and drug dependence, *the goal of cognitive behavioral therapy is to teach the person to recognize situations where they are most likely to drink or use drugs, avoid these circumstances if possible, and cope with other problems and behaviors which may lead to their substance abuse.*	• *Generally, most synergistic with The Conquer Program* • Can be done in short time-frames • Highly structured - can be provided in different formats • *Emphasizes useful and practical strategies that can be used in everyday life – even after the treatment has finished*	• May need extra work between sessions • May not be suitable for people w/ more complex mental health needs • Involves confronting your emotions & anxieties; may be un-comfortable • May not address deep or child-hood issues. [17]
Motivational Enhancement Therapy	Motivational Enhancement Programs are designed to raise drinkers' awareness of the impact alcohol has on their lives, as well as the lives of family, co-workers and society. They are encouraged to accept responsibility for past actions and make a commitment to change future behavior	• Helps get the alcoholic out of their shell – to think beyond "me" and the selfishness that comes with alcoholism	• Can be used as intensive Guilt-trip for the alcoholic—against the principles of this program.
Step Facilitation Therapy	This peer-support approach encourages people to become involved with a 12-step or similar program that complements professionally supervised therapy, e.g., go to meeting but come to my couch as well.	• Easy to find • No/Low cost (group part) • Provides sense of community	• One-Size-Fits-All/ Little Customization (in group)

Behavioral Couples Therapy

Alcohol behavioral couple therapy (ABCT) is an outpatient treatment for individuals with alcohol use disorders and their intimate partners. ABCT is based on two assumptions: Intimate partner behaviors and couple interactions can be triggers for drinking, and a positive intimate relationship is a key source of motivation to change drinking behavior.

Using cognitive-behavioral therapy (discussed next), ABCT aims to identify and decrease the partner's behaviors that cue or reinforce the client's drinking; strengthen the partner's support of the client's efforts to change; increase positive couple interactions by improving interpersonal communication and problem-solving skills as a couple; and improve the client's coping skills and relapse prevention techniques to achieve and maintain abstinence.

The treatment program consists of 2-3 hours of assessment for treatment planning, followed by 12-20 weekly, 90-minute therapy sessions for the client with his or her partner. The number of treatment sessions may be increased if sessions of less than 90 minutes are desired. Treatment follows cognitive-behavioral principles applied to couples therapy and specific therapeutic interventions for alcohol use disorders. The optimal implementation of ABCT occurs in the context of an existing clinic or private practice with certified/licensed mental health or addictions professionals who have a background in treating alcohol use disorders and knowledge of cognitive-behavioral therapy.[18]

Therapy includes providing the non-dependent partner with training on communication and support strategies that facilitate the advancement of treatment and sobriety. An integral component of couple's therapy involves developing a "contract" agreeing that:

- The alcoholic-dependent partner will commit to abstinence
- The non-dependent partner will offer continual support and reinforcement
- Neither partner will discuss past addictive behavior and its consequences
- Neither partner will discuss the future and misuse outside of the therapy sessions."[19]

Cognitive-Behavioral Therapy (CBT)

Cognitive behavior therapy is mostly used to treat depression, anxiety disorders, phobias, and other mental disorders, but it has also proven valuable in treating alcoholism and drug addiction, especially as part of an overall program of recovery. _CBT is the most synergistic form of therapy with The Conquer Program._

Cognitive-behavioral coping skills treatment is a focused therapeutic approach to helping substance-dependent people become abstinent by using the same learning processes the person used to develop alcohol and drug dependence initially.

Cognitive behavior therapy is based on the idea that feelings and behaviors are caused by a person's thoughts, not on outside stimuli like people, situations, and events. People may not be able to change their circumstances, but they can change how they think about them and thus change how they feel and behave, according to CBT therapists.

In the treatment for alcohol and drug dependence, *the goal of cognitive behavioral therapy is to teach the person to recognize situations where they are most likely to drink or use drugs, avoid these circumstances if possible, and cope with other problems and behaviors which may lead to their substance abuse.*

According to the National Association of Cognitive-Behavioral Therapists, there are several CBT approaches. These include <u>Rational Emotive Behavior Therapy</u>, <u>Rational Living Therapy</u>, and <u>Dialectic Behavior Therapy</u>.[20]

In addition, there are a wide variety of professionals that can help in behavioral-related treatment, from M.D.s to Counselor's, as seen below.

Types of Professionals Involved in Care

Many health professionals can play a role in treatment. Below is a list of providers and the type of care they may offer.

Provider Type	Degrees & Credentials	Treatment Type
Primary Care Provider	M.D., D.O. (Doctor of Osteopathic Medicine), additionally you may see a **Nurse Practitioner** or **Physician's Assistant**	Medications, Brief Behavioral Treatment, Referral to Specialist
Psychiatrist	M.D., D.O.	Medications, Behavioral Treatment
Psychologist	Ph.D., Psy.D., M.A.	Behavioral Treatment
Social Worker	M.S.W. (Master of Social Work), L.C.S.W. (Licensed Clinical Social Worker)	Behavioral Treatment
Alcohol Counselor	Varies—most States require some form of certification	Behavioral Treatment

Individuals are advised to talk to their doctors about the best form of primary treatment.

Figure 16: Types of Behavioral-Related Health-Care Professionals[21]

Another description of CBT is: "*Cognitive behavior therapy helps alcohol-dependent people acquire skills to recognize, cope and change problem-drinking behaviors. By understanding what needs are filled by drinking, the therapist can work with an alcoholic patient to find new ways to address needs that don't include drinking and modify psychological dependence on drugs. During therapy sessions, patients are taught essential coping skills to:*

- *Recognize what triggers the urge to drink*
- *Manage negative moods and emotional vulnerabilities*
- *Change social outlets and friendships to focus on something other than drinking.*"[22]

The two underlined bullets above are why CBT is the most synergistic with The Conquer Program: the first bolded bullet describes the need to understand your triggers, and the second bolded bullet describes the need to find alternative activities (defenses) for those triggers.

Motivational Enhancement Therapy (MET)

Motivational Enhancement Therapy (MET) is based on principles of motivational psychology and is designed to produce rapid, internally-motivated change. <u>This treatment strategy does not attempt to guide and train the client, step by step, through recovery, but instead employs motivational strategies to mobilize the client's resources.</u> MET consists of four carefully planned and individualized treatment sessions. The first two sessions focus on structured feedback from the initial assessment, future plans, and motivation for change. The final two sessions at the midpoint and end of treatment provide opportunities for the therapist to reinforce progress, encourage reassessment, and provide an objective perspective on the process of change.[23]

The above description from the NIAAA seems reasonable if a bit vague. Another description I found states: *"These [Motivational Enhancement] Programs are designed to raise drinkers' awareness of the impact alcohol has on their lives, as well as the lives of family, co-workers and society. They are encouraged to accept responsibility for past actions and make a commitment to change future behavior."*[24] <u>In short, MET tries to "Guilt" the hell out of you.</u> The Conquer Program advocates *ignoring* Guilt, as it is a very hard trigger to design defenses for, but for some people MET may be effective.

Step Facilitation Therapy

This peer-support approach encourages people to become involved with a 12-step or similar program that *complements* professionally supervised therapy, e.g., go to Alcoholics Anonymous meetings but come to my couch as well. To a certain extent this begs the question as to what kind of therapy is used in the private/personal part of the therapy (e.g. CBT, etc.)? This could work well if the private therapy (regardless of type) tries to capitalize on and extend what the addict learned in the group meetings.

More broadly, twelve-step facilitation therapy is an active engagement strategy designed to increase the likelihood of a substance abuser becoming affiliated with and actively involved in 12-step self-help groups, thereby promoting abstinence. Three key ideas predominate: (1) *acceptance*, which includes the realization that drug addiction is a chronic, progressive disease over which one has no control, that life has become unmanageable because of drugs, that willpower alone is insufficient to overcome the problem, and that abstinence is the only alternative; (2) *surrender*, which involves giving oneself over to a higher power, accepting the fellowship and support structure of other recovering addicted individuals, and following the recovery activities laid out by the 12-step program; and (3) *active involvement* in the 12-step meetings and related activities.

★ ★

Is The Conquer Program a 12-Step Program?

No. While initially it might not seem much different (e.g. one more number), it is quite different. 12-steps programs like AA's are strictly a *process*, which implicitly presumes you will not reach longer-term sobriety until after you have completed *all* 12 steps. The Conquer Program, while having some process elements, is about putting together a series of defenses, any <u>one</u> of which can be very effective in getting and staying sober.

More broadly, the key difference is that step programs—particularly AA—are *faith-based.* You are turning yourself over to God (or a "higher power") to help you get sober. While there is nothing inherently wrong with that (if it works), the issue is that there is no in-depth analysis of the *motivations* behind your drinking. The AA 12-Step programs are "one-size-fits-all", with no recognition of an alcoholic's history or particular circumstances.

In contrast, The Conquer Program is trigger-focused, identifying the *root causes* and developing very specific, very *custom* mental (and physical) defenses to that individual.

★ ★

There are many 12-step programs, with only two specifically related to alcohol: Alcoholics Anonymous (AA) and Al-Anon (for loved ones of alcoholics). Each follows some variation of the "first" 12-Step program, Alcoholics Anonymous:

The Alcoholics Anonymous Twelve Steps

1. We admitted we were powerless over alcohol—that our lives had become unmanageable.
2. Came to believe that a Power greater than ourselves could restore us to sanity.
3. Made a decision to turn our will and our lives over to the care of God *as we understood Him*.
4. Made a searching and fearless moral inventory of ourselves.
5. Admitted to God, to ourselves, and to another human being the exact nature of our wrongs.
6. Were entirely ready to have God remove all these defects of character.
7. Humbly asked Him to remove our shortcomings.
8. Made a list of all persons we had harmed, and became willing to make amends to them all.
9. Made direct amends to such people wherever possible, except when to do so would injure them or others.
10. Continued to take personal inventory, and when we were wrong, promptly admitted it.
11. Sought through prayer and meditation to improve our conscious contact with God *as we understood Him*, praying only for knowledge of His will for us and the power to carry that out.
12. Having had a spiritual awakening as the result of these steps, we tried to carry this message to alcoholics, and to practice these principles in all our affairs.

There are several keys to these kinds of step facilitation programs, most notably their emphasis on faith/spirituality/God/religion (depending on your interpretation).

The full list of 12 Step programs (with links) includes:[25]

Table 11: Twelve Step Programs

AA – <u>Alcoholics Anonymous</u>	MA – <u>Marijuana Anonymous</u>
ACA – <u>Adult Children of Alcoholics</u>	NA – <u>Narcotics Anonymous</u>
<u>Al-Anon/Alateen</u>, for friends and families of alcoholics	N/A – <u>Neurotics Anonymous</u>, for recovery from <u>mental and emotional illness</u>
CA – <u>Cocaine Anonymous</u>	Nar-Anon - for friends and family members of <u>addicts</u>
CMA – <u>Crystal Meth Anonymous</u> <u>Co-Anon</u>, for friends and family of <u>addicts</u>	NicA – <u>Nicotine Anonymous</u>
CoDA – <u>Co-Dependents Anonymous</u>, for people working to end patterns of dysfunctional relationships and develop functional and healthy relationships	OLGA – <u>Online Gamers Anonymous</u>
COSA – an <u>auxiliary group of Sex Addicts Anonymous</u>	PA – <u>Pills Anonymous</u>, for recovery from prescription pill addiction
COSLAA – <u>CoSex and Love Addicts Anonymous</u>	SA – <u>Sexaholics Anonymous</u>
DA – <u>Debtors Anonymous</u>	SA – <u>Smokers Anonymous</u>
EA – <u>Emotions Anonymous</u>, for recovery from <u>mental and emotional illness</u>	SAA – <u>Sex Addicts Anonymous</u>
FA – <u>Families Anonymous</u>, for relatives and friends of addicts	SCA – <u>Sexual Compulsives Anonymous</u>
FA – <u>Food Addicts in Recovery Anonymous</u>	SIA – <u>Survivors of Incest Anonymous</u>
FAA – <u>Food Addicts Anonymous</u>	SLAA – <u>Sex and Love Addicts Anonymous</u>
GA – <u>Gamblers Anonymous</u>	SRA – <u>Sexual Recovery Anonymous</u>
<u>Gam-Anon</u>/<u>Gam-A-Teen</u>, for friends and family members of <u>problem gamblers</u>	UA – <u>Underearners Anonymous</u>
HA – <u>Heroin Anonymous</u>	WA – <u>Workaholics Anonymous</u>

Alcoholics Anonymous and its 12 Steps are covered more in Level 7—Join a Community, along with other communities that use some variation of the Steps concept.

How Do I Select a Therapist?

Overall, the key is to find the right doctor with the right type of therapy and demeanor for you, and for the appropriate amount of time. Remember, the key to your Therapist is to be *synergistic* with the broader Conquer Program. This means you want help in:

- Identifying your triggers
- Exploring those triggers in detail (particularly their root causes)
- Determining their priority, and
- Figuring out defenses to suit your personality.

Therapy can also be very helpful in figuring out your trigger history (how they have changed over time) and in general to bounce ideas regarding your alcoholism off someone impartial and sympathetic.

That said, demeanor is particularly an understated but important criterion; after all, you are telling this person your deepest secrets, so you should have *some* sort of connection with them. For example, my first therapist said practically nothing during our sessions, which was extremely frustrating—in hindsight I *wanted* his insights, or at least to ask me probing questions. Instead he went the "how do you feel about that?" route.

★ ★

Types of Therapist Styles

Therapists have a style like anyone else. Some will ask you specific questions (Did you want to drink at all this week? Why?). Some will be generalists (How did your week go?). Some will be even *more* general (How do you feel? What do you want to talk about?). And some will just sit there and listen to you and say hardly anything. You have to figure out which style works for you, which is not easy, and what a potential doctor's style *is*—very tough to do before seeing them. I have a personal bias towards ones that focus on asking progressively detailed questions that help you get to the heart of whatever matter you are discussing, but it is just that—a personal bias. The style has to work for <u>you</u>.

★ ★

One helpful resource that provides a great discussion of therapist styles can be found at http://alcoholrehab.com/alcohol-rehab/rehab-therapist-styles/. It discusses various therapist styles such as *"Telling Style"*, *"Teaching Style"*, *"Supporting Style"*, and *"Delegating Style"*.

★ ★

How Long Should I Stay in Therapy?

For purposes of The Conquer Program, the short answer is: as long (or short) as you need to nail your drinking triggers. That should take weeks, not years. One interesting opinion I found in my research (I learned there are no "facts" in Therapy) is that the "right" amount of time in therapy is 12 to 16 sessions. This seems reasonable on the surface; not enough sessions do not allow you to develop a rapport and "peel the onion" to get at your core issues. More sessions are probably a waste of time and money; if you haven't figured out the issues after 4 months of sessions it is probably not going to happen.

★ ★

Selecting a Therapist is similar to selecting a Rehab facility, in that you may not have much choice since your insurance carrier will likely determine the treatment options available to you. However, as noted earlier you will have some choice in theory. *The big problem today for people seeking therapy is that many, even most therapists are not accepting new patients.* They are booked solid. Good news if you a therapist, not good if looking for a therapist with somewhat scarce skills in addiction therapy.

Like for rehab facilities, there are a number of websites that help you find therapists. Note that I use the term "therapist" to cover both psychologists and psychiatrists. Some equate the term with only psychologists or even including "psychotherapists" and "counselors," that while trained are not degreed like psychologists and psychiatrists.[26] While all are trained professionals, only psychiatrists are Medical Doctors (M.D.); thus, they are the only ones that can prescribe medications. However, that does not necessarily mean one is better than another; both require many years of training and education. In the end, it may be the intangibles such as style that make the most difference in your therapy, not the number of diplomas on the wall.

There are two online sources for therapists from Psychology Today, a respected industry publication. One for psychologists is at http://therapists.psychologytoday.com/rms/prof_search.php. A similar site (http://psychiatrists.psychologytoday.com/rms/prof_search.php) is available for psychiatrists. The problem with these sites is that they key off your zip code only, so you then have to search individual doctors for their specialty. However, each doctor describes their approach at least a little, which may give you some indications in terms of specialty area and the elusive "style". There are also other commercial specialty (for addiction) sites that may be helpful, including one from The Association for Addiction Professionals at http://www.naadac.org/sap-directory.

UNCONVENTIONAL TREATMENT APPROACHES

If there is one overall answer to the question *"What should I do to stay sober?"* it is *"Whatever works!"* If standing on your head for an hour a day keeps you sober (and sane), I'd say go for it. While a silly example, it doesn't mean there aren't other somewhat unusual methods that you can use as a defense or safety net; a few of the higher potential ones are discussed here. You can do one or more of them in addition to the more "traditional" rehab and therapy methods described earlier. Or you can do one instead, or not at all. But at least consider them; again, the mantra is **_Whatever Works!_**

The essence of this section is that a) there are a variety of more unusual treatment approaches for alcoholism, b) while some border on quackery, some of them have enough success they are worth considering, though c) the likelihood of them working is likely small, but d) what is important is if it works for you.

All of the programs/treatments below have been around at least a few years, and have persons who swear by (or at) them, so you still might consider at least investigating them as a possible extra defense against one or more triggers, or to help your overall sobriety.

Acupuncture

Western medicine has proved to be highly effective in the treatment of many diseases and conditions. However, it is not always effective or only partially so. Thus, people will often turn to complementary treatment approaches for a solution. Acupuncture, through its use of tiny needles, is one such treatment approach and probably the most widely used.

Acupuncture is said to be effective in preventing and curing many physical, as well as mental conditions. It has been used for at least 2,000 years in China and other parts of Asia.

Acupuncture is based on the idea that physical and mental symptoms are caused by imbalances within the body. Chinese medicine views such imbalances as leading to blockages of Qi. The ability of Qi to move unimpeded is important because this is the life force. When this force gets trapped, it leads to mental or physical symptoms. There are 14 major energy paths in the body, and these are called *meridians*. Along these meridian paths are hundreds of acupuncture points. Acupuncture uses tiny needles to promote the flow of Qi. These needles are placed in specific acupuncture points depending on the problem.

Acupuncture and Addiction Treatment

Acupuncture has been used in the treatment of addiction since at least the early 1970s. *While Acupuncture is not viewed as a complete treatment for withdrawals, it has proved to reduce the strength some of the more unpleasant symptoms.* Acupuncture is believed to be beneficial because it promotes:

- Less severe withdrawal symptoms
- Reduced experiences of craving
- Improved ability to sleep at night
- Reduced anxiety and depression.

The primary benefit appears to be in helping with the withdrawals process, *particularly as a complementary therapy*. Many rehabs now offer such treatments to clients. A good unbiased source of information can be found at http://www.webmd.com/fibromyalgia/tc/acupuncture-topic-overview.

Aversion Therapy

Aversion Therapy is considered by some as a non-traditional, even fringe-type of therapy, *but it can be very effective if done right*. At its heart is an approach that looks to make you *physically sick* when you drink alcohol. This concept plays a key part in Level 11—Make Yourself Sick of Alcohol (with major modifications and enhancements), but I introduce it here to expose alcoholics to a significantly different concept in trying to get sober.

At the core of aversion therapy is the concept of breaking the association between alcohol and pleasure, and establishing a new association between alcohol and pain and misery.

You may have heard little or nothing about aversion therapy. There is a good reason for this: there are relatively few hospitals/clinics that offer this treatment, and they are all expensive—generally well into the five-digit territory. While they profess to take insurance, the bald fact is that insurance, usually, will not take *them*. Typical insurance plans nearly universally cover only traditional types of outpatient/inpatient substance abuse help.

So, what is Aversion Therapy? It is a form of psychological treatment in which the patient is exposed to a stimulus while simultaneously being subjected to some form of discomfort. The primary goal of aversion therapies is to produce an aversive reaction to alcohol by establishing a conditioned response to cues associated with drinking. The conditioning can be accomplished by using electric shock, apneic paralysis, chemical agents such as Disulfiram/Antabuse (discussed shortly), or negative image-based[27] techniques.[28]

This conditioning is intended to cause the patient to associate a stimulus with unpleasant sensations in order to stop the specific behavior. In other words, *give you something to make you sick while you are doing something you want to do, but are not supposed to be doing.*

The *premise* of aversion therapy with respect to alcoholism assumes the brain has, over time, directly "learned" that drinking alcohol equals some very positive physiological benefits, such as relaxation, reduced stress, and pleasure in general. We alcoholics thus come to rely on drinking for these benefits; to the point that we feel we cannot achieve them <u>without</u> alcohol. Thus, there is a need under this premise to unlearn or "break" this association and consequential behavior (drinking), <u>essentially by punishing you</u>. The main way of doing this in a clinical session is combining certain drugs with drinking, often with a drug called Disulfiram.

★ ★

How Disulfiram (Antabuse) Works in Aversion Therapy?

<u>Disulfiram</u> changes the way your body breaks down (<u>metabolizes</u>) alcohol. If you drink alcohol while you are taking disulfiram, you will experience uncomfortable symptoms, including severe <u>nausea</u>, vomiting, and <u>headache</u>. These symptoms discourage you from drinking alcohol by making it unpleasant.

The effectiveness of Disulfiram varies. When taken as directed, it can help you completely stop drinking by increasing the number of days you go without a drink. It works best if you are motivated to stop drinking and you take the medicine as directed.

The effects from Disulfiram are <u>intentionally unpleasant</u> to help encourage you to remain sober. Disulfiram effects generally last from 30 minutes to 2 hours. When you take disulfiram and do not drink, the main effect is drowsiness. Use caution when you drive or operate machinery while taking this medicine.[29]

★ ★

Disulfiram (also known as Antabuse) is by no means a miracle drug for alcoholism; indeed, <u>no such drug exists</u> (See Level 11 for more information on drugs for alcoholism). The typical benefit achieved is a short-term stoppage of drinking, which combined with other mechanisms (like this program) may help build the momentum for long-term sobriety.

Many individuals who take Disulfiram describe feelings of being liberated when taking this medication as it makes the option of drinking not a pleasant one. However, *if you stop and the root causes of drinking have not been addressed, you are essentially right back where you started.*

One of the most well-known Aversion Therapy clinics, at least in the western U.S., is Schick Shadel Hospital, based in Seattle (*http://www.schickshadel.com*).

Problems with Aversion Therapy

While aversion therapy proponents claim it is a relatively successful method for dealing with alcohol addiction, there are a number of issues associated with it. First, long-term compliance is needed as an individual may be expected to take nausea-inducing drugs for <u>many years</u>. Also, alcoholics can just quit Disulfiram or a similar drug if they wish to return to their addiction. There are high dropout rates. It may only be effective for a specific type of alcohol, not alcohol in general. It accentuates the negative with no positive reinforcement.

While in its <u>traditional</u> form, aversion therapy does little to address the underlying craving for alcohol and its associated triggers for the individual alcoholic. ***But***, as utilized it in Level 11—Make Yourself Sick of Alcohol, its target purpose is modified for specifically dealing with the triggers of Proximity, Smell, and Taste. I have personally found it to be extremely effective for those triggers, but as the process can be physically risky, Level 11 is optional.

Hypnosis

Hypnosis, also known as hypnotherapy, as an addiction treatment is gaining some credibility in the medical and psychiatric communities. It can be of help for those who have gone through the initial stages of rehabilitation cope with cravings and stave off relapse. Before attempting Hypnosis, the alcoholic has to detoxify his or her system completely. (The need for complete detoxification before attempting hypnotherapy is repeatedly emphasized in every source I researched).

A medical professional offering hypnosis as a treatment for addiction is a hypnotherapist. This person guides the recovering alcoholic into a trance-like mental state in which the person is more susceptible to ideas and suggestions. In this state, those being hypnotized can become more imaginative and better at problem solving. In short, they are in prime position to sort out strategies for conquering their own addictive behaviors.

★ ★

What Does Hypnosis Really Feel Like?

The experience of a *hypnotic trance* is not so unusual or strange. To the contrary, it feels vaguely familiar to countless other moments in your life where you were absorbed in a zone, lost in thought, enthralled by bliss, or perhaps simply meditating. Meditation is the closest you can come to a state of trance without being guided there as you would experience in hypnosis.[30]

★ ★

However, _the only way that hypnosis can be effective as a treatment for addiction is if the person being hypnotized wants to give up their destructive habits and behaviors_. The treatment does not change minds or induce new outlooks. Instead, it helps to hone and refine a preexisting mindset.

It is important to understand that hypnosis is not a cure-all for addiction, but it can serve a *complementary* role in the treatment. It's considered particularly useful in helping recovered alcoholics stay on the right track, e.g., as a kind of maintenance therapy.

During this relaxed state, the person being hypnotized is more open to exploring the mechanics of their addiction to alcohol. This openness allows them to explore the ebb and flow of their cravings (with the goal of putting together strategies to overcome them) without any stress or feelings of guilt getting in the way. Author's Note: The "mechanics" to me sound very much like the underlying causes of drinking, e.g. your triggers.

In some cases, the hypnotherapist may also train their patients to practice self-hypnosis in their daily lives. Going into a lightly hypnotic state is an excellent way to overcome a craving in real time.[31]

Meditation

When the word *meditation* is mentioned, most people will get a mental image of somebody sitting cross-legged with their eyes closed humming some sort of mantra nonsense. While it is true that this is how some meditators practice, it is certainly not by any means the full story. It is possible to meditate in a number of positions including sitting, standing, and lying down. It is even possible to meditate when doing everyday movements or physical activities such as walking, running, and even karate! But what the hell does it have to do with addiction treatment?

★ ★

What is Meditation?

Meditation is a practice often associated with Eastern traditions but is present in almost every world culture in some form. Traditionally a part of spiritual practices in India, China, Japan, and other Eastern cultures, Western versions of meditation are often more focused on relaxation and stress reduction.

There are *thousands* of specific meditation practices. Some practices focus on quieting and clearing the mind to experience a deep sense of presence in silence and connection to the spiritual world. Others bring the mind's focus to a single, specific thought or intention. The practice is, usually, self-guided and can involve the use of music, chant, breathing techniques, specific postures, or focus on a visualization or external image. [32]

In essence, it is a way of clearing and/or relaxing one's mind, helping to discard troubles of the day and helping put you "in a better place," mentally, for a period of time ranging from many minutes to as long as several hours, and possibly even days.

★ ★

Meditation for Addiction

A small but growing body of research is lending support to meditation's effectiveness in treating addiction, either alone or in combination with other more conventional treatments.

Some of these studies have shown meditation's effectiveness at decreasing substance use and relapse in several settings. The changes in thought processes and brain function that accompanies meditation also have contributed to scientists understanding of the biological addiction process.

The point of the above is not to assert in any way that meditation by itself can overcome alcoholism. However, there is enough evidence to justify considering meditation as <u>an additional tool</u> to add to your overall Conquer Program defenses. The results (if any) will vary greatly by individual, as well as type of meditation, discussed next.

Types of Meditation

There are many different types of meditation, <u>which all work to slow down the chatter of the mind and promote relaxation and mental clarity</u>. The different types of meditation techniques that have evolved from Hinduism, Christianity, and Buddhism can be classified under five categories: Concentration, Reflective, Heart-Centered, Creative, and Mindfulness Meditation. [33]

Mindfulness Meditation seems to have the highest potential specifically for addiction. In the main book, I cover all the main types of meditation. It is my view that for *any* meditation to be effective as a Conquer Program defense, you have to:

a) Give the concept the benefit of the doubt (meaning don't bother trying it if you think it is a joke)

b) Find a meditation type that works for your personality type. There are a ton of different ones that use different methods, so don't try to force fit yourself into something that feels silly or awkward for you—try a different one.

c) Fully understand your triggers and if/how one or more might benefit from meditation, and

d) Give it a *meaningful* try in terms of attempts, time, and attitude (meaning don't do it half-assed—it won't work).

Item c) is, of course, the trickiest part of using meditation of any kind to help alcoholism, at least in the context of The Conquer Program. My view is that while most triggers could theoretically benefit from meditation, it is the ones that cause physical distress, such as a jump in blood pressure, which could benefit the most. These include Anger, Anxiety, Extreme Emotions, Frustration, Health (Pain), Noise, Stress (physical), Yelling, and Zeal (Excitement). These are ones where it seems common sense to take a step back to try and calm down, and meditation seems a great way to do so. Insomnia and being Tired could also benefit as well.

Mindfulness Meditation

Mindfulness meditation is considered one the most powerful and alternative meditation techniques, which emphasizes cultivating a highly receptive mindful attention toward any action or objects within your sphere of influence. It emphasizes a simple thing: to pay attention or be "mindful". This type of meditation is known to provide pain relief and help for those suffering from anxiety and depression.[34] It is also considered to be the most successful category of meditation in helping addiction—to the extent it can and does help. Of all the types of meditation described here, Mindfulness Meditation has the most synergies with The Conquer Program, for reasons described earlier.

There are several different types of Mindfulness Meditation techniques, including:

- *Vipassana meditation.* In <u>Vipassana meditation</u>, one does not try to deny or ignore thoughts related to addiction. Rather, when a thought or craving to use arises, it teaches one to *observe* and *accept* the presence of the thought while not over-identifying with it. This type of meditation is appealing to some because it avoids blame and stigmatization related to the addictive thought process while also acknowledging its reality.[35]

- *Movement meditation.* This is usually yoga, <u>t'ai chi</u>, <u>qi gong</u> or another physical mind-body exercise. This type of meditation involves focusing on your bodily sensations, breathing and mindfully watching and perhaps letting go of whatever thoughts and emotions arise as you practice. Slow *walking meditation* is another possibility.

- *Breathing meditation.* Many meditations involve focusing on the breath. Two variations of breathing meditation techniques include *Breath Awareness* meditation and *Stillness in the Breath* meditation; the second builds on success with the first. Both are what they sound like, but take a bit of practice; you can find step-by-step instructions at <u>http://www.meditationoasis.com/how-to-meditate/simple-meditations/breathing-meditations/</u>. A video showing a third variation—deep breathing meditation—can be found at http://www.youtube.com/watch?v=hD2eGsGTldc. Another variation is Breathing Space meditation.

- *Body scan meditation.* Often done lying down, but you can use any posture you like. This meditation involves becoming aware of your bodily sensations in a mindful way, step by step. You can start from the top of your head and move downwards, or at your toes and move upwards, or even from your heart outwards in a spiral.

- *Visualization meditation.* Visualization techniques work well for those who find it difficult to focus on a mantra or a particular topic, and/or for people who mostly imagine negative things instead of positive (e.g. alcoholics). It involves generating an image or idea in your mind, such as love or joy or a positive, then building a visual image of what that might mean.[36]

A good overall description of visualization meditation can be found at http://www.project-meditation.org/a_mt4/meditation_visualization_techniques.html.

* * *

While there are many types of meditation, it only takes one to possibly help. All of the above meditation types could provide potential benefits to alcoholics seeking a great sense of tranquility and relaxation, though again there is no definitive proof of such benefits. Like so many things in life, the benefits you receive will be in direct proportion to the effort you make.

The Salvation Army

The Salvation Army is a charitable organization operating in 126 countries known for a variety of charitable works and its charity stores. It operates with a quasi-military structure (e.g., "Army" is no accident in the name). It is characterized as a Christian organization, primarily Methodist in its beliefs although distinct in government and practice. Its objectives include "the advancement of the Christian religion… of education, the relief of poverty… beneficial to society or the community of mankind as a whole".

Sobriety and abstinence from alcohol is an important cornerstone of SA's beliefs and activities. <u>It does not believe alcohol has *any* positive effect in any society</u>. As part of this philosophy, the SA has established its Adult Rehabilitation Centers (ARC), which are in large part focused on combating substance abuse but also in providing work therapy; life skills training; and individual, group and family counseling.

Each person considered for admittance into the Salvation Army Adult Rehabilitation Center must:

- Admit the need for rehabilitation to overcome problems
- Be in good physical health
- Be willing to participate in the entire program
- *Commit to a six-month period of rehabilitation (inpatient in nearly all respects)*
- Be free of intoxicating drugs, including alcohol, upon admission
- Have a desire to rebuild a lifestyle free of chemical dependency.

During the stay, each man (not usually women)[37] is offered counseling, group therapy, spiritual guidance, educational programs, work therapy, chemical dependency classes, Christian living classes (practical application of Christian ethics), Bible study, literacy education, medical screening, and help with anger management and relapse prevention.

<u>Work therapy is a major part of the program.</u> When possible, men are placed in an assignment compatible with past work experience and abilities. In many work therapy areas, fundamental training is provided to prepare

136

men for entering the job market. Chemical dependency classes have guest lecturers and film viewing sessions showing all aspects of addiction including many classic symptoms and emotional phases through which the disease progresses.

SA provides access to other support groups including Alcoholics Anonymous and Narcotics Anonymous.[38]

Author's Note: As you might imagine, this program is probably best suited for _men_ *who have hit* _complete_ *bottom, are very open to incorporating religion into their daily regimen, and in general need a completely new start in nearly every aspect of their life.*

* * * * *

As you can tell by now, anyone who suggests you "need therapy" or should "go to rehab" without any education or experience into what is involved, doesn't know what the hell they are talking about. But that shouldn't dissuade you from trying them; you just need to go into the process educated on what they are about and with the right set of expectations.

What is the right set of expectations? For rehab (particularly inpatient), it is an expectation that you are entering a "safe harbor" that will protect you (*for a time*) from the temptations of alcohol while you get your head wrapped around a future without it. If you are doing it while reading this book, it will give you time and an opportunity to explore your triggers and possible new defenses without worrying about an unexpected attack.[39] In addition, any rehab program will provide a certain level of "baseline" education on the nature of alcoholism and how you can combat it, which can only help.

The discussion on therapy also shows how just throwing around the term "go to therapy" or "see a shrink" is insufficient. You need to investigate possible therapists thoroughly; in particular examining what kind of therapy they practice and how much experience they have in treating alcoholics.

Finally, recognize that even with the best rehab and/or therapy, _they will not be enough to keep you sober longer-term_. Eventually the defenses they provide you will begin to weaken, or attacks will come from other areas where rehab/therapy did not provide much in the way of defenses to begin with. If you expect this reality, and treat rehab/therapy as just two levels of defense in a much bigger fortress of protection, then you will make the most out them and they will serve as a valuable part of your long-term defense. If you expect that either will be sufficient by themselves long term or will provide some sort of "cure," you are <u>completely</u> deluding yourself.

Therapy and in particular Rehab are where many alcoholics are introduced to the concept of an alcoholic "community", discussed next.

LEVEL 7—JOIN A COMMUNITY

Whether you first do rehab and therapy, and then join one of the support communities discussed here such as AA or Women for Sobriety (WFS), or you join a community first and then do rehab and therapy, really doesn't matter. _The key is to join at least one community that you can turn to as part of your overall defense building efforts and support structure._

There are numerous support organizations that have been established over the years to help alcoholics achieve and maintain sobriety. Many of these were established to support specific recovery/rehabilitation programs, often formulated by the organization's founder(s). The most well-known is Alcoholics Anonymous (AA), but there are others with various focuses (e.g., Women-only) and/or philosophies (with or without religion/spirituality, viewing or not viewing alcoholism as a disease), etc. Some of the more well-known ones are listed here in alphabetical order: I strongly encourage you to do a thorough research for alcoholic communities to join at least one.

Why?

We introduced the concept and importance of building a _support network_ in Level 4—Engage Friends and Family. This Level is the next logical extension of this concept. Now that you have Detoxed, and perhaps been introduced to the concepts of support programs in Rehab, Therapy or during your Detox, you are ready to extend your support network to a new group of people—other alcoholics looking to become sober or who are already sober.

A <u>critical</u> aspect to recognize is that most if not all of these programs view themselves as *stand-alone* treatment/support programs, e.g., that your sobriety begins and ends, succeeds or fails, <u>with them</u>. That is NOT a view that this program endorses. Not because it is not a worthy goal; rather it is because *<u>few of these programs work on a stand-alone basis for most of their participants</u>*. Statistics vary depending on the program and the effectiveness methodology, but <u>few if any</u> of these programs has anything approaching a double-digit success rate. An extensive discussion of treatment success rates is included in the main *How to Conquer Your Alcoholism* book.[1]

With The Conquer Program, you should view these other programs more broadly—as a *Community extension* of your support network. These programs are there to help you defend against alcohol when other methods are not working that day for that particular trigger or circumstance. In those situations, a fellow community member or going to a meeting may be just what you need, not necessarily to hear about step 4 of the AA 12 steps, but to hear from others who know about the daily struggles with alcoholism.

WHAT TO LOOK FOR IN A COMMUNITY

There are four key things to look for in an alcoholism community: Relatability, Demographics, Convenience, and Variety.

"Relatability"

The most important thing you want in your community is what I call Relatability, which is your ability to "relate" to the persons attending the same meetings as you. Also known as "identifying," this refers to the degree that you see some of yourself and your background in them. This is important because if you think a person has nothing in common with you about how they became an alcoholic, what their triggers are (even if they do not call them that), what their daily life is like, etc., then frankly you will not listen to them let alone feel like they are people with whom you feel comfortable sharing your own stories.

You don't want them to be *exactly* like you by any means; you just want them to be enough like you to identify with. These elements include their personalities, their "back stories" (history), and their general attitudes towards getting and staying sober, both individually and how they express themselves in a group. As you might guess, Relatability can vary *greatly* between groups. Some groups are informal and very outgoing, while others can be strictly business, with a specific agenda and process. While outward appearances will give some indication of relatability, e.g., demeanor, dress, gender, age, you have to spend time with the group (at least a couple meetings) to get a sense of the real nature of the group and the people who attend.

Demographics

Don't discount the importance of demographics; it can be extremely important, particularly when it comes to *gender* and *age*. As discussed shortly, some women have issues with certain aspects of certain alcoholic communities, so ones that offer women-only groups/meetings may be attractive. Same for age—youth is often greatly underrepresented in many groups and meetings and feel much more comfortable expressing themselves in groups focused on their younger age. Other variations include groups that are blue-collar (e.g., vs. professional/white collar) which may be important for some, and certainly as it relates to Job-related issues.

Convenience

Some communities, particularly AA, seem to have meetings everywhere, all the time. This availability can be of enormous help, because for many people if a meeting is at all <u>in</u>convenient then that is an easy excuse not to go! Some are moving towards online meetings to address the convenience issue (it also helps anonymity), but you should recognize there is <u>no</u> substitute for face-to-face interaction when it comes to Community for the purposes of <u>this</u> program. You want someone you personally know to be able to help you or just to talk to when you are in a pinch regarding a crisis or tough situation.

Variety

There is no denying it: some meetings can be incredibly boring, particularly if they cover the same topic in the same style every time, like "Big Book" readings, with the same people talking about the same things after the readings. I fully recognize my reaction may just be because of my personality. Some people likely find great comfort in that predictability and routine, but for me I just need more variety. That's one of the reasons I like speaker-type meetings so much. You never know what the story is going to be for these individuals; some are extremely fascinating in what they went through during their drinking and how they clawed their way out if it. There is no right way, just what fits your personality and even daily mood.

Note: if one of your triggers is Boredom (or Loneliness), then I'd encourage you to explore a wide variety of programs/groups/meetings. If on the other hand Change is a trigger, then you may be better off choosing one program/group/meeting and sticking with it.

* *

Combining Other Alcoholism Community Program Teachings with   The Conquer Program

For some of you, the teachings, steps, or other parts of programs advocated by an individual community may *alone* be enough to get you sober. If that is the case, great! Recognize that you will be one of the relatively small percentage for which this is so, making it even more important to adhere and diligently practice over time the concepts and steps contained in that particular program.

However, I would strongly encourage you to *also* continue following The Conquer Program. Not only does it not preclude or conflict with any other programs that I am aware of, its very nature can make it very complementary to those programs, such as discussions of triggers (whether they are called that or not) and the use of spirituality.

There are always exceptions of course. Some programs take a very strong stand against spirituality, or refuse to treat alcoholism as a disease, or negatively view the use of rehabs, therapy, or other medical practices in alcoholism treatment. My view is that these programs are few and generally operate at the fringes of accepted medical practice. Even so, much of The Conquer Program can be done in coexistence with these programs, and at a minimum can serve as a backup in case your program of choice fails for some reason some day.

* *

ALCOHOLISM COMMUNITIES

The following provides an overview of some Alcoholism Communities to consider for this Level. It is by no means an exhaustive list, but they are some of the more well-known ones. I lead with Alcoholics Anonymous (AA), not just because it is first alphabetically but because it is by far the most well-known and convenient Alcoholism Community available.

I recommend that you try at least a few AA meetings to get a feeling for what the seemingly big deal of AA is, but for many different reasons it may not be for you. Frankly I don't care which Community you join, **but you need to join at least one**—to provide that extended part of your support network defense if and when you need it to combat particular alcohol-related situations that your other defenses cannot do that day. Or just to have a safe place to relax knowing you are in a completely alcohol-free environment.

Alcoholics Anonymous—The Gorilla in the Support Room

Alcoholics Anonymous (AA) is the most well-known program in the world for addressing alcoholism. It is the "big kahuna;" the 800-pound gorilla in the alcoholic treatment/support program world. Why? Perhaps because it was one of the first such programs, founded in 1935. But there can be no doubt that it has successfully kept sober many individuals over the years. Every alcoholic seeking sobriety should try it—at least attending a few meetings. That said, AA has several aspects that can be problematic for many people, most notably it being essentially faith-based and also because it has a much lower success rate than generally believed. While not covered in depth here, two articles that cover some of the perceived downsides of AA can be found at http://www.conqueryouraddiction.com/case-for-change-at-aa.html and https://www.theatlantic.com/magazine/archive/2015/04/the-irrationality-of-alcoholics-anonymous/386255/.

What is AA?

AA was founded in 1935 by a couple of men frustrated by their inability to stay sober.[2] They formulated a "12-Step" program (discussed earlier in Level 6), and over time developed a variety of teachings and other guidance captured in what has come to be called *"The Big Book."* These steps and readings from *The Big Book* form the basis of most AA meetings.

AA as an organization views the thousands of meetings that take place each day as the work of autonomous groups, responsible for supervising themselves.[3] While there is no actual count, one AA chapter estimate has overall AA "membership" in the US at approximately 2 million people in almost 100,000 Groups. Groups are local chapters that coordinate and conduct their own set of meetings.

For example, a self-named "New Life" group may organize Monday 7:30 pm, Wednesday 7:30 pm and Friday 8 pm evening meetings at the local Baptist church. Another group with a different name may organize its own meetings on Monday evenings at 6 pm, Wednesday afternoons at noon, and Saturday mornings at 8 am in another venue a few miles down the road. The only coordination involved is passing organizational info to regional AA organizations that maintain a master list of all groups and meeting times/types for publication on websites and other forums. There is NO data captured on the individual identities or other personal information of members/attendees. The whole program is based on anonymity.

★ ★

What Are AA Meetings Like?

AA is based on anonymity, with "members" (really, anyone who shows up) identifying themselves only with their first name, so there is absolutely no reason to think you have to attend one meeting over another. That said; there are "specialized" meetings, such as women/men-only, Open (alcoholics and non-alcoholics invited), and Closed (only alcoholics) being some of the most common variations. There are no statistics available about the demographics of AA participants. My observation is that it is skewed towards older men, but that is just my personal experience (based on several hundred meetings across about 50 groups in half a dozen states). Participation, without exception, was majority male in every single meeting I attended (exception: those meetings I went to while in Inpatient Rehab were predominantly female, which is weird in retrospect). A safe bet is that with the exception of Women-only meetings the majority of participants (in "outside" meetings) will be male most of the time.

Meetings generally start with a quick overview of what AA is about (often called the "preamble"), including its anonymous nature. Then the meeting focuses on a particular topic, usually a particular Step in AA's 12-Step program and/or reading from a chapter from "The Big Book," which is in effect a much more detailed discussion of a particular alcoholism issue or step. Some meetings are "speaker" meetings, where a specific person (usually not a regular member of the group, and often a total stranger to the attendees) talks about his or her experiences with alcohol. Personal note: speaker meetings were my favorite, since they allowed me to relate to someone else's situation in great detail, and were often very interesting in general.

After the readings or speakers, the remainder of the meeting is "open discussion," where anybody who wants to can talk about his or her thoughts on the particular topic or what is bugging them that day in general. Cross-talk, e.g., more than one person at a time talking is not allowed. At the end of the meeting (usually 1 hour) the meeting is often closed with <u>The Serenity Prayer</u>.

Tip: when trying out AA for the first time try a few different groups and/or meeting times, not just the one closest to you at the most convenient time. While it can be hard to precisely define, different groups and different meetings can have different "personalities" in total and of course in the individuals who attend, even in the same geographical area.

★ ★

Finding a group that you are comfortable with and decide to attend regularly is the most important decision in pursuing AA—at least as it applies to the Conquer Program. The reason is that the Community nature of this Level is not just having warm bodies around you—it is getting to know at least some of the other attendees (even if you never find out their last name!). There may be ones you can call in a crisis and maybe even ones who you feel comfortable asking to be a sponsor if you decide you want to try the AA program to its fullest.

★ ★

What Is an AA Sponsor?

Newcomers to AA are encouraged to find an experienced fellow alcoholic, called a sponsor, to help them understand and follow the AA program. The sponsor should preferably have experience in all twelve of the steps, be the same gender as the sponsored person and refrain from imposing personal views on the sponsored person.[4] There is no "qualification" or certification of any kind required to be a sponsor; anyone can show up and offer to be one, though generally only AA "old-timers" offer to be one. It is very likely that your sponsor will expect you to try and "work the steps," meaning for you to make an earnest effort at trying 12-Steps.

★ ★

This group can (it does not have to) become your "home group," which really only means that you can (not must) put your name (just your first name and initial of your last name) on a roster list and indicate whether or not you are willing to sponsor other alcoholics. You can get emails about announcements as well, e.g., a meeting postponed, an upcoming treasurer meeting, a member death, etc. (you do NOT get on any sort of spam list, and you do not get emailed about trivial matters). Nothing prevents you from selecting multiple groups as your "home" group, or from selecting any group as one at all. It is just a label for a group whose meetings are the ones you go to the most.

Groups are self-supporting, generally on a shoe-string. During the meeting, a basket is passed around for those who want to put one dollar in—there is no obligation. This money is used to buy supplies (e.g., coffee, cookies) and pay rent (meetings are often held in local churches, either for free or at a very low rate).

<u>If you are not comfortable with one group of people, then try another.</u> However, all the ones in my experience were/are universally friendly, supportive, and very open to helping new members.

Bottom Line: AA is most likely to help (beyond its community appeal) <u>if</u>:

- You enter the program with an open affinity and willingness towards religion or at least spirituality, <u>and</u>

- You are willing to have God become a key part of your life going forward, <u>and</u>

- You are willing to set aside a good chunk of your longer-term life going to weekly or even daily meetings,

But for most of you, *<u>joining something like AA, Women for Sobriety (discussed shortly), or similar step programs will be mostly helpful in broadening your support network and filling key defense needs in vulnerable times</u>*. You may also find that many of their topic discussions mesh well with various parts of this program, such as certain triggers. Always bear in mind that the Conquer Program is a multi-level program, and joining a Community such as AA is just one of thirteen.

Remember: There <u>will</u> be circumstances and triggers where going to a meeting or calling Community friends may be at the top of your list for best dealing with a bad situation, so you want to have those defenses ready to go when needed.

* * *

The balance of this Level discussion provides an overview of some other types of Community programs you might want to consider. Some take an AA-type approach, while others are expressly anti-AA. I encourage you to consider them and any others of which you might become aware. Frankly it does not matter too much which one you select—<u>but, again, you need to select at least one</u>, so you have this kind of alcoholic Community defense ready if and when you really need it.

Rational Recovery

While most alcohol support programs, including Alcoholics Anonymous, focus on providing a softer approach to battling addiction. Rational Recovery takes a no-nonsense, hard-core attitude that an individual must quit their excessive drinking or be forced to lose everything. It is also one of the most vocal anti-AA groups out there. Key dimensions include:

- Rational Recovery does <u>not</u> regard alcoholism as a disease, but rather a voluntary behavior.

- Rational Recovery discourages adoption of the forever "recovering" drunk persona.

- There are no Rational Recovery support groups (although meetings were held throughout the country during the 1990s).

- Great emphasis is placed on self-efficacy.

- There are no discrete steps and no consideration of religious matters.

At the core of Rational Recovery (RR) is its Addictive Voice Recognition Technique (AVRT). The program is offered for free via the Internet and through books, videos, and lectures. The Rational Recovery program is based on the premise that the addict both desires and is capable of permanent, planned abstinence. However, the Rational Recovery program recognizes that, paradoxically, the addict also wants to *continue* using. This paradox is because of his belief in the power of a substance to quell his anxiety; an anxiety that is itself partially substance-induced, as well as greatly enhanced, *by* the substance. This ambivalence is the Rational Recovery definition of addiction.

According to this approach, the primary force driving an addict's predicament is what [the founder] calls the "addictive voice," which can physiologically be understood as being related to the parts of the human brain that control our core survival functions such as hunger, sex, and bowel control. Consequently, when the desires of this "voice" are not satiated, the addict experiences anxiety, depression, restlessness, irritability, and anhedonia (inability to feel pleasure). In essence, the RR method is to first make a commitment to planned, permanent abstinence from the undesirable substance or behavior, and then equip oneself with the mental tools to stick to that commitment. Most important to recovering addicts is the recognition of this addictive voice, and determination to remain abstinent by constantly reminding themselves of the rational basis of their decision to quit. As time progresses, the recovering addict begins to see the benefits of separating themselves and their rational minds from a bodily impulse that has no regard for responsibility, success, delayed gratification, or moral obligation.

Overall, the RR program is based on recognizing and defeating what the program refers to as the "addictive voice" (internal thoughts that support self-intoxication) and dissociation from addictive impulses. The specific techniques of Addictive Voice Recognition Technique (AVRT) are concerned with demonstrating to the practitioner that the practitioner is in control of the addictive voice, not the other way around.[5]

The AVRT approach is not inconsistent with that of the Conquer Program, with the "addictive voice" being not that different from our drinking triggers, though on a much more limited and general basis. Its emphasis on dissociation is also consistent; the Conquer Program spends a great deal of time in breaking old, destructive associations and building new, more positive ones.

Attitude Towards AA

Different non-AA communities have varying attitude towards AA and its 12-Steps. To say Rational Recovery is very anti-AA is to put it mildly. The program is founded on the belief that 12-Step programs such as AA, and many clinical treatment methods, such as rehab centers, are both scientifically and spiritually "incorrect." It goes further with AA, stridently opposing several of its core dimensions such as its heavy reliance on God, attitude towards relapses, and often forced nature of attending AA meetings.

Rational Recovery also strenuously objects to the regular habit of our (the U.S.) court system in mandating participation in AA. I have some sympathy with this view because the courts seem to have a greatly exaggerated sense of AA's effectiveness. As a general observation, Rational Recovery will not suit those searching for a friendlier approach to dealing with addiction and certainly not those who believe it is a disease or want to include some spiritual element in their getting sober. In fact, RR tends to view alcoholism as an indulgent behavior that can only be made worse by programs such as AA or clinical rehabilitation.

As you might expect, RR has a narrow appeal in general and practically no appeal to established institutions like religious groups and our judicial system (it has sued, unsuccessfully as far as I can tell, to protest rulings making individuals attend AA). As you might guess, I'm not going on record as recommending this program. However, I did not want to limit the possibilities to consider, and RR certainly gives you a perspective on the range of options to consider when considering Community programs. All have a worthy end goal but sometimes radically different approaches to try and achieve it.

Secular Organizations for Sobriety (SOS)

Secular Organizations for Sobriety (SOS) (*http://www.sossobriety.org/*), also known as Save Our Selves, is a non-profit network of autonomous addiction recovery groups. It emphasizes rational decision-making and is not religious or spiritual in nature, specifically avoiding spiritually-based addiction recovery programs philosophies. At its core are a number of guiding principles:

- *SOS is not a spin-off of any religious or secular group. There is no hidden agenda, as SOS is concerned with achieving and maintaining sobriety (abstinence).*

- *SOS seeks only to promote sobriety amongst those who suffer from addictions.*

- *As a group, SOS has no opinion on outside matters and does not wish to become entangled in outside controversy.*

- *Although sobriety is an individual responsibility, life does not have to be faced alone. The support of other alcoholics and addicts is a vital adjunct to recovery.*

- *In SOS, members share experiences, insights, information, strength, and encouragement in friendly, honest, anonymous, and supportive group meetings.*

- *To avoid unnecessary entanglements, each SOS group is self-supporting through contributions from its members and refuses outside support.*

- *Sobriety is the number one priority in a recovering person's life.*

- *As such, he or she must abstain from all drugs or alcohol.*

- *Honest, clear, and direct communication of feelings, thoughts, and knowledge aids in recovery and in choosing nondestructive, non-delusional, and rational approaches to living sober and rewarding lives.*

- *As knowledge of addiction might cause a person harm or embarrassment in the outside world, SOS guards the anonymity of its membership and the contents of its discussions from those not within the group.*

- *SOS encourages the scientific study of addiction in all its aspects. SOS does not limit its outlook to one area of knowledge or theory of addiction.*[6]

SOS recognizes genetic and environmental factors contribute to addiction, but allows each member to decide <u>whether or not alcoholism is a disease</u>. SOS holds the view that alcoholics can recover (addictive behaviors can be arrested) but ultimately it is *never* cured and relapse is always possible. SOS does not endorse sponsor-type relationships. They also do not take a stand about alcoholism as a disease, which is a bit strange given their stated emphasis on pursuing addiction science.

SMART Recovery

Standing for *Self-Management and Recovery Training,* SMART Recovery focuses on empowering participants to abstain from drinking and create a more positive lifestyle. It is more science-based than other programs and looks at addiction as both a physical and a mental disorder and condones the use of the appropriate medication and psychological treatments. The following is from the website *www.smartrecovery.org*:

> *Our participants learn tools for addiction recovery based on the latest scientific research and participate in a world-wide community which includes free, self-empowering, science-based mutual help groups.*
>
> *The SMART Recovery 4-Point Program® helps people recover from all types of addiction and addictive behaviors, including: drug abuse, drug addiction, substance abuse, alcohol abuse, gambling addiction, cocaine addiction, prescription drug abuse, and problem addiction to other substances and activities. SMART Recovery sponsors face-to-face meetings around the world, and daily online meetings. In addition, our online message board and 24/7 chat room are excellent forums to learn about SMART Recovery and obtain addiction recovery support.*

SMART is built around a 4 Point Program that offers tools and techniques for each program point:

1: Building and Maintaining Motivation

2: Coping with Urges

    3:   Managing Thoughts, Feelings and Behaviors

    4:   Living a Balanced Life.

Like many non-AA programs, Smart Recovery tries to distinguish itself clearly from that program. They consider their differences to be summed up by the following:

- SMART Recovery is not an ideology but focuses on rational analysis and action.

- It does not consider that all addicts are alike. Thus, no one "solution" fits all.

- It does not claim that it is the best program for everyone with addiction problems, and in fact encourages trying other programs if it does not work.

- It emphasizes personal choice and responsibility for one's actions, versus being "powerless."

- It does not view religious and spiritual beliefs as essential in solving the problems of addiction.

- It does not consider "alcoholism" a life-long preoccupation.

- There is no single "alcoholic personality" type or profile.

- SMART Recovery meetings are self-help groups, not support groups.

- There is no definitive and incontrovertible text, such as AA's *Big Book*.

I confess I like a lot of the above. While their 4-Point Program is extremely general, a lot of the underlying details are well articulated, and I can see how that can translate into usable help. I also never tried it so I can't vouch for it personally. The fact that it says its program can work on *all* addictive behaviors is a bit concerning, despite saying elsewhere that all addicts are not alike, and no one solutions fits all. While this generality implies a lack of focus on the nuances of alcohol addiction specifically, its philosophy makes it worth consideration.

Women for Sobriety (WFS)

Women for Sobriety (*http://womenforsobriety.org*)is the USA's first national program specifically designed for women alcoholics, founded in 1975. It aims to deal with the many issues that women have when it comes to excessive drinking or a dependency on alcohol, and was influenced by a mix of medical and feminist principles. It asserts that alcohol dependent women have fundamentally different needs in recovery than do men. *Author's Note: I wholeheartedly agree with this philosophy for numerous reasons, including alcohol's more severe impact on women's health, the different nature of (some of) their key triggers, and the historical ignoring of women in treatment programs (particularly AA's overwhelmingly male-centric writings).*

While still premised on alcoholism as a disease and using the Self-Help support group model, WFS has some major differences from Alcoholics Anonymous (though it positions itself as more of a complement to AA than an alternative). It never mentions God or a "Higher Power". Instead, women are helped to determine why they became so dependent—an approach very consistent with The Conquer Program. Participants are assisted to become self-empowered and to change their thinking.

Lapses are more tolerated in WFS, with no need to begin at day one of sobriety again, and openly talking to other members during meetings is allowed (unlike in AA that have no cross-talk rules). Another difference is the greeting; instead of announcing and labeling oneself as an alcoholic, members introduce themselves by stating, *"Hi, I'm [name], and I'm a competent woman."* There's no concern about being egotistical or the need to be humble (like AA emphasizes). Instead, WFS asserts that for most women with an alcohol problem there is a need to <u>emphasize</u> empowerment and increasing self-worth.

WFS has 13 affirmations in its *New Life Acceptance Program*. They are:

1. I have a life-threatening problem that once had me.
    I now take charge of my life and my disease. I accept the responsibility.

2. Negative thoughts destroy only myself.
    My first conscious sober act must be to remove negativity from my life.

3. Happiness is a habit I will develop.
    Happiness is created, not waited for.

4. Problems bother me only to the degree I permit them to.
    I now better understand my problems and do not permit problems to overwhelm me.

5. I am what I think.
    I am a capable, competent, caring, compassionate woman.

6. Life can be ordinary or it can be great.
    Greatness is mine by a conscious effort.

7. Love can change the course of my world.
    Caring becomes all important.

8. The fundamental object of life is emotional and spiritual growth.
    Daily I put my life into a proper order, knowing which are the priorities.

9. The past is gone forever.
    No longer will I be victimized by the past. I am a new person.

10. All love given returns.
    I will learn to know that others love me.

11. Enthusiasm is my daily exercise.
    I treasure all moments of my new life.

12. I am a competent woman and have much to give life.
    This is what I am and I shall know it always.

13. I am responsible for myself and for my actions.
    I am in charge of my mind, my thoughts, and my life.

WFS asserts the following: *"To make the WFS Program effective for you, arise each morning fifteen minutes earlier than usual and go over the Thirteen Affirmations. Then begin to think about each one by itself. Take one Statement and use it consciously all day. At the end of the day review the use of it and what effects it had that day for you and your actions.*[7]

From my research, I found Women for Sobriety has more testimonials than any other group except for AA, and they are predominately positive. They do not appear to have a critical mass of in-person meetings like AA does, relying more on online forums. I had an opportunity to talk with one of the officers of WFS, who gave me some valuable insight into female-specific alcoholism issues as well as pointing me to additional material that I reference throughout this book. They did not let me join WFS, however, being very strict on it being women-only.

Also from my research, it becomes apparent that alcoholism hits women in substantially different ways than men, from the triggers involved to medical issues. WFS takes this viewpoint even further, saying that _women need their own program to successfully overcome the female-specific issues that come with alcoholism_.

I highly recommend WFS for its positive approach and recognition of the additional burdens of female alcoholics. Additional information can be found at:

- Blog Site: http://wfsorg.blogspot.com
- Daily Inspirations on Twitter: https://twitter.com/WFS4C
- Facebook: http://www.facebook.com/WomenForSobriety
- Catalog Site: http://www.wfscatalog.org/

Online Communities

All of the above communities have various types of online forums for supporting their members. Some, like AA, do not focus much on electronic information, whereas others (particularly those with relatively few or no face-to-face meetings), rely very heavily on online tools and forums to supplement their literature and other support capabilities.

In addition, there are online-only resources that can be of great help, such www.alcoholism.about.com. An excellent overview of support groups can also be found at http://www.cigna.com/healthwellness/behavioral-awareness-series/coping-with-substance-abuse (a good example of their webinars is http://www.cigna.com/assets/media/audio/behavioral-health-series/substance-abuse/2014/march2014-substance-abuse-replay.mp3).

An ongoing, up-to-date of online resources can be found at http://www.conqueryouraddiction.com/key-web-resources.html. Throughout this book there are many other online sources that provide elements of support in various dimensions and perspectives of alcoholism.

* * *

Hopefully, this Level has provided insight into what types of alcoholic communities are out there to support you in general, and provide critical defenses for specific triggers at key times. *It is very important that you give at least one of these a try.* Even if the tenets of a specific program are not successful by themselves (which is likely), remember that *the* goal here is to get to know other alcoholics looking to become and stay sober. Those alcoholics and the meetings they attend can really help you out in certain situations where your defenses are otherwise vulnerable.

LEVEL 8—BREAK BAD HABITS

There is absolutely no question—<u>developing or adopting new hobbies is an</u> <u>*absolute necessity in a* new life of sobriety</u>. Becoming sober means you are freeing up an <u>immense</u> amount of time that you formerly spent obtaining, using, and recovering from alcohol. But before we get to hobbies, let's talk about habits, particularly *bad* habits. In my view, <u>adopting a new hobby</u> <u>(particularly one that involves interacting with others) while still carrying</u> <u>around a bunch of bad habits is a recipe for trouble in reaching and</u> <u>maintaining your sobriety</u>.

In the worst case, <u>the continued existence of drinking-related bad habits</u> <u>in sobriety can cause a risk of relapse</u>. Bad habits can cause conflict and turmoil in your head and everyday life that you and others just don't need. Odds are that you either developed or made far worse some bad habits while you were drinking that made life uncomfortable, if not downright unpleasant, for many people around you.

First, we need a clear definition. Like many words used when discussing alcoholism, the word "habit" is familiar without necessarily meaning the same thing to different people. Hence, an unambiguous definition is in order. *Thefreedictionary.com* defines a habit as:

> *Habit: A recurrent, often unconscious pattern of behavior that is acquired through frequent repetition; An established disposition of the mind or character; A customary manner or practice.*

Habits, of course, can be good or bad, or "just there." Your routine before you go to bed is an example of one that is "just there," with some positive overtones: you make sure the doors are locked, dishes are washed, kids are asleep, lights are out, brush your teeth, read a book, go to sleep. You may be thinking about other things that have nothing to do with those activities; they just happen.

While locking the doors, checking on the kids, and brushing our teeth can easily be viewed as "good," most of our habits are likely skewed more toward the Dark Side of habits. Unfortunately, bad habits—ones that have a detrimental impact on you and/or others—seem to be developed much easier than good ones (in my opinion) and are usually very hard to break (in nearly everybody's opinion). Most importantly, we don't recognize many of our bad habits (even when sober), as they can lurk in the background and make our lives and the lives of the people around us unpleasant, with us not understanding why! And an unpleasant environment is <u>not</u> good for the newly sober; we are very fragile and vulnerable, and any negative situation may throw us back into the abyss, e.g. unpleasant situations easily caused by annoying, obnoxious, or downright unpleasant bad habits.

Of course, many "bad" habits are minor, and many may be totally irrelevant to a sobriety discussion. Examples include chewing with your mouth open, belching (without saying "excuse me"), cracking your knuckles, fidgeting, and chewing your fingernails. But others are <u>not</u> so trivial. Let's focus on the ones' most likely to been affected by your drinking.

Alcohol-Related Bad Habits

There are several bad habits that many alcoholics seem to have in my experience, and more importantly can have a negative impact on the newly sober due to their potential for creating a negative or hostile environment by or around the alcoholic. These are:

- (Deliberately or unconsciously) alienating others
- Attention-seeking behavior (Look at me! Look at me!)
- Chronic lateness, procrastination
- Constantly complaining, being argumentative
- (Excessive) cursing
- Eavesdropping
- Freeloading
- Gossiping
- Impulsive behavior to the point of recklessness
- Interrupting
- Lying, exaggerating
- Monopolizing the conversation
- Nitpicking, being critical and controlling
- (Deliberate and excessive) non-conformity, often for its own sake
- Reacting quickly and often without thinking to various things, often with bad consequences
- (Not) smiling when the situation clearly calls for it
- Smoking
- Whining.

It is very possible—indeed *probable*—that you developed or worsened one or more of these bad habits while you were drinking. It is also very possible that some of these habits will get worse once you are sober, if you are not aware of them beforehand. That certainly happened to me with respect to nitpicking! I started picking out flaws in everything I saw once I became sober. It was extremely annoying to those around me; fortunately, once pointed out it could be easily fixed, as can most of the ones listed above.

So, as you enter this new and wonderful phase of life, it is worthwhile to step back and do an honest assessment of what kind of bad habits you've had. You can then make a very conscious effort to stop, eliminate, or reduce them as best as you can. This is one area where <u>engaging your friends and family</u> can have an early payoff by getting them to point out to you when you are "indulging" in the habit, since much of the time you are probably not even aware of it. You and everyone around you will be much happier, and you will find it that much easier to stay sober!

Tips for Breaking Drinking-Related Bad Habits

I'm not going to cover all the habits listed above in great detail. I have listed websites for each in the resources section (Break Bad Habits subsection) at the end of this book that may help. Here, I am going to address those I think are likely caused or severely aggravated by drinking, <u>and</u> not likely to immediately disappear or diminish in severity once you stop drinking.

Deliberately (or Unconsciously) Alienating Others

For many active alcoholics, deliberately alienating others is a "popular" strategy, as it keeps away many people who would otherwise comment on your drinking. There are different ways of doing this; in my case it was by being a rude son-of-a-bitch when I was drinking. I certainly was not violent, but was unpleasant nonetheless.

One thing you will want to find out once you are sober is how you behaved *before* you got sober, both before and after drinking on any given day. If you were a happy and relaxed drunk, great; you don't have to worry about this habit. But if you were a mean, obnoxious person to your friends, family, coworkers, grocery store cashiers, people who bumped into you (you get the idea)—even when you were not drinking—this is a habit you <u>have</u> to be aware of, as it may not immediately end when you stop drinking. Being sober doesn't automatically make you feel good all the time mentally and physically, particularly early on. There will be significant stretches where you flat out don't feel well, and the temptation to take it out on others may be very strong, particularly if were a nasty drunk-type.

At the very least, you will have a major perception problem on your hands if people a) didn't know you were an alcoholic or b) don't believe that you have really stopped drinking.

There are several common-sense things to do to break this habit. First, find out <u>what kind</u> of drunk personality you were, and <u>who</u> you took out that behavior on the most and in what forms. Asking family and friends who know about your alcoholism *and* know you are committing to a life of sobriety is the best way to do this (and another example of the importance of Level 4—Engage Friends and Family). This may be a difficult set of conversations to have, but worthwhile.

Beyond that, it is up to you on how you try to repair those relationships based on the specifics of your interactions. This activity is a distant cousin to the "making amends" step in Alcoholics Anonymous, but with a key difference: you are not necessarily making apologizes for your drinking or even acknowledging what you did to those people. You are just behaving a lot better towards them: friendlier, politer, or more sensitive, or more helpful. They may immediately recognize this new behavior and wonder what is up (particularly if they don't know about your alcoholism), but too bad for them. You don't have to explain yourself if you don't want to. Eventually, they will accept it as a new (and much happier) norm.

Chronic Lateness, Procrastination

As their alcoholism progresses, many alcoholics find themselves going to bed later and getting up later (when possible), while having ever decreasing amounts of energy. All of this can translate to a very unproductive lifestyle of lateness and procrastination. If this sounds like you, recognize that this is not going to go away immediately after you stop drinking for good. It can take a great deal of time to fix.

Personally, once sober I endured several months of feeling that my head was stuffed full of cotton, which made me both lethargic and forgetful much of the time. I found that making and keeping lists of things to do and places to be was very helpful, as I could no longer rely on my memory. The good news was that this "cotton head" feeling eventually went away as did my lethargy. My memory also (slowly) improved. Over time I started getting up progressively earlier in the morning. If this happens to you, there is probably not much you can do to shorten this cycle (other than caffeine), but just recognizing it upfront can avoid most of the pitfalls that are possible (e.g. forgot appointments, lost car keys, etc.)

Constantly Complaining, Being Critical, Argumentative, Interrupting, and Nitpicking

One of the "downsides" of being sober is that much more of your brain is active as are your senses, enabling you to see much more of the world around you than you did before. Unfortunately, you may not like a lot of what you see and have a strong compulsion to make others aware of it, sometimes mid-sentence when the other person is talking. Complaining, being critical, arguing, interrupting and nitpicking are cousins to alienating others above, and are often hard to realize you are doing it much of the time. Asking your friends and family to point out this behavior <u>at the time you are doing it</u> the best way of identifying this behavior. You will be able to make the "real-time" adjustments that over time will help eliminate this habit.

Lying and Exaggeration

One of the biggest and worst habits to break—one often perfected while drinking—is lying. Alcoholics are almost universally less than honest about the when, where, how, why and how much they drink. In addition, they lie about when or how long they have *stopped* drinking.

Unfortunately, for many alcoholics lying is not restricted to drinking—it became a part of everyday life; as natural as talking. Some therapists even go so far to say that lying is the number one negative aspect of alcoholism, and even a *cause* of alcoholism.[8] While I don't believe that lying can <u>directly</u> cause alcoholism, a case can be made for it indirectly *contributing* to it. Lying helps a person hide increasing alcohol consumption for so long that the person becomes physically dependent before anyone else notices and calls them out on it. Certainly, lying is one of the very negative dimensions that comes hand-in-hand with alcohol abuse.

There are many resources such as Wikihow (http://www.wikihow.com/Stop-Lying) for good mini-steps and tips for dealing with lying. In reality, the first step in dealing with lying is understanding about what, when and how you lied when you were drinking—on topics other than drinking. This knowledge will show you the extent of the problem and what areas are particular ones to focus on remedying. Here again is when friends and family are invaluable, by them telling you in real-time when they think you are full of shit either in terms of exaggeration or out-right lies. In fact, you can even make a game out of it. There is a card game called "Bullshit" (http://www.wikihow.com/Play-Bullshit) that you modify into a reality game where you get a point every time someone calls you a liar and you prove you were not. Dinner is on them if you reach 5 points in a month, but on you if you were caught five times. A possible new hobby!

Reacting Without Thinking

Reacting to an unexpected event or comment without prior thought can often result in unpleasant consequences—no surprise there. Alcoholics, since they are consciously or sub-consciously not particularly happy individuals to being with, often react unpleasantly. This is especially true for alcoholics that tend towards the nasty side, but it is not limited to them.

Being reactive can continue long after you become sober, particularly when it comes to certain triggers; this was the case with my eX-wife. Long after we were divorced (and well after I got sober) I found myself "instinctively" reacting to her jibes and negative comments, usually in the form of a burst of anger. The best way I found to address my reactiveness was actually a two-parter.

First, I would try and pre-program myself to *ignore* any such comments. One way I did this was eventually not talking "live" with her if at all possible. I would avoid her calls, and if she would text me or email me with what I thought of as silly, stupid, or irrelevant topics I would ignore them completely. I found that often whatever the issue was went away on its own. Second, if it were a topic I could not ignore, I would *delay my response*, usually by waiting a day or two. I found this delayed response was often different (and better) than the one that first came to mind. Once it became clear that I would not immediately respond, the overall volume of her negative comments also went down as an added bonus.

* * *

The Hands-and-Mouth Problem

While not exactly a bad habit, many drinkers (particularly those that smoke when they drink) often face a much-underestimated problem associated with breaking alcohol (and smoking) addictions: *What do I do with my hands and mouth?* That is not a joke—it can be a major issue for some.

One possible solution is "hand hobbies" such as gardening or knitting, but those are by their nature constrained in opportunity, skill required, and/or duration—there is a need for "anytime" hand *and* mouth activities. One such solution is to have a replacement beverage, with a beverage that you can have many times a day. Tea is one such beverage. A list of herbal, relaxing teas can be found at http://thedailytea.com/wellness/calming-soothing-and-relaxing-herbal-teas/, and a broader discussion of the benefits of tea can be found on www.ConquerYourAddiction.com. The herbal tea benefit trifecta of being hand-and-mouth occupying, a replacement (and tasty) beverage, and relaxing to boot can be very powerful.

* * * *

If one of your bad habits is not one specifically listed above, consult the website resources at www.conqueryouraddiction.com or at the end of this book. Plus, do your own research; it seems like there are plenty of people with ideas on even the most obscure habits.[9] It is worth mentioning again the potential benefit of aversion therapy (to break bad habits by associating them with something unpleasant); in other words, really *break* them. I'd suggest studying in depth Level 11—Make Yourself Sick of Alcohol to see if it generates any ideas for breaking any particularly unusual bad habits you might have picked up over the years.

While making yourself physically ill is not the answer for many habits, a less extreme yet still effective method is to try to *think* of something unpleasant/sick/gross when you find yourself doing something you know is a bad habit. If you do this often enough, you may well find it very effective in stopping you doing a bad habit, or at least doing it less often.

* * * * *

The bottom line here—always treat the process of becoming sober as an opportunity to build a better future, *not* as something to dread. By breaking bad habits, you make yourself far more attractive to others than you have been while you were drinking, which in turn can have only positive benefits on how you enjoy your new life.

LEVEL 9—DEVELOP NEW HOBBIES

The essence of this Level is simple: <u>you *have* to find new hobbies to enjoyably fill the *gigantic* time hole in that your life that *not* drinking frees up</u>.

When I was drinking, I spent somewhere between 4-8 hours a day, *every* day, planning, obtaining, using, and recovering from alcohol (or recovering in the morning from the night before). My *actual* drinking was done over 3 to 6 hours, but there was overhead! Recovering the enough to function took at least an hour of extra time in the morning and caused productivity issues for the first portion of the workday.

Of course, I was not drinking continuously during that 3-6 hours, but *every* activity was centered around it; a glass or bottle was never far from hand during that time. Planning would be involved if I were in an unfamiliar city.[1] If I was in my normal drinking area (e.g. at or near home), I spent a lot of time rotating my alcohol purchases across different places (so they wouldn't think I drank too much).[2] I lived in Connecticut for much of this time, which limited where hard liquor could be sold. So rotating my hard liquor purchases was not easy. This liquor store hopping was further complicated by the fact that I usually bought my alcohol the day I drank it, in the belief it would help limit my consumption.[3] Bottom line: Drinking took a lot of time!

Take a minute to figure out how much time you spent that is related to drinking; I guarantee you will come away convinced that huge amounts of your daily life were spent with booze one way or another.

Once you become sober, this time will not fill itself. If you don't <u>proactively</u> figure out ways to spend this newly free time, your mind will start to wander back to alcohol. You need ways to refill that time with sober, mind- and body-occupying activities.

So what hobbies might make sense for you personally? Some might be obvious, such as ones you had and enjoyed before you became an alcoholic like bowling, gardening, reading, or walking, while others may be ones you have only idly thought of at various points. I suggest you try as many as possible as your tastes and interests may have evolved over the time while you were drinking, and you were not even aware of it!

While there obviously are many hundreds of potential hobbies, you should look for ones that have several of the following attributes:

- Mind occupying
- Physically challenging
- Not depressing (Exception: Volunteer work)
- Generally *not* boring (there are exceptions)
- Requires creativity
- New to you and/or has a high learning component
- High social interaction
- High laughter component
- Relaxing
- Relatively low financial commitment.

In addition, if you have a what-do-I-do-with-my-hands problem described in the previous Level, add a "high usage of hands" or "Hands-On Usage" (HOU) need to the above list.

Potential Hobbies From A to Z

Numerous examples of hobbies that address many of these attributes are listed below. Many of these hobbies can be used to address numerous triggers. Some of the more obvious ones are listed, but do not limit those hobbies for only those triggers. A few of these hobbies, particularly Exercise, Meditation, Pets, and Volunteering, can be "designed" to help in almost any trigger defense!

Table 12: Potential Hobbies from A to Z

Hobby	Trigger(s)/Need	Hobby	Trigger(s)
Aerobics	Anxiety, Insomnia (e.g. exhaustion), Loneliness and Social Situations (group classes)	Meetings (Alcoholic Community—Real or Online)	All, particularly Holidays, Peer Pressure, Relatives, Social Situations
Antiques (Buying, Selling)	Fun, Mid-Life Crisis, Reminders	Models (Building, Displaying)	Fun, Kids, Hands-On Usage (HOU)
Aromatherapy	Anxiety, Depression, Insomnia, Smell	Movies (Going To)	Boredom, Change, Escape
Art/Arts and Crafts (Many examples, such as Beadwork, craft-show crafts)	Many, incl. Anxiety, Depression, Hands-On Usage (HOU)	Movies (Making, and posting on Internet/ Facebook/ YouTube))	Boredom, Escape, Kids, Media, Relatives, UnFun
Biking	Escape, Fun, Weather/Seasons	Museum visiting (Cultural Attractions)	Many, incl. Boredom, Noise, Reminders, Social Situations (in group)
Bird watching (Observational hobbies)	Escape, Weather/ Seasons (different bird habits by season)	Music (Listening)	Anger (angry music) Job (at work), Media, Music, Noise, Yelling
Bowling	Depression[4], Fun, Peer Pressure, Social Situations, Weather	Music (Making, and posting on Internet/ Facebook/ YouTube)	Boredom, Escape, Fun, Media, Music
Bug Hunting (finding computer programming errors)	Boredom, Money (many software firms pay everyday users)	Nail Polishing (hobbies requiring some skill and specific temperament)	Loneliness, Money, Social Situations, HOU
Camping	Escape, Fun, Insomnia, (physical) Stress, Weather/Seasons	Online-Blogging	Frustration (of others not listening to you), Powerlessness
Carpentry (incl. Home remodeling)	Money, HOU	Online-Chatting	Boredom, Loneliness, Social Situations
Cave Exploration (or similar isolation-type hobbies)	Anxiety, Depression, Escape, Fun, Noise, Zeal	Online-Dating, Social	Anxiety, Powerlessness, Relationships, Sex, eX
Clubs, Groups, and Lodges (active) – Many forms	Many, particularly Fun, Social Situations	Online-Games	Boredom, Escape
Coaching (or Refereeing)	Guilt, Kids, Job/Money, Social Situations	Organize (Schedule, Filing, Closets, etc.)	Anxiety, Change, Disorder, Times of Day

Hobby	Trigger(s)/Need	Hobby	Trigger(s)
Collecting (e.g., cans, fossils, stamps, autographs, etc.)	Boredom, Fun, Insomnia, Reminders	Origami, Paper Crafts	Disorder, Kids, Money (cheap), HOU
Cooking (includes watching Food shows and trying their recipes)	Anxiety, Hungry, Proximity (e.g. cooking wine), Smell, Social Situations (cooking classes), Taste, HOU	Pets[5]	Many, part. Anxiety, Boredom, Depression, Fun, Guilt, Health, Kids, Loneliness, Relationships, Social Situations, (physical) Stress, UnFun
Crocheting, Embroidery, Knitting, Leather Working, Jewelry Making, Needle-pointing, Quilting, Sand Art, Sewing, Sculpting/Pottery	Anxiety, Boredom, Depression, Fun, Money, Loneliness/ Social Situations (in groups), HOU	Photography	Anxiety, Depression, Escape, Relationships (bonding through photographs)
Dancing (many sub examples)	Many, particularly Social Situations	Piano (Learning, Playing)	Media, Music, HOU
Dog Training	Anxiety, Depression, Loneliness, UnFun (interesting to others)	Prayer	Many, particularly Anxiety, Change, Frustration, Powerlessness
Drawing/Sketching, Painting	Anxiety, Depression, Victim (as therapy), HOU	Racing – Real or Virtual	Escape, Zeal (Excitement)
Driving	Escape, Hand-Usage	Radio (Ham)	Peer Pressure, Social Situations
Exercise (many sub examples)	All, particularly Anxiety, Boredom, Depression, Escape, Insomnia, Loneliness (when in group)	Reading	Many, part. Anxiety, Boredom, Depression, Escape, Fun, Insomnia
Fantasy Sports	Boredom, Fun	Recipe Collecting	Hungry, Smell, Social Situations, Taste
Fashion Designing	Sex (body type), Peer Pressure, Social Situations	Renovations (incl. Home design)	Change, Money
Feng Shui	Change, Disorder	Rock Climbing (e.g. dangerous, strenuous activities)	Escape, Fun, (physical) Stress, Zeal (Excitement)
Financial Planning[6]	Boredom, Change, Money, eX	Running[7]	Many, particularly Anger, Anxiety, Escape, Health, Insomnia, physical Stress, Zeal
Fishing	Escape, Fun, Noise, Insomnia, Weather	Sailing/Boating (incl. water ski, Jet Ski, etc.)	Escape, Fun, Weather/ Seasons, Zeal
Floating (particularly in professional, sealed chamber)	Anxiety, Health, Noise, physical Stress	School (Go back to)	Many, including Boredom, Change, Powerlessness
Floral Arrangements	Anxiety, Depression, Smell, HOU	Scrapbooking	Kids, Reminders, HOU
Foreign Language (learning one)	Boredom, Change, Mid-Life Crisis, Powerlessness	Sculpting/Pottery	Boredom, Victim (Self-Esteem) HOU
Games (many sub categories)	Many, particularly Boredom, Fun, Insomnia	Skating (Rollerblade)	Escape, Fun, Weather/Seasons, Zeal
Gardening	Anxiety, Depression, Escape, Fun, HOU	Skiing (Snow-downhill, cross)	Insomnia, Weather/Seasons
Genealogy	Mid-Life Crisis	Singing	Fun, Media, Music, Noise, Reminders
Golfing	Escape, Fun, Weather/ Seasons	Sports (PLAYING - many examples)	Many, incl. Anger, Boredom, Frustration, Fun, Health, Insomnia, Loneliness, Social Situations, physical Stress, Weather/Seasons
Gym (go to – not necessarily to Exercise)	Depression, Social Situations	Stretching/Deep Breathing	Many, incl. Anger, Anxiety, Health, physical Stress. Tired
Hiking	Escape, Fun, Weather/Seasons	Swimming	Fun, Health, Insomnia, Zeal (competitive swim)
Hunting	Escape, Fun, Weather/Seasons	Table sports (Ping-pong, Air Hockey)	Fun, Job (at work tables)[8], Social Situations
Ice Skating	Boredom, Fun, Weather/Seasons	Teaching/Tutoring	Many, part. Kids, Social Situations, UnFun

Hobby	Trigger(s)/Need	Hobby	Trigger(s)
Irish Dancing (popular form of family dancing)	Fun, Kids, Relatives	Toastmasters (Public Speaking Club)	Social Situations, Yelling (dealing with Conflict, Debate)
Jamming/Jarring (e.g. jarring food)	Hungry, Smell, Taste, Hands-Usage	Traveling/Trekking	Many, incl. Escape
Journaling	Anxiety[9], Reminders	Unicycling (and other strange "sports")	Physical Stress, Zeal (Excitement)
Junking (e.g. Antique, Craft Shows–Buying, Participation)	Escape, Fun, Reminders, Social Situations (via participation)	Volunteer Work (many examples)	Many, incl. Boredom, Depression, Fun/UnFun, Envy, Guilt, Insomnia, Loneliness, Mid-Life, Overconfidence (vol. at rehab centers), Mid-life, Power, Powerlessness
Karate, Kickboxing, Other Martial Arts	Anger, Fun, Frustration, Health, Insomnia, physical Stress	Walking	Many, incl. Anger, Health, Insomnia, (physical) Stress
Kayaking	Escape, Fun, Weather	Web Site (Creation, Editing, Learning How to Do)	Many, particularly Media, Money. Also HOU
League Sports, Games	Boredom, Fun, Social Situations	Wood Carving/Wood working (incl. Carving)	HOU, Boredom, Frustration, Money Victim (Self-Esteem)
Loitering (People Watching)	Peer Pressure, Social Situations	Writing (many sub examples)	Many, incl. Boredom, Media, Victim, HOU
Magic (Learning and Performing)	Escape, Kids, Money, UnFun, HOU	Yoga	Anger, Anxiety, Depression, Job (related stress), Loneliness (in classes), physical Stress
Massage Therapy	Anger, Anxiety, Job (stress), physical Stress	Yo-Yo Tricks (Learning, Doing)	Kids (Children), UnFun, HOU
Meditation	Many, incl. Anger, Anxiety, Change, Depression, Loneliness, Victim	Zoos (visiting, Volunteering at)	Depression, Escape, Fun, Kids, Loneliness

A convenient reference for many of these hobbies can be found at http://www.buzzle.com/articles/list-types-of-hobbies/. For some really unique groupings by topic as well as some unusual ones (caring for virtual pets, or beetle collecting anyone?) go to http://www.buzzle.com/articles/list-of-hobbies-interests.html. An excellent resource for finding and coordinating with others with similar interests is www.Meetup.com.

Not all hobbies are created equal of course, and for newly sober alcoholics the choice of hobbies can be very important in terms of time and emotional investment and return. In my view, the most important factor in choosing one or more hobbies—besides having a natural interest—is that you can do them often, and they last for substantial periods of time, each time. Bowling is an example; with multiple people and at least three games it can last for 2-3 hours. It is also relatively cheap.

You need to *align* your triggers with your hobbies. If one of your major triggers is Times of Day (say early evening hours), and you are on a limited budget (e.g. Money is an issue), bowling in a league (to also help with Social Situations) might be an excellent choice. Note, most bowling alleys have a bar, and many league bowlers seem to be beer drinkers (particularly men-only leagues), so it might not be a smart choice for those affected by Proximity and Smell triggers. **These little details can make a big difference.**

The Best Hobby: Exercise Anyway You Can!

The single, most impactful hobby you can do is _Exercise_! This will help practically <u>any</u> trigger, and in general vastly help your mental and physical health—both of which likely took a beating after years of abuse.

★ ★

Endorphins and Exercise and Alcohol

<u>Endorphins</u> are released from the body after a great workout and can result in feelings of great pleasure. Indeed, there is even a term for it—the "runner's high." One theory on alcohol abuse has Endorphins playing a major role,[10] which in turn may explain why some people can supposedly get "addicted" to exercise. But it also explains why exercise can be a great *substitute* for drinking.

★ ★

Specifically, the benefits include:

- Improved brain function and decision making
- Improved sleeping habits and patterns
- Stress reduction, particularly stress that has manifested itself in the muscles
- More positive demeanor (at least for a few hours after exercising).

While there is likely not much reason to worry about too much exercise in the newly sober, there are some causes for concern. Too much exercise can lead to injury, burnout, and possibly even long-term health problems.

Exercise does <u>not</u> equal having to go to the gym or other "work-like" activities. Practically anything that gets your butt off your couch and moving around qualifies. Walking the dog, gardening, (brick-and-mortar store) shopping and even playing some video games[11] qualify! Your list of hobbies **must** include at least one or two that give you some significant physical movement, particularly every day in early sobriety. It helps <u>greatly</u> to wear yourself out physically as much as you practically can, from pre-empting feelings of Anxiety or Depression to removing Insomnia from your list of post-sobriety concerns.

In fact, exercise in the appropriate form can be used in defending against nearly any drinking trigger, at least in part. The trick, of course, is matching the exercise type with the trigger and the specific situation. Angry? Go outside for a walk if it's a cool night and literally chill out. Bored? Go play an outdoor sport. Depressed? Play with a pet by throwing a ball or playing tug-of-war with them. Noise? Go for a quiet viewing in a museum, or walk in a park. Indeed, you can turn anything that does not involve sitting on the couch into some form of exercise. And there are hundreds of types of exercise; how you apply them to your triggers is limited only by your imagination.

Exercise both takes your mind off of alcohol—particularly your triggers—and sometimes also replicates the "buzz" you felt while drinking. What more incentive do you need?

* * * * *

We have now reached the end of Phase 2. For some of you, Phases 1 and 2 may be enough. They provide the essential foundation for understanding alcoholism in general and how it is impacting *your* life <u>specifically</u> (Phase 1). You will have a great set of starter tools and tips to draw on and guide you using the best that existing treatment methods have to offer (Phase 2). I would encourage you to re-read these first two phases, and in particular Level 2, to make sure you are getting <u>everything</u> you can out of what is described there. There is a huge amount of material, and it may be hard to digest all of it in one go.

But, I suspect that for most of you reading this book Phases 1 and 2 will *not* be enough. You need something *really* new. Hence, Phase 3 that describes new ways of approaching "old" ideas, such as spirituality and aversion therapy. You will also find some completely new stuff— particularly Level 13, where you learn how to integrate all of the tips, tools, defenses, and other ideas of the previous twelve Levels, making them *much* stronger than the sum of their individual parts.

Phase 3 may take some time to digest and may require re-reading as well. But again, I have tried to stuff as many interesting and fun items as I can into it, so your attention and energy builds and by the end you are <u>excited</u> about what is coming up in your life. Enjoy!

LEVEL 10—CONSIDER SPIRITUALITY

One way of looking at Phases 1 and 2 is that while much of it was new in terms of details and structure, it still was based on "conventional" methods used in other treatment programs, e.g. Rehab, Therapy, AA, etc. The Conquer Program sought to use the best of these methods and techniques.

Phase 3 however is different. Starting with Level 10, it uses new, unorthodox, and even controversial methods to solidify your sobriety, <u>for the long-term</u>. While the first two phases make up most of the program—or fortress, as below—it is Phase 3 that makes The Conquer Program unique.

PHASE 3 – Complete Your Fortifications

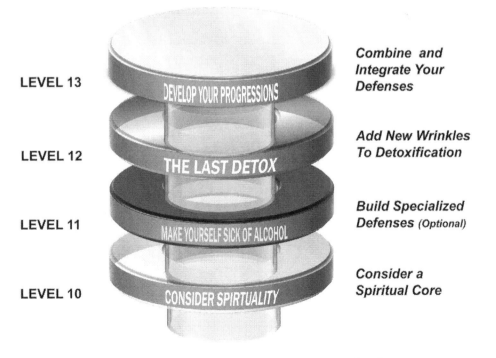

LEVEL 13 DEVELOP YOUR PROGRESSIONS	*Combine and Integrate Your Defenses*
LEVEL 12 THE LAST DETOX	*Add New Wrinkles To Detoxification*
LEVEL 11 MAKE YOURSELF SICK OF ALCOHOL	*Build Specialized Defenses (Optional)*
LEVEL 10 CONSIDER SPIRITUALITY	*Consider a Spiritual Core*

Figure 17: Phase 3—Complete Your Fortifications

Before we get into the main discussion of possibly using spirituality in your sobriety, it is worthwhile calling attention to Figure 17. Notice there is a kind of light-colored tube, connecting all of the different Levels.

While the primary purpose of the tube is to illustrate how Level 13 connects and integrates all the Levels of The Conquer Program, "integration" can also occur in *this* Level with respect to spirituality and its potential for tying together otherwise distinct elements of defense. Some people who are successful in incorporating spirituality into their sobriety find that it is not only a tool but a platform for their way of life, tying together otherwise disparate, unconnected pieces of their life. Keep that in your mind as you consider the potential for spiritualism in your sobriety.

In the main *How to Conquer Your Alcoholism* book, I extensively cover different ways to "get spiritual": from becoming involved in various organized religions, reading literature, reflecting on spiritual events in your life, and overall considering the "preponderance of the evidence" to *possibly* accept spirituality/God into your life in some form, in general or at least for purposes of being sober. In this book, I'll keep it simple: **to get or stay sober, it is *helpful* to be spiritual, but _not_ a necessity.** Hence the word "Consider".

★ ★

Why Is This Level Optional?

It is not only very difficult to "make" someone spiritual or religious against their will, I personally believe it is nearly *impossible*. Even worse, forcing (or very strongly urging) someone to "get religion" is actually counter-productive. Since much of religion/spirituality is based on faith (vs. hard facts), debating its merits has to be done at an emotional plane, not a factual one. If someone is not open to such concepts, then hard-edged, my-way-is-the-only-way-type arguments are likely to result in irritation, resistance, and possibly even anger—certainly not in adoption.

Thus, this Level is optional.

★ ★

That said, let's briefly explore ways that might help you become a bit more spiritual, and how it might help you in sobriety.

★ ★

Reasons to Try Spirituality in The Conquer Program

It boils down to two reasons: 1) Spirituality in many forms can help you "offload" the pressures' of life, in general and with respect to specific triggers, and 2) It can be considered an extension of your support network.

Programs like Alcoholics Anonymous specifically have God (or a "higher power") as central to its steps; actually putting the burden on Him (or Her) to help achieve sobriety. That approach <u>can</u> be effective, as evidenced by the thousands of sober AA-ers.[1] *Whatever works*, and for some, faith-based programs like AA <u>do</u> work.

Since The Conquer Program is trigger-based, the question becomes: "how can spirituality help with my drinking triggers?" The answer is that while it won't help with some triggers, it can with others. While spirituality is less likely to help with "physical" triggers (Hungry, Noise, Proximity, Smell, Taste) and "situational" ones (e.g. Boredom, Job, Peer Pressure, Social Situations), it *can* help with triggers that have to do with some form of "mental anguish" or pressure. These can include Anger, Anxiety, Extreme Emotions, Frustration, Guilt, Powerlessness, Victim, and Yelling. These mental anguish-type triggers can benefit from "knowing", and even praying to, a spiritual entity to help you deal with those types of anguish—without alcohol.

Indeed, a different way of looking at spirituality is as an *extension* of your support network. As was emphasized in Levels 4 and 7, **you cannot do this alone**. In a sense, spirituality is about expanding your contacts and community, just in a different way—the spiritual realm! It's really just redefining what "support" actually means and includes. Even if you're uneasy with such an expansive definition, (human) members of spiritual-communities can be a valuable extension to your support network.

At the end of the day not only can spirituality not hurt, it can add an extra layer of defense and support in resisting the temptations of alcohol.

★ ★

There are many ways to adopt and practice some form of spirituality, and doing so is not by any means an "all or nothing" proposition. There are many ways to do Spirituality Lite! I've categorized them into four categories: Organized Religion, Spiritual Literature and Teachings, Spiritual Epiphanies and Events, and "Preponderance of the Evidence",

Organized Religion

The short answer to the question of *"Can Organized Religion help me be sober?"* is: *"It depends"* — on the specific religion and particularly the people involved, and how in combination they approach addiction as a religious community.

Specific Religions and Alcohol

The world's religions have very differing relationships with alcohol. Many religions (Islam, Southern Baptists, Mormons) forbid alcohol or see it as sinful. Others have allocated a specific place for it, as in the Catholic practice of drinking Communion wine. There are other indicators of acceptance, such as monastic communities having brewed beer and made wine for centuries.

Within those religions that allow alcohol, the practical *attitude* can vary greatly. Alcoholic beverages appear frequently in the Bible (though drunkenness is condemned, for example by the stories of Noah and Lot). Some Christians including Pentecostals and Methodists today believe one ought to abstain from alcohol, but don't forbid it. In Hinduism, wines are sometimes used as medicine.[2] There are even variances within religions; for example, Southern Baptists are much stricter about alcohol than other Baptist denominations.

In other words, <u>alcohol is all over the map when it comes to how it is viewed (and even used) by organized religion</u>. It can be useful, something to be avoided, or outright banned, depending on the <u>specific</u> religion or denomination. *All* seem to recognize that there is a danger in drinking too much alcohol and have incorporated it into their teachings in one form or another.

Community Support within Organized Religions

While religious institutions have differing perspectives on alcohol use, the positive news is that to some degree all have teachings against alcohol abuse. There is even some research that shows people who are active in their faith are less likely to have problems with alcohol.[3]

However, research also indicates that in some religions and associated communities it can be very difficult for addicts to *seek* help when have a problem, particularly when a community views addiction/ alcoholism as a problem of human "sinfulness" that can be overcome by "free will."[4] Even worse are those groups that consider addiction as a sign of "moral weakness" or even "the work of the devil."

The question thus becomes whether the religion's attitude is just one of *opposing* alcohol abuse versus actively and constructively *helping* in its treatment. Unfortunately, such attitudes can vary as much by geography as by religion, with some areas having the local social norms outweighing whatever the "official" religious stance. Thus it can be very difficult on the surface to single out any particular religion/denomination as better or worse than others when it comes to addiction support—it becomes a matter of the beliefs of the individual religious community.

To Get a Religious Community Involved in Your Sobriety, Or Not?

The good news here though is that the attitudes towards addiction in your local church can usually be readily identified by some discrete asking-around. An ideal situation is to find a local religious community that understands the complexity of alcoholism (for example, the genetic and social factors that contribute to the disease), and that seem to be more open and matter-of-fact about its existence (versus addiction being treated as a deep dark secret to be kept hidden at all costs). Even within a small geographical area there can be a great variety of such attitudes. If you have the flexibility, you may want to "shop around" to identify if there are any viable possibilities in your area.[5]

As you consider a religious community, you will also want to see how possible communities treat the <u>family members</u> of alcoholics/addicts, as in more backwards communities they can extend distain and disgust towards the addict onto his or her relatives, who in turn may isolate themselves out of fear of what other people will think, gradually disappearing from the social arena of community and church. **In other words, it is possible that having your addiction known in your religious community results in a backlash onto your relatives.** That said, joining a caring religious community can be of great help, as research indicates being part of such communities can help alcoholics come to terms with their addiction and provide family members and friends with critical support.[6]

<u>**Bottom Line: Religious communities can be of significant help, or hindrance, when it comes to your alcoholism, depending on the specifics of your religion, denomination, and local community**</u>. If you believe your particular religion and/or its local community falls into the "helpful" category, seek support there to add to what you developed in Level 4—Engage Friends and Family and Level 7—Join a Community. If you think they are in the "not helpful" category, <u>do not</u> feel obligated to try—you will be <u>much</u> better off excluding such religious groups from your sobriety plans.

* * *

As we move from an organized religion discussion to a broader spirituality one, it is worth noting the concept of "Quasi-Religious" alcoholism treatment organizations—ones that focus specifically on alcoholism/addiction and include a heavy emphasis on God in their treatment. While some consider The Salvation Army and even Alcoholics Anonymous (discussed in Levels 6 and 7, respectively) to be such organizations, there are numerous others. These are what I call "specialty" organizations—mostly Christian-based—that combine elements of organized religion and alcoholism treatment. These include organizations such as <u>Addictions Victorious</u>, <u>Alcoholics for Christ</u>, <u>Celebrate Recovery</u>, <u>Christians in Recovery</u>, and <u>Strawberry Ministries</u>, to name a few—there are many of them. I have no specific opinion on the capabilities or structure of such organizations/programs,[7] but if you want to try to merge your beliefs (in Christianity) with alcoholism treatment, they might be worth investigating.

Spiritual Literature, Teachings, and Testimonials

If you ask a dozen people what "spirituality" means, you will get 12 different answers. Some possible definitions:

- Oxford English Dictionary: *The quality or condition of being spiritual; attachment to or regard for things of the spirit as opposed to material or worldly interests.*
- National Cancer Institute: *Having to do with deep, often religious, feelings and beliefs, including a person's sense of peace, purpose, connection to others, and beliefs about the meaning of life.*
- Neurobehavioral: *Spirituality means any experience that is thought to bring the experience into contact with the divine (in other words, not just any experience that feels meaningful).*

The best definition I have found, at least for purposes of The Conquer Program, is:

Spirituality refers to the beliefs and practices by which people live. These beliefs are varied and may include the presence of a divine being, a higher power or other spiritual beings. Spirituality plays a key role in guiding people and bringing inner peace, self-awareness and a purpose in life.[8]

One way to "get" spirituality, or even a specific religion, is in the study of it. Of course, there are a <u>huge</u> amount of texts, teachings, and stories of a spiritual or religious nature dating back centuries and even millennia, including the Bible (Christianity), the Tanakh (Judaism), and the Koran (Islam) to name a few of the over 20 major religions in the world.

I'm not about to go into a detailed study of the role of alcohol in individual religious practices, but as you can guess there are tons on the topic. To summarize (admittedly a very dangerous practice when it comes to religion), it is reasonable to say that religion's viewpoint on alcohol ranges from embracing it to equating it with the worst of evils, with most wandering in-between, even *within* a religion.

So, unless your religion explicitly teaches that it is wrong to drink alcohol (<u>and</u> you believe and accept that), it may be hard to find clear guidance on dealing with your alcoholism, even if you were brought up within and still actively practice the religion. If this latter applies to you, I would strongly encourage you to speak with leaders of your church or equivalent about your problems with alcohol and see what kind of <u>specific</u> guidance the religion can offer (subject to the concerns described in the Organized Religion section earlier). But it is probably not likely that they will be able to give you *specific*, <u>useable-on-a-daily-basis</u> help for your particular situation. *You will likely have to do it yourself.*

Even if your religion/religious community does not offer specific guidance on how to deal with alcohol problems, its literature may still provide you with an excellent grounding in how spirituality can play a role in your life. If you believe in some form of higher power (God, angels, etc.)—now is the time to use it. It is <u>your</u> task to apply those teachings and beliefs to bear specifically to <u>your</u> alcoholism.

★ ★

What is a Higher Power?

Higher Power is a term coined in the 1930s in <u>Alcoholics Anonymous</u> (AA) and is used in other <u>twelve-step programs</u>. It is also sometimes referred to as a *power greater than ourselves*. It can used to refer to a <u>supreme being</u> or <u>deity</u>, or some <u>conception of God</u>,[9] but in reality a Higher Power can be *anything*: a pet that has passed on, an inanimate object, a philosophy—*whatever works!*

The concept of a Higher Power can be very helpful for people who want to embrace spirituality, but are uncomfortable with Organized Religion or opposed to explicitly naming God as that source of spirituality. Testimonials abound about the "usefulness" of a Higher Power:

> *I have found something better and much safer in my higher power. Alcoholism is a living hell. I appreciate just getting up in the morning not sick and needing a drink.*[10]

The main benefit of using the words *higher power* is that it cannot be easily defined. This means that people can interpret the concept as they wish. It makes it possible for a Christian to follow the steps alongside a Buddhist or even an atheist. Most people interpret *higher power* as meaning "a" deity, but it does not have to be interpreted this way. It is left up to the individual to decide how they wish to define it. There are no rules except *that this power has to be greater than the individual*.

One of the biggest *practical* benefits of incorporating a higher power into a newly sober life is that it can provide a new or renewed sense of purpose. This new approach to life—a kind of clean slate approach—can strengthen a person and reduce the risk of relapse. Those who follow a spiritual path claim that it brings a great deal of happiness to their life. It can also have related benefits such as introducing the person to a new set of activities (e.g. attending spiritual group meetings, volunteer efforts) that can provide key defenses for specific triggers such as Boredom.[11] Thus the use of a Higher Power is consistent with and supportive of The Conquer Program.

★ ★

The study of spiritual literature can be an excellent place to bring in what you found out about yourself in the foundation building Levels 1 through 3. Level 2—Know Your Triggers is particularly important. Since you specifically and in great detail determined what causes or tempts you to drink, you can look to spiritual literature and leadership for help and teachings on those specific topics.

However, you may have to "translate" the triggers of this program into the "language" of your religion, with some triggers being harder than others (Change, Job, Sex, and Victim immediately come to mind). Specific teachings on your triggers may make much more of an impact on you and your drinking than any broader teachings on alcohol. However, it may require consulting with someone especially familiar with such texts and teachings (e.g. a minister or scholar), who may be able to help point you to specific texts and passages.

Fortunately, there are many religious/spiritual texts to choose from if you want to go the route of reading/teaching yourself. Unfortunately, there are *many* religious/spiritual texts to choose from if you want to go the route of reading/teaching yourself.[12]

First you have to select your religious denomination or spiritual approach. There are over a hundred to choose from, each with at least one major text, according to https://en.wikipedia.org/wiki/Religious_text (Wikipedia).[13]

Where to start? Probably the easiest way is starting with those texts you are using today (if at all) or those with which you were brought up. You may not have read them much, but even if you have, you did not with a specific eye towards alcoholism and/or triggers. You also might try some religious/spiritual-based addiction programs (generally Christian, discussed earlier in this Level) to see what texts they use. If you have no preference, you might try to do a side-by-side comparison of all the different types out there; with http://www.religionfacts.com/big_religion_chart.htm being a good starting point. [14]

Spiritual Event or Epiphany

I call this *Spirituality by being Scared to Death*.

Many of us—particularly older adults (not necessarily alcoholics)—have encountered life-threatening situations. Maybe a severe illness, a car accident, or a near disaster that left us physically intact but mentally traumatized, at least for a while. In those situations, you may have said to yourself "If I get out of this I'll be a better person" or some similar variation, even a vow to become more religious. A common phrase for this is "there are no atheists in foxholes." [15]

The same source for the definition of spirituality earlier also provided this perception of a Spiritual Event:

A spiritual experience can be described as an event or moment where a feeling of a purpose, a defined moment of clarity, or even of seeing angels, ghosts or spiritual beings occurs. It is believed that this experience changes a person's direction in life and has been linked to individuals giving up a life of abusing alcohol or drugs. Some individuals use this experience to find a new sober path in their life. [16]

The challenge, of course, is that many people forget such events as time goes on, or the pain or trauma "wears off" so we forget the vow or the determination to do things in our life differently. My view is this is often because many of these promises are often too vague or general, thus difficult to put into action on a day-to-day basis. Instead, if/when these occur, you should <u>very specifically</u> use the situation to focus on your alcoholism, and even on a specific person you want to prove your new resolve to:

> *I ended up in hospital in serious condition from drinking and, of course, not eating. I was a total physical, emotional and spiritual wreck. I hated myself so much that the only thing to do seemed to be drinking to oblivion. A doctor came by my bed twice a day to tell me I was a drunk and only I could change that. I found out much later this doctor was a godsend to many alcoholics. I was so angry with him I thought, I'll show him I can quit.*[17]

* * *

> *I finally hit rock bottom! I have been in and out of AA, in and out of institutions, rehabs and got really sick and tired of myself playing games to my mind. I blamed people, I blamed my family, most of all I blamed God for all of my wrong doings. I had a traumatic brain injury due to my chosen sport, this was the time to learn about me, a chance to get myself clean and sober. I have a purpose in living and knowing what's true, right and correct.*[18]

Many of these experiences happen at the same time, or are caused by, depending on the specifics—as a feeling of having hit "rock bottom." *Rock bottom* is the feeling that—except for death—your life can't get any worse. For some people it is a failed marriage, lost job, severe accident, DUI, or another traumatic event (usually related to alcohol (that finally convinces them that they <u>have</u> to get help).

You don't have to be in physical danger or life upheaval to feel this way of course. It may be some other peril or event that suddenly causes you to think about life in a different way. This is often called an "epiphany"[19] or an "a-ha" moment, when something that has been lurking in your brain that you have been unable to articulate suddenly becomes clear—sometimes called "a moment of clarity".

I decided to stop drinking after I was charged with a DWI in Missouri. This was the "a-ha" life altering moment for me. I realized I needed to stop before I hurt myself, or more importantly, my family...This was the low point for me...

For some, it may be that in the back of your mind you "knew" the end of your drinking was coming, but you just needed a kick-in-the-head to get you over the hump:

...It became clear to me that I needed to quit when I was in the holding cell at the jail, which was almost 3 years ago. I had never been to jail in my life, and that scared the hell out of me. I was court ordered to participate in outpatient therapy. And, I was ready to quit because I knew it would happen that way. So I took it seriously, I showed up for every session, and soon I started really believing that I was an alcoholic. I always knew I was, but I didn't fully accept it until I was forced to! [20]

In my research, it seemed most such testimonials were not overtly spiritual, most did have some elements of "feeling a bit" spiritual, particularly as described by the earlier definition. Spirituality <u>does not</u> need to have God or some form of deity, nor even a higher power; it just needs to result in some *inner peace, self-awareness and a purpose in life.* I call this "Spirituality Lite." It's good and good for you.

It doesn't even have to be a specific experience or situation that causes you to have an a-ha/kick-in-the-head moment. Even a bit of self-reflection on what alcohol is doing to your soul may do the job:

It wasn't being homeless, or losing my family or even my career of choice, a professional golfer. None of that mattered, and I later learned why, but what changed one day, having tried to drink myself into oblivion, even death, was how empty my soul felt and how completely alienated [I felt] from life, from myself and from everything that mattered. [21]

Some people cannot dissociate spirituality from religion—which, of course, is absolutely fine. Some even approach it very aggressively, in deciding to view alcohol and alcoholism as evil, and the way to deal with it is from the other side of the coin—God.

Alcohol I hate you! U are destroying me! I am blind to see the truth! But I see it now! God please break this evil yoke! Upon my life! Jesus u paid for my future healings and sins I accept your deliverance today! Forgive my sin to drink and let it destroy me slowly! Help me to live anew life thru your help! Change me make me anew person thru you lord, I'm weak but you are strong! Give me total control and power to overcome this addiction! Then renounce alcohol.[22]

There are many, many variations on this. You may feel at some time that God is speaking to you while you are actually awake and aware. Why not? Again, *whatever works!*

The main point of the above testimonials is that there are <u>many</u> ways you can introduce spirituality in your life, and a significant event in your life is a great way to start the process. Be on the lookout for such situations or events, and figure out the best way <u>for you</u> to get a bit of spirituality to help with your other defenses in conquering your alcoholism.

Preponderance of the Evidence

Do a search on "scientific evidence of God." There will be smart-ass links, such as *rationalwiki.org*'s compilation of <u>all scientific evidence for the existence of a deity</u> (2 tumbleweeds) and *godlessgeeks.com*'s <u>hundreds of proofs of gods existence</u>.[23] A more detailed search finds many articles about "evidence," including some well thought out pieces ranging from intelligent design, the creation and expansion of the universe, to dissecting Albert Einstein's theory of relativity. But, for better or worse, there is no definitive evidence that screams out—*Yes there is a god!* You have to take a different approach when it comes to evidence-building.

★ ★

A Note on Spirituality and Death

As discussed in Level 3, there are some alcoholics who drink because they have an active suicide wish. But there are likely many more who don't care one way or another, as strange as that sounds. This is particularly common for those individuals who have active health problems and know that drinking is a very bad idea—but they do it anyway. There are even some who drink *because* they have a fear of death, particularly the elderly. But if these alcoholics can introduce spirituality into their lives in some form, odds are that it will help in some form and to some degree. Try it!

[★ ★

Probably one of the simplest, even easiest ways of believing that there is something beyond your life is the evidence before your own eyes: <u>you are still on this earth, even when by all logic you should be *dead* from your drinking.</u>

> The physical withdrawals got worse and worse after shorter and shorter binges. It came to the point where only a 3-day binge would put me in the ER to detox from withdrawals. Whereas before, it would take 2 weeks, and before that, 2 months. Over 50 ER visits in 12 years? I'm lucky. By the grace of my HP.[24]

Extending this type of evidence to near-death stories from hundreds of individuals can provide in total a powerful argument for life after death and by inference to a power great than ourselves. One of the best overall descriptions of the afterlife I found was in a *Newsweek* article titled "<u>Proof of Heaven: A Doctor's experience with the Afterlife</u>" by Dr. Eben Alexander. Dr. Alexander looks to prove from a medical/scientific perspective based on his own near-death experience that heaven exists.[25]

There are many similar stories and many sources for such stories. One good source is the *Chicken Soup for the Soul* series (visit <u>www.chickensoup.com</u> for a list of titles). Depending on the specific title and category, the Chicken Soup books can offer many testimonials about the impact of spirituality in some form on their lives, including various miracle-type and near-death/after-life experiences. Individually, they might be easy to dismiss, but collectively they get you thinking.[26]

* * *

There is no reason not to combine some or all of the four categories of ways to get spiritual together—in fact, together they may be far more powerful. That is my personal experience.

In the end, it is up to you to determine what, if any, role a deity and/or other ways of looking beyond your life play in conquering your addiction and your life in general. I'm not here to proselytize one way, or another. My only suggestion is that you keep an open mind and consider it—it could provide a formidable set of additional defenses against alcohol for you!

LEVEL 11—MAKE YOURSELF SICK OF ALCOHOL

Warning: This Level poses a potential health risk. Be sure to consult your doctor before utilizing. This Level is **optional,**[1] though I'd encourage you to read it regardless as it provides very interesting information on why alcohol affects you like it does.

Why is this Level optional? Because depending on how you do it, it can be physically risky. So why even consider doing it? The bottom line for me was that I found the potential defenses I described earlier for some triggers—particularly the evil trinity of Smell, Taste, and Proximity—were just not complete enough for me.

In particular, I didn't just want to avoid those triggers (which is almost impossible anyway) I also wanted to function *completely* in those aromatic, tasty, buzz-beaconing, just-an-arm's-reach-away environments without having to worry about relapsing. That I also had occasional desires to "get buzzed" or "checkout" added to my relapse worries. I ultimately concluded that a form of aversion therapy (making myself sick of alcohol) might provide the additional defenses I needed, and it did.

This Level not only describes the techniques I developed to get sick of alcohol, it also includes a brief discussion of the rationale and science behind such aversion therapy—the underlying philosophy of the "getting sick" techniques described. The main *How to Conquer Your Alcoholism* book goes into much more detail, but the key points are provided here.

Aversion Therapy and The Conquer Program

Aversion Therapy was introduced in Level 6 as an unconventional treatment approach. It is revisited here because at its heart is *breaking the association* between alcohol and pleasure, and *re-associating* it with pain and misery—the goal of this Level.

Aversion therapy as it has typically and historically been applied has had only limited success. However, I believe that if done somewhat differently, it can be done more effectively and not necessarily only in the setting of a formal alcoholism treatment facility.

Aversion Therapy Refresher

Aversion therapy is a form of addiction treatment that uses behavioral principles to eliminate unwanted behavior. In this therapeutic method, the unwanted stimulus is repeatedly paired with discomfort. The goal of this conditioning is to make the individual associate the stimulus with unpleasant or uncomfortable sensations.

During aversion therapy, the person may be asked to think of or engage in the behavior they enjoy while at the same time being exposed to something unpleasant such as a bad taste, a foul smell or even mild electric shocks. Once the unpleasant feelings become associated with the behavior, the hope is that the unwanted behaviors or actions will begin to decrease in frequency or stop entirely.

★ ★

The Relevance of Pavlov's Dog

Ivan Petrovich Pavlov was a famous Russian physiologist. The concept for which Pavlov is famous is the "conditioned reflex" he developed jointly with an assistant in 1901. He came to learn this concept of conditioned reflex when examining the rates of salivations among dogs.

Pavlov discovered that when a bell was rung in subsequent time with food being presented to the dog in consecutive sequences, the dog would initially salivate when presented with food. The dog will later *come to associate* the ringing of the bell with the presentation of the food and salivate upon the ringing of the bell. His writings also record the use of a wide variety of other stimuli, including electric shocks, whistles, metronomes, tuning forks, and a range of visual stimuli.[2]

★ ★

The overall effectiveness of aversion therapy can depend upon a number of factors, particularly the methods used and whether or not the client continues to practice relapse prevention after treatment is concluded. The specific issue with (the few) institutional practitioners of alcohol-related aversion therapy today is that the methods used (primarily drugs) to induce "aversion" may not have a long-lasting effect on some individuals, particularly as those drugs are not continued long-term once inpatient treatment is completed. Also, the fact that the vast majority of insurers do not cover aversion therapy makes its extensive, long-term use out of reach for all but the most well-off individuals.

A more radical approach is needed, one that makes the sight, smell, taste, and feel/effect of alcohol actually *disgusting* to the alcoholic, discussed next.

Getting Sick—The Proximity Trigger

Let's start with the Proximity trigger. Is there a way to make the mere *sight* of alcohol (or anything related to it), make you feel unwell? The answer is maybe; I was able to do it, and some variation of it might work for you.

The possibility of sight-based "aversion therapy" first started to click with me as a result of colon problems I'd suffered for many years, and unfortunately in a negative way. Without getting too graphic, problem colons can be very sensitive to a variety of factors and in turn cause unpleasantness, or at least emergency trips to the bathroom. While I had experienced various instances of this over the (30!) years, they were for the most part manageable and controllable. It wasn't until after recovering from colon surgery that I realized this sensitivity wasn't just limited to what I ate or did physically, but also to what I thought and sensed — sight in particular.

I could be perfectly fine colon-wise, even recently having gone to the bathroom. However, I still found that the mere *thought* of going to the bathroom or even random musings on my intestinal health would cause a great uptick in the urgency to go again. I even found that if I was in a store, feeling perfectly fine, and saw a sign for "Restrooms" that I would have a sudden and urgent need to get there. <u>Fast</u>. And I needed to be faster as I got physically closer and closer to said restroom.

This urge had happened to me before but never so insidiously. After thinking about it for a while (enjoyably lying in my hospital bed after surgery), I came to the conclusion that this kind of mind-body connection could be created for <u>positive</u> purposes, namely my alcoholism. Once I was released, I started trying to think negative thoughts <u>every</u> time I saw the word "Liquor" on a store front or sign, and especially every time I saw a bottle of vodka (my long-time drink of choice and horrible nemesis).

In particular, each time I saw these I would think of how hideous I felt in the lead-up to my going to the hospital, and <u>try to actively associate these bad feelings with the sight of alcohol</u>.[3]

To my amazement it worked. After a couple of weeks of doing this (with probably about 100 "sightings" of alcohol signs and immediate thinking about my hospital pain and nausea) I would start to feel queasy whenever I happened across the word "Liquor" or sight of a vodka bottle. I was even able to extend the feelings to other types of alcohol. I felt I had broken (or at least seriously bent) the Proximity trigger! No longer did the sight of alcohol make my mind weaken and my mouth water! This feeling still continues several years later. While I no longer start to get physically sick at the sightings, I have absolutely no temptation to go near anything that resembles alcohol in any form.[4]

Getting sick at the sight of alcohol is helpful. However, the real potential for aversion therapy is in the reduction of the impact of Smell and Taste as triggers, and the potential elimination of "Buzz-Rush" as a desired feeling or outcome, discussed next.

Getting Sick—Smell, Taste, and the "Buzz-Rush"

Here is where The Conquer Program's version of aversion therapy can get complicated, and is ***totally optional and at your own risk***.

Odds are there is some food or beverage that during some point in your past made you violently ill. Maybe you choked on popcorn once and can't bear the smell let alone taste of it. Maybe you have an allergic reaction to onions or nuts. Maybe there is some food that just tastes hideous to you (like lima beans—the most hideous vegetable ever created). You might even think back when your mom put something gross on your thumb to make you stop sucking it. Or perhaps some alcoholic beverage that you had such a horrible experience with that you vowed never to drink it again—and stuck to it![5]

Those kinds of feelings are what we are trying to replicate here (at your own risk). In my case, it involved drinking <u>purely</u> for the purpose of getting sick, combined with a food that I was allergic to (red onions) to aid in the process.

★ ★

Foods That Can Cause an Allergic Reaction

According to mayoclinic.com[6], there are eight foods included in food allergy labeling, accounting for an estimated 90 percent of allergic reactions. These eight foods are: Milk, Eggs, Peanuts, Tree Nuts (such as almonds, cashews, walnuts), Fish (such as bass, cod, flounder), Shellfish (such as crab and shrimp), Soy, and Wheat.

Other specific sources of reactions include Avocados, Bananas, Caffeine, Cheeses (aged in particular), Legumes (beans and peanuts), MSG, Onions, Peanut Butter, Pickled products, Pizza, Processed Meats, Yeast-based products, and Yogurt. Hopefully, it is obvious, but I'll state it here: *If you have a serious allergic reaction to anything here (such peanuts), do NOT use them if you attempt the approach described shortly.* The assumption is that you have a _mild_ reaction to them, or that they regularly or predictably cause some indigestion, heartburn, or queasiness.

★ ★

First, the prerequisites. These are <u>absolute</u> requirements:

- Be at home or staying with a friend or family member

- Have that friend or family member with you at all times while you are drinking

- Do NOT drive under *any* circumstances

- You are **_not_** partying, socializing, or having a good time while you are drinking—<u>you are trying to make yourself sick</u>. That doesn't mean you can't watch TV, read a book, surf the internet, or other mildly entertaining activities. However, the focus is on making yourself vomit, break out in a hideous rash, or something similarly unpleasant (but not life threatening).

Some additional suggestions and recommendations if you can manage them include:

- Document your experiences (real-time or close to it), including amounts and times in a log, blog, or another forum.

- Try to plan on doing the aversion therapy when you can minimize personal and professional commitments. This will be difficult to do, since the therapy can be a multi-week process, but do your best.

- Take some "selfies," before and after in the bathroom mirror, at various points in your drinking each night. Since you will likely be drunk and pass out, you might not remember what you looked like if you breakout in a rash or your skin becomes heavily flushed (which is actually a sign of the therapy working).

<u>Last, but absolutely not least, run this approach by your doctor.</u> If he or she says no, ***don't do it***.

★ ★

The Author's Extreme Approach to Making Myself Sick of Alcohol

1. Five days/nights drinking for the <u>sole</u> purpose of drinking (vodka in my case, which by this time in my drinking "career" was pretty much the only thing I drank in volume). <u>No</u> fun, entertainment, parties, or socializing involved. *I was drinking only to try to make myself sick.* I included introducing my allergic-reaction inducing food (onions) into the mix, eating them right before I started drinking.
2. Five days/nights NOT drinking. I didn't do anything special during these days besides not drink. And yes, I essentially went through detox again. I then repeated the process (including the associated detoxes[7]), with shorter time intervals:
3. Four days/nights drinking
4. Four days/nights NOT drinking
5. Three days/nights drinking
6. Three days/nights NOT drinking
7. Two days/nights drinking.

By this point, I was sick of drinking and had no desire to do more. Also, I did not experience much in the way detox symptoms after the last round of drinking besides a few shakes that first subsequent day of not drinking. I kept on thinking my desire to drink would come back, but it did not. I finally decided to do one final drinking session as a final "test," about 2 weeks after my previous drink, using a different type of alcohol (Margaritas). I felt nauseous after one drink, and two was enough to make me vomit.

I make absolutely no guarantee or warranty that this will work for anyone else. I do <u>not</u> recommend trying it, particularly if you can find some other way of defending against the Smell and Taste triggers and any desire for "Buzz-Rush".[8]

★ ★

As I "progressed" in the above approach my reactions to alcohol changed. While the "rush" was still ok (only lasting a few minutes), the "buzz" period got progressively shorter before I reached the "numb" state, which is when I started to experience queasiness and finally vomiting. Note that I *wanted* to vomit—and did *nothing* to prevent it, and even *encouraged* it when I was borderline. I was even able to "progress" to having a facial then full body rash break-out towards the end—I looked like I had the chicken pox a couple of times. I also passed out ("checked-out") drinking less and less the volume that I had always consumed before. After my final "test" drinks, which I forced, *I have had no desire to smell or taste alcohol since, and when I do, it does not bother me, other than occasional light nausea (which is a good thing).*

This process also increased my aversion to the sight of alcohol as well, using a variation of the visual aversion process described earlier. Last, but not least, I came to <u>dislike</u> the *effect* of alcohol. Instead of the "pleasure" of a rush/buzz/numb/checkout, drinking was now associated with being woozy, light-headed (not in a good way), nauseous, puking my guts out, gross rashes, and overall feeling of "yuk."[9]

Over time, the physical nausea when I came near alcohol went away, but the *indifference* remained—<u>I can ignore the presence or smell of alcohol</u> in any circumstance, often with a degree of disgust when I smell it up close. When, years later, I *tasted* alcohol, it had absolutely no appeal.[10] I have continued to "test" myself in many other ways and forums, such as packed bars during the NCAA tournament, dozens of drunken students in college graduation parties (including even buying booze for someone else, and smelling the drinks), and walking down the liquor aisles when I go grocery shopping, and I am not tempted by it <u>at all</u> (the smell of wine in particular brings instant nausea).

I have no idea if my specific approach is replicable or not, other than various "formal" medical-clinic aversion therapy testimonials, which frankly are kind of a mixed bag.[11] But that doesn't mean you can't find your <u>own</u> way to accomplish the same thing:

> *What I have to do for myself if a fleeting drinking thought comes to mind is to make it a point to "think the drink through" to its logical conclusion. These days it is HIGHLY unlikely that stopping off at a bar and drinking would net me any young, compliant, ego-stroking young women, but it likely WOULD net me yet another opportunity to try on some ill-fitting orange clothing......The thought of wearing ill-fitting orange clothing and the attendant humiliation and loss of personal liberty goes a LONG way toward quelling the "euphoric recall". For others who do not have the advantage of having experienced a stay in the local drunk tank, their own personal version of hell will, no doubt, do nicely.[12]*

You don't have to go through what I did, nor go to prison to make yourself sick of alcohol. At the end of the day, it really is all about reminding yourself of your own personal version of hell and <u>continually associating</u> it with alcohol. Make its Smell, Taste, nearness (Proximity), and effect (rush/buzz/numb/checkout/Fun/Escape) equate to pain, misery, sickness, even death. With practice, you may be very pleased with the results and will have added another major defense in Conquering Your Alcoholism!

LEVEL 12—THE <u>LAST</u> DETOX

Hopefully, you have successfully detoxed by the time you reach Phase 3, using the knowledge gained in Level 5, or have become heartily sick of alcohol using the aversion therapy-type approach described in Level 11. But odds are there is a significant percentage of you for which this is not the case. Perhaps you are scared to make an attempt (perfectly understandable), or perhaps you did try your best, and it just did not take hold for you. That is what this Level is about: to give you additional ideas to make this Detox the LAST you ever do.

In particular, this Level is relevant for you if:

- You skipped Level 11—Make Yourself Sick of Alcohol, and you are still drinking; or
- You did parts of Level 11, but did not include actions to physically make you averse to the smell, taste, sight, and the effect of alcohol; or
- You did do Level 11 completely, but it did not work for you sufficiently such that you are still drinking.[1]

Regardless of the above, this Level 12 is <u>only</u> for people who have tried to detox in some form in the past, e.g., during Level 5 or during some other program.[2] Assuming this is the case (and if not then go back to Level 5 in Phase 2), you've got some idea of what is coming at you. Maybe you are dreading it like the plague, or perhaps you are looking at it with trepidation or resignation, but also a large amount of skepticism that nothing is going to change. Regardless, with <u>this</u> detox, things are, hopefully, going to be different.

The Trick is Do It While You're Sick

The essence of this Level is to _detox while you are sick with something else_. _This is totally optional and at your own risk_. The core idea is to combine the <u>misery of detox</u> with the <u>pain and unpleasantness of your other aliment</u> and blame _both_ on alcohol. You are attempting to obliterate any association between alcohol and pleasure, and _replace it_ with an association of misery and agony. In essence, this is a type of the aversion therapy used in Level 11.

In my <u>personal</u> experience, the sicker you do this the "better"—even being sick enough with your illness to be in the hospital. No, I'm not nuts. This was my situation, and it helped greatly believe it or not. I was in the hospital for what turned out to be a hole in my colon, with the symptoms being intense abdominal pain. This situation had several "advantages," including:

- Considering the pain I was in before entering the hospital, I had already not drank for a couple of days—a kind of running start.

- With the pain I continued to suffer in the hospital, the last thing on my mind was getting a drink (except for water).

- There was absolutely no liquor around anyway.

- It was a tightly controlled environment, to the point of dictating my every movement. Comforting in a strange way, knowing there was nothing I could do about my situation including obtaining alcohol.

Having made absolutely sure they knew I was a raving alcoholic (my words to them), the doctors and staff were <u>very</u> conscious of how they prescribed medicines and were very sensitive to monitoring my vital signs for any potential detox complications. As such, I was killing two birds with one stone in terms of hospital admission: intestinal problems and alcohol detoxification. This was a great side benefit in terms of with time and cost.[3]

As mentioned numerous times before, *lack of control* over alcohol is one of the four cornerstones of alcoholism. Being (bed-ridden) ill in a strange way provides you a degree of safe control over alcohol—at least until you are well (and particularly if you are in the hospital). My theory is that one of the big reasons inpatient rehabs (including ones with detoxification services) are so attractive and successful (in the short term), is that the alcoholic has no control over their drinking situation—other people do. In my hospital situation, it was strangely beneficial knowing that there was *nothing* I could do to obtain and drink alcohol, which after the initial panic and worst of the withdrawal turned out to be very comforting.

My experience would explain why so many people relapse after they leave rehab. There is no longer the structure and (involuntary) discipline to prevent them from drinking other than what they can generate on their own. Unfortunately, this is often not enough, particularly as more time goes by and more alcohol "attacks" occur.

It was during this time of hospitalization (overall about two weeks from symptoms to discharge) that I started to develop this program in general and this Level in particular. At every turn, when my pain medication started to wear off (particularly when there were hours until my next dose), *I would blame the agony on alcohol—over and over and over again*. And it worked! I came to view alcohol more often as a cause of misery than I did a means of pleasure. Ever since, I try at every opportunity to mentally associate *any* pain I have with alcohol.

You don't have to be in the hospital for this to work, but in my opinion you do have to be in major pain or at a minimum extremely uncomfortable, "ideally" for a significant period of time. In essence, this is another version of aversion therapy discussed in Level 11. That's the key for this (hopefully) last detox: _associate the pain and misery of it, and all pain and misery you experience—with alcohol_. <u>Break</u> any lingering association alcohol has with fun or pleasure and <u>replace it</u> with discomfort and even agony! This "re" association might come easy, or take much "practice," but it if you can do it you will find it a <u>very</u> effective deterrent to many kinds of alcohol attacks.

If you decide to try the any of the above, ***consult your doctor first***. While it is hard for me as a lay person to conceive of any illness where your doctor _wants_ you to continue drinking, it is possible. For example, he might worry that possible side effects of <u>not</u> drinking (e.g. DTs) may introduce too much risk into the treatment prescribed for you for your illness.[4]

Other Tricks to Help Detox

Of course, it may be quite a while before you get sick, or you may not get sick at all (the ultimate good news-bad news scenario). In that case, the best advice is to go back to Level 5 and try again. Perhaps use a medically-supervised approach (if you tried to do it yourself before), or use a different facility if the first one did not work or you. Also reread Level 11, to see if it may provide insights you missed the first time, and perhaps (at your own risk) try that approach again if you haven't already.

It may be you are the sort of person that needs some of the most unorthodox approaches to problem solving for them to work on you. If so, my research found a variety of other tricks and tips that _may_ help with your Detox process. I have not personally tried any of these and so cannot vouch for their effectiveness or even safety, but one may give you additional ideas to make this your LAST Detox:

- Detox while there is something you absolutely <u>love</u> on television, for long periods of time, such as the NCAA Tournament or the Olympics. Watching it can help you occupy your mind and channel your distress for long periods of time over multiple days. "Binging" on certain TV programs (such as Breaking Bad or Game of Thrones) may also serve this purpose, and is very easy to do in the age of Netflix.

- If you are going to self-detox, do it (<u>with someone else with you</u>) in a *remote location* and/or where alcohol is not sold within at least 100 miles (e.g. at least a couple hours' drive one-way). This distance can provide a great way to resist urges since it is logistically difficult (and likely for someone to notice you being gone). Make sure medical treatment is <u>*close by*</u> however.[5]

- Drink lots of fluids. Try to "taper off" to beer.[6]

   I've detoxed over 7 times, 3 of them were fully successful, with two of those successfully being medically treated and supervised.[7] If you are detoxing, stay calm and make sure you have someone with you, at least in the house so you can be checked on frequently. Taper off the alcohol if you can to the point where you are only drinking beer, and if you are already only drinking beer see if you can get yourself down to a place where you're not having the shakes. Keeping hydrated is most important. Drinking Gatorade or putting very light salt in your water will help your cells retain it. If you have the ability, try to exercise. Get out into the sun or outside and try to stretch and move around. Eating is most difficult, though if possible will help you rebound and means you are on the road to recovery.[8]

- Try to get into a rhythm on how you start and end your day.

   I have been starting each day with hot water and lemon juice and taking melatonin at night to help me sleep. I feel lucky that my withdrawal symptoms haven't included shakes, or vomiting.[9]

- Give up alcohol for Lent.

   I am a 65-year-old woman who has drank most of her life and has quit more times than I can tell. Lent is coming up and I will try one more time to quit for good.[10]

- Ask your doctor about drugs, including various vitamin supplements.[11]

   The morning of the 2nd and 3rd day after I stop is the hardest. Severe tingling, anxiety, nervousness. Like a panic attack. I take a mild sedative (low dose Xanax)[12] by 9am, and that will eliminate the withdrawal symptoms. After 4 or 5 days of no drinking, my system seems to function OK and I don't need the benzodiazepine meds. But let me tell you, those attacks are very real and very scary![13]

- Exercise intensely; including hiring a personal trainer (it will likely be less than the cost of your booze).

- Juicing!

  Juicing and drinking lots of water daily helps cleanse the body and liver of toxins. Research juicing for detox of the liver [such as] juicing 2 beets, 1 apple, 3 celery, small piece of ginger, one dandelion root.... juicing helps with getting to sleep. Juice daily at least twice a day.[14]

Again, please **consult your doctor** before trying any of the above (except for perhaps the Lent and Juicing ideas). It is unlikely that any single one of these might be the magic bullet that helps you succeed when everything else failed, but you never know!

* * *

If you are <u>still</u> drinking after all the previous Levels (including this one), but you see <u>strong</u> signs of improvement and potential for stopping drinking entirely, then you have a great chance of succeeding completely. If you have *not* seen much improvement by now, I strongly encourage you to go back to Level 1 and literally start over. This time with <u>much</u> more attention to detail, in particular in Level 2 where you identify your triggers.

The next and final Level in The Conquer Program: Level 13—Develop Your Defense Progressions—is where we put together all of what you've learned so far in an even more powerful way to complete your fortifications against the attacks of alcohol.

LEVEL 13—DEVELOP YOUR

DEFENSE PROGRESSIONS

We are almost at the end! By now you should feel that you have *many* ways to defend against alcohol attacks, and perhaps have already successfully used at least some of them in a variety of circumstances.

★ ★

You Think You Have Made Progress, BUT...

...you still feel there is a lot more you can do. Maybe you are still drinking, and/or just not comfortable with what you have learned about yourself so far.

If so, go back and re-read this book, or at least Level 2—Know Your Triggers. That Level is the heart and soul of The Conquer Program. I recommend *all* readers re-read this book at least once. Besides picking up on elements you missed, or identifying helpful nuances to a particular tip, you will also see humor and interesting facts that will make it even more entertaining (and thus more apt to stick in your mind) the second time around!

★ ★

Level 13 looks to do what many, if not most alcoholism treatment programs do <u>not</u> do, which is *integrate* and *coordinate* all the tools that you have learned, to get all your defenses <u>to work together.</u> For the best overall defense, individual defenses should be optimally structured, grouped together, integrated and coordinated, to get them to work their best in the worst of circumstances and *all* circumstances in general. Using the war analogy, it is to get all your defenses to work together as a cohesive army, not as a bunch of individual weapons and soldiers just milling around, waiting for a fight. Level 13 is where all the power the individual phases and Levels of the Conquer Program can be brought to bear to defend against the most stubborn, most varied, most intense alcohol attacks, in one impenetrable fortress, as illustrated in Figure 18 below.

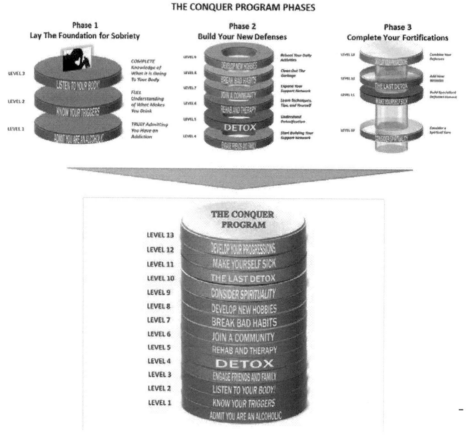

Figure 18: The Complete Conquer Program

Let's re-review the underlying philosophy of The Conquer Program. At its core is that **no one single** method, idea, tool, tip, level, or approach will work <u>all</u> the time, for <u>all</u> triggers, for <u>all</u> situations and circumstances. You **_must_** have multiple defenses. But just having multiple defenses will not be enough sometimes. In these circumstances or situations, how you _structure_ the defenses may be even more critical than the strength of any individual defense.

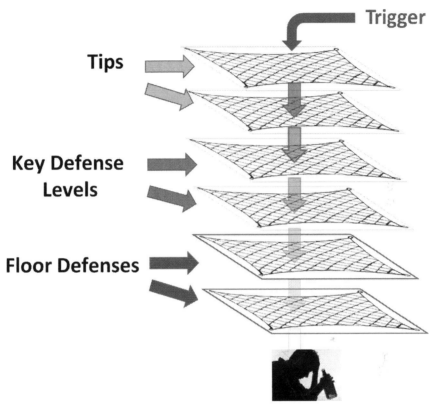

Figure 19: Trigger Safety Nets

Figure 19 above illustrates the end result of Level 13. You identified your triggers and a variety of tips and Key Defense Levels in the earlier chapters. Now is the time to put them together in a <u>structure</u> so that they form a *series of safety nets* in between a trigger occurring and you relapsing. Each individual net serves not only as a way of potentially completely rebuffing a trigger attack, but even if *not* fully successful a way of partially diminishing the trigger's impact. This will make it much more likely that the *next* safety net will fully stop the attack (illustrated by the slowly vanishing downward arrows).

What do I mean by structure? Mostly it has to do with the *order* that you think and/or do the tips and defenses. When being attacked by alcohol (in the form of a trigger) what do you do to resist? Do you call so and so first, work on Hobby #3, go to a meeting, or jump online to website B? Which one will be the most effective way of not drinking <u>right now</u> for the situation or feelings I'm dealing with <u>right now</u> and how I think I am most vulnerable <u>right now</u>?

And what happens if that first method doesn't work? *"I called so and so and still feel like drinking." "I did Hobby #3 for an hour and <u>still</u> feel like drinking." "What do I do next? And what after I do those <u>and I still</u> feel like drinking?"* Addressing these challenges is where the concept of defense *progressions* comes in: to methodically yet intuitively structure all your defenses in the order right for you.

WHAT ARE PROGRESSIONS?

While perhaps an unfamiliar word, in reality <u>everyone</u> has been doing progressions in some form all their lives. It is what we do in everyday life in "reading" and responding to complex situations, such as driving a car or even walking and talking and eating (particularly at the same time). We are taking in the situation(s) around us, and acting/reacting accordingly with the options (e.g., often defensive in nature) available, which could constantly be changing. This is similar to reacting to treacherous driving conditions or complex social/job situations where you have to "keep on your toes" to deal with the ever-changing and often unforgiving environment.

For example, in bad road conditions we may constantly veer or change lanes, accelerate or brake, look in the mirrors, use turn signals, and look in all directions so fast that it seems we are doing it all at the same time. We may use similar techniques but in a completely different order depending on the conditions. We "read" the situation and immediately implement a set of actions to keep us safe from that situation while changing the radio station the whole time!

Here "reading" means seeing, hearing, touching, reading, and maybe even smelling and tasting[1] the situation. All of our senses are constantly at work in "reading" our situation, and sending information to our brain to process and act/react accordingly.

For many of these everyday activities we don't <u>consciously</u> think about doing them, we *subconsciously* do. It took education, training, and experience to get these kinds of activities to become embedded in our subconscious, so we do them automatically or nearly so. This kind of automatic reading and responding to threatening circumstances, such as what we do when we drive in dangerous traffic conditions or walk on uneven and slippery terrain, is what we seek to also achieve in dealing with the threats of alcohol.

The general concept of progressions can be learned and applied at any age by anyone. One example where "reading the progression" is used is in (American) football with the quarterback "reading" the opposing players and consciously AND subconsciously analyzing and adapting to the circumstances of the play (more info at "<u>Reading The Progression</u>"[2]). The Conquer Program draws on this concept (without your being a football fan or player) so you can retrain/rewire your mind and body in how it deals with the threat of alcohol.

Of course, the football analogy does not translate directly to defending against alcohol trigger attacks. For one thing, there are more than 11 possible triggers (attackers on the opposing side) that can come at you. There are also lots more on the bench just waiting to drive your head into the turf! More weapons too; an attack can be not just physical but mental, emotional, and environmental. They can vary by time of day, day of the week, month, season, even year. Or even hourly! Your defenses can vary too; some of the time you might be in full pads and protection coverage and other times running around in your shorts.

So how do you develop <u>your</u> defense progressions with the seemingly endless possible ways to be attacked by alcohol?

DEVELOP YOUR DEFENSE PROGRESSIONS

While the concept of progressions might seem like it might include dozens or even hundreds of possibilities reflecting all the different ways and times that triggers can manifest themselves, <u>simplicity</u> is the key. If you can't remember, and eventually *instinctively and intuitively* know, what to do in a certain trigger situation, it's not going to do you any good much of the time.

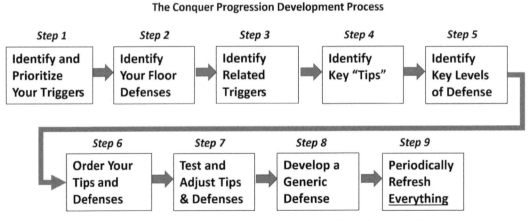

Figure 20—The Conquer Program Progression Development Process

214

Figure 20 above depicts a 9-step, trigger-centric process to develop your progressions. The <u>very</u> good news is that you have probably done most of the hard work for most of these steps—and if you haven't, you have learned enough that doing them should be relatively straightforward. So, while developing your progressions may *seem* complicated, the reality is not as harsh. The steps are:

- Step 1—Identify, Inventory and Prioritize Your Triggers
- Step 2—Identify Your "Floor" Defenses
- Step 3—Identify Key Related Triggers
- Step 4—Identify Key "Tips"
- Step 5—Identify Key Levels of Defense; Get <u>Specific</u>!
- Step 6—Order Your Tips and Defenses
- Step 7—Test and Adjust your Tips and Defenses
- Step 8—Develop a "Generic" Trigger Defense Progression
- Step 9—Periodically Refresh <u>Everything</u>

Step #1—Identify, Inventory and Prioritize Your Triggers

In Level 2 you identified all your triggers. Here you step back, inventory all the ones you identified (making sure they are <u>major</u>, <u>direct</u> triggers), and prioritize them, ranking them from most impactful to least. As described in Level 2, "major" triggers are those that <u>really</u> make you want to drink, <u>more often than not</u>. "Direct" means they cause you to want to drink by themselves, not just in combination with other triggers (those are referred to as "related triggers").

The first time you inventory all your triggers you may find you have 10, 15, or even more. This number should not be surprising at all. Over the course of the Alcoholism Process and its ever-increasing dependence on alcohol, we are likely to associate alcohol with "dealing with" more and more triggers as time goes on.

Your inventory should list *all* of your triggers, even if you are not sure of some. Then go through each trigger discussion again to see if it <u>really</u> is a major trigger (one that makes you want to drink more often than not) as well as being a direct (and not a related) trigger.

Try to get this list down to between 5 and 12 major triggers if you can. There is nothing magical about this range. However, if you have fewer than five, you may not be breaking down the triggers in sufficient detail. A great example: "Stress" may be two or three more specific ones such as your Job, Kids, or Money not the narrow physical stress and strain of the Stress trigger.

More than 12 triggers probably indicate you are categorizing "minor" triggers (ones that only occasionally make you want to drink) as major ones, or you are listing several Related Triggers when they are all rooted in the same 1 or 2 major triggers.

That said, more triggers are much better than fewer ones. It only takes <u>one</u> undefended trigger to screw things up, particularly early in sobriety.

Prioritizing these triggers will be very helpful as you think through things and possibly eliminate (or even add) certain triggers. What is prioritizing? It is just what it sounds like: which triggers hit you the worst? More specifically, it is those triggers whose *severity* and *frequency* make them the worst for you in terms of desire to drink. Is Boredom #1 in terms of the severity and frequency, or is it #4? Does Depression top all other contenders, or is it more the desire to Escape from the pressures of everyday life? Is Stress really at the top, and if so what <u>kind</u> of Stress?[3] Think about these priorities, but don't *over*-think it. Odds are your first thought of your #1 trigger will truly be your top priority. Prioritizing other triggers might require a bit more thought. If you are uncertain about whether a trigger is a major one or not, the easiest thing to do is place it at the bottom and come back to it later. Consider dropping the ones at the bottom of the priority list as really being minor triggers, not major ones.

It can be <u>extremely</u> helpful in both identifying and prioritizing your triggers if you try and map them out *over time*. Doing so really helps get to the root causes of how you first became an alcoholic—those triggers likely continue to this day. Then examine the roots of triggers you've added relatively recently—are this really alcohol triggers, or just short-term problems that you've been dealing with recently?

The author's historical triggers can be seen in Figure 21 below. Since I have been an alcoholic for a very long time before I got sober, I split my drinking time into 3 periods: Early, Middle, and Late Alcoholism.

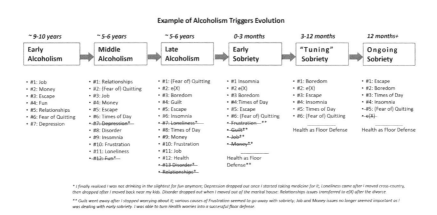

Figure 21: The Author's Stages of Alcoholism and Sobriety

There are several key observations from my history that might be helpful as you put together your prioritized inventory. These are:

- Two key triggers were there at the start and continue to this day: Escape and Fear of Quitting. Odds are you also have at least one or two triggers that have been with you since the beginning;

- "Fun" was there at the beginning, but quickly dropped off the list as I moved deeper into The Alcoholism Process. Try and figure out how long you were drinking for "Fun" (or if you still are);

- More triggers were added as I progressed through the years, a result very consistent with The Alcoholism Process. Odds are good that something similar happened to you (particularly if you have been an alcoholic for many years). The good news is that several triggers dropped off my list the longer I was sober;

- One trigger—Relationships—morphed into its "close cousin" eX once I got divorced. Look for similar "cousins", but make sure they are not actually Related Triggers. Examples include Boredom or eX turning into Loneliness, Job issues turning into Money problems, etc. The reverse of these can also be possible (e.g. Money concerns making you slowly more dissatisfied with your Job);

- I converted a trigger—Health—into a floor defense (discussed next). A classic turning of lemons into lemonade—always a good thing;

- Insomnia kicked in as soon as I attempted quitting and continues as a concern to this day. Odds are that you will have Insomnia in a big way, or not at all, making it an easy trigger to identify;

- Times of Day and Boredom were very subtle triggers that took me a great deal of contemplation to realize were major triggers. They are also examples of triggers that are very hard to shake and continue to this day. In contrast, while Disorder also took some time to realize, once I did it became almost immediately fixable.[4]

- I dropped Guilt by rejecting it completely. Guilt is one of the most toxic of triggers, and in my opinion the only way to deal with it without alcohol (at least while trying to get sober) is reject it completely. You can't control what happened in the past, and if Guilt is preventing you from getting sober, *ignore it*! Most alcoholics experience strong periods of Guilt. The question is whether they were short lived or are self-fulfilling, e.g. Guilt makes you drink, which causes more Guilt, which makes you drink, which…;

218

- I dropped other triggers over time for a variety of reasons. I was able to eliminate the Frustration trigger though a new hobby (writing about my alcoholism). I also realized that for the most part it was a Related Trigger of e(X), not a major trigger by itself. Similar logic applied for dropping Money (both however had been full-fledged major triggers while we were still married). Loneliness was dropped once I moved back closer to my family (another benefit of Level 4).

This last bullet illustrates an extremely important point: that it is essential to think through and distinguish between what are truly your independent major triggers versus (often strong) Related Triggers. For some triggers, particularly close interpersonal ones (e.g. Relationships, Relatives, and eX), not clearly identifying which is which may prevent you from getting at key causes of your drinking, resulting in misplaced or totally missing defenses.[5]

Prioritization

Once I listed out all these triggers, I then prioritized them. For the most part it was just a question of a gut-feel—which ones drove me to drink most often? Key observations include:

- *Priorities change over time.* For each of the 6 time-slices (3 drinking, 3 sober), each had a different #1 priority. Two triggers (Job and Money) moved from #1 and #2 in early alcoholism down to the bottom in late alcoholism, and dropped off the list completely almost immediately after I became sober.

- *Prioritization can help identify Related Triggers.* Look at the triggers that you have far down on your list, and make sure they are not Related Triggers for ones higher.

- *Consider eliminating the last triggers in your list.* If you have more than 10-12 triggers, consider eliminating any prioritized at #11 or higher. If you have 8, consider removing #7 and #8, and so on.

The final result is a list that has been fully vetted and distilled into true root causes, *not* symptoms.

Step #2—Identify Your "Floor" Defenses

"Floor" Defenses are those that are effective for most if not all of your triggers. In addition to being a "universal" defense against many triggers, a floor defense should be very powerful. Think of floor defenses as the last safety net(s) in a serious of safety nets that prevent you from relapsing. Table 13 next provides some possible floor defenses.

Table 13: Possible Floor Defenses

Floor Defense	Reasons to Consider as A Floor Defense
Appearance	Level 3, not drinking can _greatly_ improve your appearance! Besides, your skin can dramatically improve, and the by-products of improved health by not drinking will make exercising (and the resulting appearance benefits) _much_ easier (from increased energy levels, lower blood pressure, etc.) and enjoyable. In general, it will dramatically improve how potential mates perceive you—believe me!
Children	Our children are often the most important thing remaining in many alcoholics' lives. The desire to repair or redeem one's self in their eyes can be a powerful defense. However, it can generate a great deal of Guilt if not careful. Ask yourself: "What would my children think if I drank today?" Answer: They would be <u>very</u> unhappy. So don't!
Cost	$ can be a powerful motivator. You are costing yourself dearly in terms of money, both in cost of alcohol but what it is costing you in lost wages or opportunities. Doing multiple rehabs isn't cheap either.
Health (Pain, Death)	Fear of Death can be powerful. If not death, then _pain_ can be a powerful deterrent. See Level 3—Listen to Your Body for graphic ideas on the hell you can go through if you relapse.
Inefficiency	Do you really want to go through the pain, time, and money it took to get sober in the first place, <u>all over again</u>?
Pets	Being there to take care of one's' pets can be very motivating, particularly if they are your best friend and/or there may be no one to take care of them if you are incapacitated or dead.
Self-Awareness	For many alcoholics, it has been many years (if at all) since they have been self-aware—_really_ aware of what make them "tick". The trigger identification and prioritization process (e.g. Step #1) has the by-product of drastically raising self-awareness. Not losing awareness via a relapse can be motivating for some people.
Self-Esteem	This is a floor defense that can be <u>used repeatedly</u>. Conquering alcoholism is something to be _immensely_ proud of. It is very hard to get and particularly stay sober—a GREAT achievement! Use this defense wherever you need, including boosting your everyday self-esteem in addition to "just" not drinking. Great floor defense for people with Powerlessness as a major trigger.
Spirituality	For those for whom spirituality, God, and/or religion is important, asking yourself questions like "would God be happy if I drank?" can be very effective. Can be used often and repeatedly.

The "durability" of floor defenses will vary by person. Some can be used as many times as you need without "wearing out", while others should be considered a kind of last resort (to be used only if other defenses do not work and a relapse is imminent). Thus, in choosing floor defenses try and determine how you would likely use them. Would you only be able to use them once (or very few times): a last resort in every sense of the term (a kind of "nuclear option")? Or could you use them repeatedly without diminishing their impact? Every person will be different. Try and have a least one that you think will be effective even if you use them somewhat often. Above all, you select ones that you <u>know</u> will stop you from drinking in almost any situation.

In my case I have two floor defenses: my health and my children.

I know pretty definitively that if I start drinking again, I'm going to die pretty quickly, and *painfully*.[6] It might take a few drinks (maybe even one drink), or it may take weeks or even months, but it *will* happen. I always keep this in the back of mind when I start to get tempted. I have even successfully used the fear of health problems/pain/Death floor defense a few times when none of the tips or other defenses for a particular trigger in a particular circumstance would work. Hence, the use of this fear as a "floor".

★ ★

Fear of Death as A Floor Defense

While many non-alcoholics may view fear of death as a floor for practically anybody, this is <u>not</u> necessarily the case for alcoholics. <u>Many alcoholics are consciously or unconsciously trying to drink themselves to death.</u> Even those without an active death wish—but with serious health problems that alcohol will dangerously impact—while we may know *logically* that we shouldn't drink, *emotionally* we might not give a shit at times. Thus, it is good to have at least a second-floor defense.

★ ★

Remember, if death doesn't necessarily scare you, agonizing pain before it happens very much might—a very real risk as described in Level 3.

Another floor defense is my children. They put up with a tremendous amount of crap growing up during my alcoholism and turned out great despite it. I know that they are proud that I was able to pull myself out of this deep shit-hole (via this program), but I also know they would be extremely disappointed if I fell back into it. To make them relive the hell I put them through is the <u>very</u> last thing I want to happen, so I use the thought of their reaction to a relapse as a floor defense. Since it is even more important to me than my health, I have it as second floor defense supporting even the fear of/possibility of imminent death.

Each person is different, but you <u>*have*</u> to have at least one floor defense; two if possible for the reasons described above. No reason *not* to have more than that, though I personally only have two that seem to be common to many of my triggers, and together *all* of my triggers. Spirituality (fear of God's reaction) and Appearance (fear of gaining weight, etc.) are popular floor triggers. There is no right answer; it is <u>*whatever works best for you.*</u>

Step #3—Identify Related Triggers

While identifying which triggers are major and which are Related Triggers were part of Step #1, we revisit it again now that you've identified your floor defenses, and before we identify which defenses work best for your individual triggers.

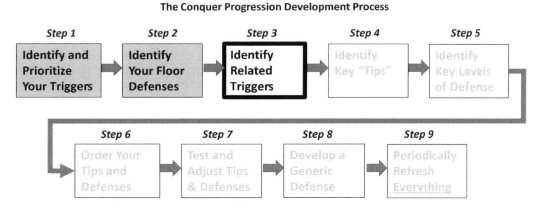

The Conquer Progression Development Process

At the end of each trigger description in Table 3 in Level 2 is a summary of key Related Triggers (RT for short) for that trigger. Revisit that list, and for each major trigger you've identified, check to see if any of their RTs are *also* on your list. If so, make doubly sure you've listed them for the proper reason: they make you want to drink, more often than not, <u>independently</u> of any other trigger. Remove those that do not fit make you want to drink <u>by themselves</u>.

Again, some of the more obvious RT relationships are Boredom and Loneliness; Job problems causing Money concerns and physical Stress; Powerlessness and Social Situations can cause Anxiety; Relationships can cause Sexual concerns (and vice versa), and so on. If for example you only get Lonely when you are Bored (or hardly ever Lonely when you are not Bored), this means Loneliness is a related trigger and should be removed as a major trigger.

Once you have distinguished Related Triggers vs. major ones, <u>do not discard</u> the related triggers. They will still be important in selecting and ordering your trigger-specific tips and defenses.

Step #4—Identify Key "Tips"

For each trigger in Table 3 of Level 2 there is a section called "Key Tips", as highlighted below for the Escape trigger.

Escape	The desire to withdrawal from the world, or exist in a completely different one (e.g. quiet, fun, relaxing, fantasy, etc.). To "escape" one's problems is the general goal and cause for drinking. Common reason to seek the "buzz-rush" of alcohol (See Level 11). **RT: "Fun".** *Key Tips: Physically escape (travel, outdoor activities), exercise, Helpful Link:* https://www.addiction.com/3276/25-ways-relax-without-using-drugs-alcohol/. *Key Defenses: Develop New Hobbies, Make Yourself Sick of Alcohol.*

These tips are one or more parts common sense and/or practical ideas for defending against those triggers without alcohol. Since some triggers literally have dozens of such ideas, a Helpful Link is also included to provide additional, easy-to-digest suggestions.[7]

In the interest of brevity, a full listing of tips for all triggers[8] was not included in this book. However, online forums are a great place for finding new ideas specifically for alcohol-related problems. In Google or Bing (Bing is great for videos), type in searches such as "Tips for [NAME OF TRIGGER] and alcoholism", and it will return many ideas. The challenge will be sorting out good ideas from general ones or just plain old bullshit. Doing this sorting is actually kind of fun.

There are no "right" or "wrong" tips—just ones that work or don't work for you. Consider them all; even try many of them—you may never know for sure what will work for you or unless you try. Odds are you will discover that at least a handful of very unlikely tips will have a major positive impact.

However, even some of the best ideas may not work for practical reasons. For example, having a pet is considered a great way of dealing with certain triggers such as Loneliness or Anxiety (e.g. Pet Therapy). Assuming you don't have an allergy and love pets, it may still not work for you at this time or at all. In the case of pets, they can come with a cost, and not just a financial one. They can, for example, contribute to Disorder (e.g., messes, smells, etc.) that may be a major trigger for you, or are just not practical for your lifestyle (traveling a lot, etc.).

The key point is that while some tips may be common sense/no-brainers, there are others that need considerable thinking through all the advantages and disadvantages before you commit, particularly if once you commit, it will be very hard to undo.

For the most part, though, most of the tips are take-it-or-leave-it. Try them, and if they don't work, then no harm-no foul. And don't limit yourself to what is listed/described; odds are that for every one listed, there are several others that might work. Do your own research, bounce ideas off of friends, family, community members. It is not that they are scarce; they just might require some digging and experimenting!

Step #5—Identify Key Levels of Defense; Get <u>Specific</u>!

The Conquer Progression Development Process

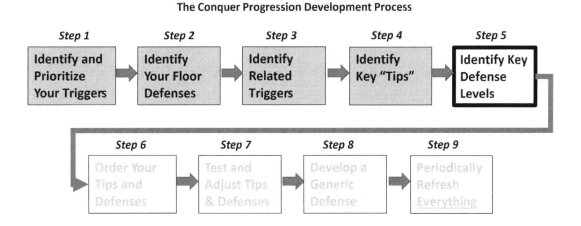

Also at the very end of each trigger summary in Table 3 of Level 2 is a list of Key Defenses (Key Defense Levels), such as for the Escape trigger, next.

Escape	The desire to withdrawal from the world, or exist in a completely different one (e.g. quiet, fun, relaxing, fantasy, etc.). To "escape" one's problems is the general goal and cause for drinking. Common reason to seek the "buzz-rush" of alcohol (See Level 11). *RT: "Fun"*. *Key Tips:* Physically escape (travel, outdoor activities), exercise, *Helpful Link:* https://www.addiction.com/3276/25-ways-relax-without-using-drugs-alcohol/. ***Key Defenses:*** *Develop New Hobbies, Make Yourself Sick of Alcohol.*

These Key Defenses refer to specific Levels of The Conquer Program, e.g. Levels 1-13, that have <u>particularly</u> high potential for helping you defend against the particular trigger attack. Some of them, such as Develop New Hobbies, are straightforward in concept (though requiring trial and error in execution). Others are more complex, such as Level 11—Make Yourself Sick of Alcohol.

As everywhere else in The Conquer Program, the key is in the specific, practical implementation. If a Key Defense Level in Level 9—Develop New Hobbies, it is the specific hobby(s) that you choose that is the key, not the concept of having a hobby in general. If Level 4—Engage Friends and Family is key for a certain trigger, it is who you identify as that friend or family member that is what is important: their personal characteristics, their willingness to help, their *availability* to help.

Why the distinction between "Tips" and "Key Defense Levels"? Two reasons. First, many of the tips may not be applicable for your situation, general lifestyle, and/or personality. So, you might not use many of them (or even any, though I urge you to find at least one).

In contrast, <u>at least one</u> Key Defense Level should be applicable for *all* of you in one form or another. Thus they are listed separately. <u>*You have to have*</u>

at least one Defense Level in <u>any</u> defense progression; otherwise the progression will be weak, meaning you would go directly from a tip to your floor defenses (or possibly *only* have a floor defense). To repeat, you only want to use floor defenses as a last resort or at least infrequently, whereas Tips and Defenses can be used repeatedly.

Again, the essence of the concept of progressions is that <u>*no one*</u> <u>*method/tip/approach/defense will work all the time for all situations*</u>. Think of progressions as a series of safety nets that are prepared to catch you if you fall off a cliff. While the first one may break, your momentum will be slowed down, such that the next one may catch you before you slam into the ground (e.g. relapse). Thus the more safety nets (tips and defenses) you have, the more chances are that you will be stopped before you hit. (To continue the analogy, the floor defense may be a cushion of foam, which depending on how much you have slowed down may or may not have a hard landing, but at least you will have survived).

Whereas a Tip is generally a simple idea to try out (in Step #7), a Key Defense may well require a great deal of experimentation, time, and/or practice to get "right." Level 9—Develop New Hobbies is one of these. Unless you have a number of hobbies that you know will work for you because of past experience, you'll have to invest some effort and even money to figure out if they work, and <u>how</u> they work, as well as when, where, and why they work. Get to as much specificity and detail as you can, down to days, times, environments/situations, and of course the specifics of the trigger and related triggers.

Step #6—Order Your Tips and Defenses

Since there are possibly several tips and at least one defense level and floor defense that should be applicable to you for <u>every</u> trigger, one big challenge is the order in which you do them. Each person is different. The same trigger with the same best tips and defenses may need a different order.

The general approach is to order your floor defenses first, weakest first, followed by Key Defense Levels (weakest first), with Tips last.

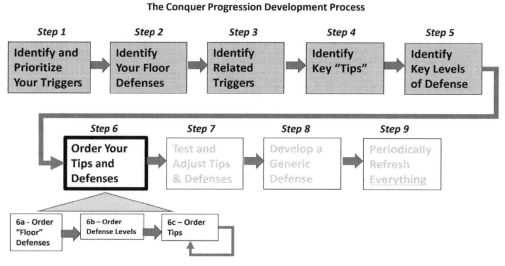

A simple 3-part mini-process will do the trick. This process will have you order your tips, defense levels, and floor defenses in reverse order.

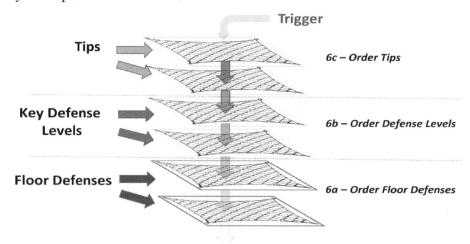

Why reverse order? Primarily because the reverse order generally mirrors the strength and importance of the various safety nets. In other words, Floor Defenses are the most important of all the safety nets, Key Defense Levels next, with Tips generally the "least" important. And while Tips will come and go fairly frequently, Defenses Levels and particularly Floor Defenses will pretty much stay the same, so you want spend time to make sure you get them right. Also, it is very possible that the Tips that you select will in some way be influenced by your Floor Defenses and Key Defense Levels.

Why weakest first, whether Tip, Defense Level, or Floor Defense? In general, it is for the practical reason that the weakest one (Tip, Defense Level or Floor), will also require the *least effort*, or put differently, *easiest to do*. The general philosophy here is that you don't want to expend more effort than necessary to repel an alcohol attack; you want to save your strength (and stronger defenses) against those <u>really</u> severe attacks when they come. And they *will* come.

The mini-process includes:

6a - Order Your Floor Defenses. In Step 2, you identified at least one floor defense. If you have more than one, put the "weakest" one first, and the strongest one last.[9] For me, Health (likely death) is the next to last one, with my children (pride/disappointment/happiness) underlying everything.

6b - Order Your Key Defense Levels. For triggers with more than one Defense Levels, the first one listed is the one best suited for that Level, but it may be that the second may be more appealing. Or for you personally that second one is easier to do, so put that first. You don't have to do more than one, but select *at least* one.

6c – Order Your Tips. If more than one, put the "weakest" one first. Next strongest second, and so on.

Other Considerations

The above, particularly the weaker to stronger ordering philosophy, is a guideline, not a rule; there are other considerations that may come into play that will change the order. These include:

- *Which one is most likely to weaken the attack the most?* In other words, which has the best chance of success to repel the attack by itself? After all, why do a bunch of things when one will work? It may make sense to put this first in their respective sub-section.[10]

- *Which will take the most out of you physically and/or mentally?* This might seem counter-intuitive; after all you are trying to *strengthen* your defenses, not weaken them! However, this is where the desire to "numb yourself" (discussed in Level 11) comes in. Numbing yourself is part of the buzz/rush/numb/checkout continuum described in that Level. There is no question that we all want to "numb" ourselves sometimes. But we can't do it with alcohol anymore, so another, even better way, is to exhaust ourselves—mentally and/or physically.

  If, for example, you listed Exercise as one of your Tips or Hobbies, consider putting that first. Draining excess energy that you otherwise might use to dwell/focus/obsess about your trigger situation will help you greatly with this "numbing" process. "Drain that negative energy" might sound like a cliché, but it is effective!

- *Which one(s) are the most distracting and/or time-consuming?* For many triggers, they are at their strongest right now in the heat of the situation, and quickly drop in intensity. Anger and Frustration are great examples of triggers where their intensity diminishes greatly with time, sometimes in as little as a few minutes. If you can wait them out, they will very likely become less intense; maybe not the underlying reasons, but how they make you want to drink right now. If you can find things that will take you at least a couple of hours to do—and even be very distracting—these are excellent candidates to put first, regardless of how "weak" or "strong" they are.

Finally, don't overthink the tips and defenses. They may be the first ones to pop into your head, ones that you think of after some thought, or even ones that come up when you talk them over with friends or family members who know you best. Ideally these should make sense intuitively to you, but it is fine if they are not—<u>as long as they work</u>.

Be prepared for some of your initial efforts to not work or work well. The result may or may not be the final, best version for you, which is the reason for Step #7.

Step #7—Test and Adjust Your Tips and Defenses

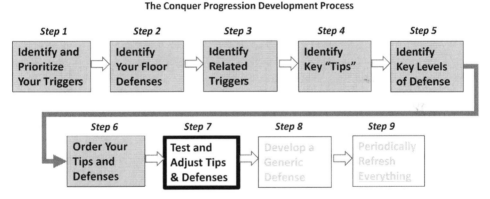

The Conquer Progression Development Process

In Missouri, where I currently live, there is no end to the opportunities to test my tips, defenses levels, and floor defenses. I swear <u>every</u> fucking store that has <u>any</u> consumable goods has a huge liquor section, and many seem to feature huge end-displays dedicated to vodka.[11] While aggravating at first, I am (now) able to ignore these displays pretty easily. On a minority of occasions, I get curious about how the pricing has changed, and occasionally I do get pretty annoyed that there are so many damn liquor displays waiting to throw themselves in my face every time I turn around. What's wrong with potato chip displays like the old days? But in the spirit of "making lemonade out of lemons" I use these displays to continually test/adjust my defenses (particularly against the Proximity trigger).

One of the places where we hold meetings in a basement is about 4 doors down from our town's liquor store. We get a lot of laughs over that one. I learned from the beginning that trying to avoid walking by there was harder than just walking by and waving to the gals that work there. They know I'm in the program and every now in then come out to ask how I'm doing. It sort-of gives me a safety net to keep them posted on my continued sobriety. They have even joked with my husband and I that Jack Daniels sales have gone down since we joined AA.[12]

Use these kinds of "tests" to determine the strength of any given tip/defense as well as their order. Do them in "safe" environments at first (like in the testimonial above), and then progress to tests that are more and more difficult and have less and less of a safety net. Such "safety net" environments include making sure you are with a trusted friend/family member, being in a situation where it is logistically impossible to give in to temptation (such as a passenger in a car), and deliberately not carrying enough money to buy booze. There are many other types of safety nets, limited only by your imagination!

Unfortunately, the best tests are those in real life, where your trigger is pounding you full force with little in the way of safety nets. It will take some trial and "error" (this does *not* include actually relapsing) to get the best mix of defenses. Just try to identify and have ready as many tips/defenses as you can that you know will work <u>at least a bit</u>, which, along with your floor defenses, should do the job until you can find better tips/defenses and/or better ordering structures.

Adjustments can take many forms as well. You may well find that a tip/defense you thought would work great works hardly at all. Don't feel wedded to it if doesn't work! Sometimes you may be *very* surprised with what works and what does not. Don't get frustrated; it can be kind of fun (sometimes) to discover how your mind actually reacts to unusual ideas!

The final progressions for several of the author's major triggers is shown in Table 14.

Table 14: Defense Progressions for Author's Triggers

	#2 E(X)	#3 Boredom	#4 Times of Day	#5 Escape
Tip #1	Text/email; NO live conversations	Vary EVERY-THING	Exercise (plan specific activities during vulnerable time slots)	Understand specific reasons for desire to escape at any given time (also make sure Related Trigger is not at core of desire)
Tip #2	Ignore Guilt, no matter how much is attempted	Read, Watch new genres	Do old/ regular activities at new (vulnerable) times	Exercise in any form possible to release endorphins
Key Defense Level A	BBH(L8) – Don't react to provocations; wait before responding	DNH(L9) – Bowling, Gardening, Writing	DNH(L9) – Hobbies likely at vulnerable times (Yoga/Gym classes, Bowling, Disc Golf)	BBH(L8) – Use herbal tea, supplements to help relax
Key Defense Level B	EFF(L4)-Vent to Girlfriend, Family	JAC(L7) – Go to AA/Al-Anon	N/A	DNH(L9) – Physically escape; long showers; relaxing (not busy) vacations
Floor Defense #1	Health (Also Level 3)	Health	Health	Health
Floor Defense #2	Children	Children	Children	Children

Note: notations such as EFF(L4) refers to Engage Friends and Family, Level 4, and so on for JAC(L7) Join A Community (Level 7), etc.

Key characteristics of the above include:

- Simplicity
- Multiple tips
- At least one Key Defense Level and one Floor Defense

Above all, the most important characteristic is *specificity*: be specific in your tips and defenses!

* * *

Steps 1-7 provide you with the progressions you need for each of your individual triggers. You are almost (but not quite) done!

Step #8—Develop a "Generic" Trigger Defense Progression

The above defense progressions will, hopefully, work for you most of the time, and even the vast majority of the time. But it is almost a certainty that they will not work <u>all</u> of the time—life throws too much shit at you for that to happen.

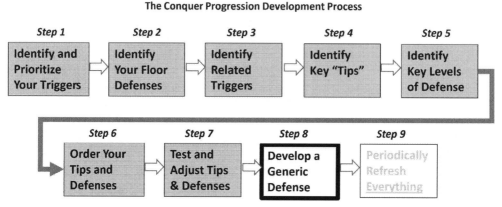

It is almost a certainty that even if you identify hundreds of defenses and dozens of progressions for dozens or hundreds of trigger/Related Trigger combinations, there will <u>always</u> be at least a few that you miss. Murphy's Law[13] is a law for a reason.

> *One of the scariest things about cravings for me is that they can appear out of nowhere. Things may be going well for me in recovery but the urge to drink or use drugs pops into my head. Very frustrating.*[14]

Since it is pointless to try to plan/develop/implement dozens of progressions, you need to develop at least one "generic" progression. A generic progression is a "catch all" set of tips/defenses that will deal with unanticipated trigger episodes, ones so unusual that they might as well be brand new triggers, or happen when you are just completely unprepared for them. You might also view a generic progression as another kind of "floor" defense—whatever the best way is for you to think about it <u>instantly</u> when such situations as the above occur.

In addition, as discussed earlier in this Level, there are trigger "events" that do not last a long time—perhaps as little as a few hours or even minutes. This is when you just need to buy some time to let *time* take care of the problem. Perhaps some road rage, or an argument with your girlfriend, or a bad Reminder on the radio that causes you to get really Depressed. These are all examples of trigger circumstances that will go away with a bit of time. These kinds of events are particularly dangerous early sobriety stage, when you haven't really tested and adjusted your defenses, or you even missed the trigger entirely.

Super-simplicity is the key here. 2-4 tips and/or defense level specifics at most. You just need enough to let you get your bearings and regroup when faced with totally unanticipated trigger events (being fired is a "great" example)—followed by your floor triggers. The author's generic progression is shown in Figure 22.

Generic Progression Example

	Tip/Defense	Description
#1—Do a general "mini-meditation" (breathing, catchy phrases/philosophies)	General "Mini" Meditation	Take several deep breaths; remember *shit happens*. Reflect with a non-alcoholic calming beverage (hot tea)
#2—Call a Family Member (default to parent/sibling)	Call Family Member Y	"Y" depends on situation (knowledge of situation, physical proximity)
#3—Take a Walk, Exercise (what type depends on the situation and *immediate* opportunity)	Take A Walk, Exercise	Go to Gym if possible and nearby, otherwise take a walk
#4—Have an overall (Examples: "count your blessings," or "things could be worse," etc.)	Mini-Meditation: Count My Blessings	Particularly when that situation hasn't happened before/happened often
#5—Floor Defense #1	Listen to Your Body!	Booze = Death/Great Pain
#6—Floor Defense #2	Engage Friends and Family	Remember My Children (Kiids will be VERY disappointed)

Figure 22: Author's Generic Progression

The key to remember for the use of a generic progression in most situations is that all you are doing is buying time so you can get your shit together to develop a new progression specific to that new/unusual/out-of-the-blue trigger and/or circumstance, <u>fast</u>.

Step #9—Periodically Refresh <u>Everything</u>

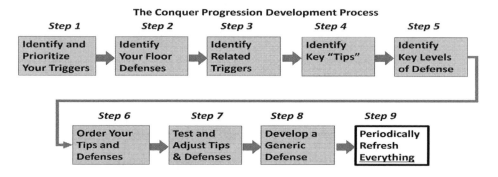

One of the 12-Steps of Alcoholics Anonymous that I never fully understood until I started writing this chapter was their Step 10: "*continue to take personal inventory of ourselves.*" I now can see the benefit to that concept, adapted for this Level.

Even if/when you finally find the "perfect" set of Tips/Defenses/Progressions for your triggers, you can <u>not</u> count on their staying that way forever. Alcoholism is patient; you can be sober for many years, thinking you are just fine, when it will try to strike again seemingly out of the blue. If your defenses are not up-to-date, an attack may succeed. As the late, great Robin Williams described his addiction to alcohol:

> "*It waits. It lays in wait for the time when you think, 'It's fine now, I'm O.K.' Then, the next thing you know, it's not O.K. Then you realize, 'Where am I? I didn't realize I was in Cleveland.'*"[15]

To avoid complacency and to be ready to defend against alcohol attacks at any time, it is critical to "refresh" everything in this Level, particularly all of the previous eight steps, at least a couple times a year, *for the rest of your life*. A rule of thumb is to refresh once a month early in sobriety, every 3-4 months for the next two years, and once every six months after that.

You should also refresh everything *immediately* when you have major changes in your life, as those changes could not only add new triggers to your life or change the priorities of existing ones, they could throw into chaos some stable dimensions of your life that you never thought of when you originally put together your defense progressions. In other words: Murphy's Law—What can go wrong, WILL go wrong.

Examples of out-of-the-blue changes in your life is a sudden firing; a spouse blindsiding you and leaving overnight for someone else; the sudden death of parent, sibling, or child; a diagnosis of cancer, etc. While all of these can be covered somewhat by other triggers (e.g. Job, Relationships/eX, Extreme Emotions, etc.), it is the *suddenness* and *unexpectedness* of these events that can really threaten to overcome whatever existing defenses and progressions you might have.

★ ★

What Do You Do If You Relapse?

First, don't panic! Odds are it is no big deal, relatively speaking. Second, stop drinking (again) if you haven't already. Go back to Level 5 (or 12) and detox again. If you had some significant sobriety (e.g. a few months) under your belt before you relapsed, <u>and</u> your relapse is a day or two (not weeks), then the detoxing process should not be too bad.

The most important thing, of course, is to figure out *why* you relapsed, and how you can prevent doing so by adjusting your defenses and/or progressions. Figuring this out will likely be harder to do than the detox since your first pass through this program did not result in preventing the relapse to begin with.

Redouble your efforts by rereading Level 2 and figuring out exactly where you "went wrong". I use that term because other people might do so, but in reality, it wasn't "wrong", it was just "inadequately identified and defended". Finally, revisit all the steps in Level 13.

★ ★

* * *

Remember…

… Most of the activities in this program will take time and practice to refine and "optimize." Besides obviously being worthwhile, it <u>will</u> get easier and easier to do. With enough refinement, time, and practice, you may not have to <u>do</u> all of the tips/defenses in your progressions; you may merely need to think about them, consciously or even sub-consciously. That is the nirvana end-goal of this program — that not only do not have to obsess about not drinking, you don't have to even think about not drinking — indeed being able to ignore alcohol as irrelevant to your new life.

* * * *

I characterize the result of this Level, and The Conquer Program as a whole, as equating a glass, can, or bottle of alcohol with a can of motor oil. Thinking about alcohol should become as insignificant to you as passing by a display of oil in the store. You will have taught your mind and body — with the help of ALL the tips, Levels of defense, and progressions that you have built — to react to the thought of alcohol just as it would to the thought of opening, smelling, and drinking that can of motor oil... by turns disgusted, incredulous, contemptuous, nauseous, and perhaps even a bit amused, but with the bottom line of it being *irrelevant* to your life now and forgotten by the time you get to the next aisle! When you are finally able to reach this kind of state and everyday reaction to alcohol, you will know as a whole that you have **Conquered Your Alcoholism!**

CONCLUSION

Let's summarize the most critical points:

- Unless you convince yourself you are an alcoholic, <u>no</u> program will help you;

- Understanding <u>your</u> drinking triggers is absolutely essential to the success of this program, and sobriety in general;

- No one defense will guard against <u>all</u> alcohol attacks, <u>all the time</u>; thus,

- *Building <u>multiple</u> defenses, personalized to your life's circumstances is the key to staying sober in the long-term.*

In the end, sometimes great summarizations can come from strange places:

If you're an addict, it controls your life and your life becomes uncontrollable. It's boring and painful, filling your system with something that makes you stare at your shoes for six hours. (Singer/songwriter James Taylor)

James Taylor is a well-known poet and singer, but sometimes even better characterizations of alcoholic life can come from the rank-and-file:

"I felt like Walking Death."[1]

Instead of ending on such a negative, I think there is a far better perspective on the whole deal:

"Sober people are the bravest people I've ever met. They are authentic and compassionate, and they exist in the truth. It is a beautiful, beautiful place to live.
Come join us. It's amazing here."[2]

Appendix A: Building Your New Defenses—A Trigger Example

In the main *How to Conquer Your Alcoholism* book, a very large amount of time is dedicated to exploring the nature and nuances of each trigger, and in identifying a more comprehensive list of alcohol-free tips and defenses for each. The one for Boredom is shown below.

I would encourage you to explore the deeper aspects of each one of your major triggers, and experiment with as wide a variety of "tips" as you can (in as detailed a fashion as for Boredom below) as you build and refine your overall defenses and associated progressions. Besides the main book, additional resources are found for most triggers in Table 3 of Level 2, as well as in Appendix B of this book.

★ ★

Tips for Dealing with Boredom without Alcohol

The good news is that there are many ways to theoretically alleviate Boredom. The not-so-good news is that it can be very tough to figure out what works. As I say repeatedly in this program, <u>finding new hobbies is absolutely key for alleviating boredom</u>, as well as help dealing with many other triggers.

> *"The boredom should get better over time. I think lots of people's problem is not replacing your addiction with something else. I've heard of stories of people who smoked, and being obsessed with the internet or a sport has caused them to quit smoking or basically not give them time to smoke. Try to find something to replace drinking if you can."*

Not all hobbies are the same, particularly when it comes to not drinking. You will want to enjoy them, but none <u>more</u> important are the following:

- *They need to be time-consuming.* This can mean eating up a bunch of time in one "session," such as an all-afternoon hiking excursion, or it can mean adding up to a lot of time, such as walking 45 minutes three times a week.
- *They need to be mentally occupying.* Doing only physical activities alone won't cut it; you need to keep yourself from dwelling on the particular triggers-of-the-day. Challenging games can do this, by focusing your attention on something other than your triggers, and gradually slowing down your thought processes as you begin to tire from the challenge. Another (strange) way of achieving this is by doing <u>very</u> boring activities such as cleaning your house, balancing your

checkbook, or even listening (in a vague way) to very boring music. You are essentially negating Boredom by *overloading* on it. This is also a counter-intuitive way of Escaping or getting "numb".

- *Admit (and accept) that sometimes you just want to be "numb."* A big reason that people often want to drink/use drugs is the ability to literally "numb" their brains/bodies to their problems. You can achieve something similar that if you can drain away the excess energy in your body (e.g., exercising, hiking, etc.) and mind. You might even supplement it with a nice cup of tea (or other nonalcoholic beverage) that you can come to associate with this new, and far better way, of numbing yourself.

Don't limit the above tips to just "formal" hobbies; use the same concepts in other, more everyday activities such as running errands, playing with your children, or driving to/from work.[2]

Other Ideas for Dealing with Boredom without Alcohol

- *TV Repeats!* If you are like me, you forgot many of the details of your favorite TV series or movies while you were drinking. Take another run at viewing them. It's almost like seeing them for the first time, with the added benefit of knowing you are going to like them (even if you don't remember exactly why). In this age of Netflix, Hulu, and DVDs sold everywhere there is practically nothing you can't find no matter how old or obscure.

- *"New" Shows!* You might also try viewing "new" shows that you never had time for while you were drinking. This can also be helpful in a strange way if you think you have a bit of an addictive personality—you literally have *years* of episodes you can watch, and even if you try to cram them into a few weeks, it still can take up a bunch of time while being tons of fun!

- *Variety!* Pay attention to and seek out variety. While drinking, odds are you fell into at least one or two "ruts" of activities whether it was going to the same sushi restaurant or bowling in the same league on the same day with the same people. While this routine can be comforting in many ways, it can also be boring— particularly now that you have more mental "cycles" available to think about them. Try different restaurants; occasionally bowl at a different alley, and just in general mix things up a bit. It does not mean stop doing what you are used to; instead, it is just a new way of appreciating what, how, and why things entertain you and/or make you comfortable.

- *More Variety!* Indeed, you might consider trying to do nearly *everything* in your average day differently, at least for a while. Take a different route to and from work, go to different grocery stores, etc. If you like to take walks, don't just walk the same route around your house; go to various parks. No one of these, of course, is going to alleviate boredom all that much, but in total it might take a good part of the edge off it.

Lemons into Lemonade Tip: If you are <u>really</u> bored, use this "free time" to try something you would normally never be likely to do otherwise. I am talking about new (to you) forms of recreational activities, such as bowling or playing squash if you have never done them before. Go rent a convertible for the weekend; drive to a summer festival <u>way</u> out of your way; get some Indian or Korean food if you never have tried it, etc. Even if some don't turn out great, consider them as having broadened your newly sober horizon. You will be sure to find several that you enjoy so much you will want to do again.

Overall Tip: <u>In order to prevent relapse from Boredom, it is critical that the newly sober develop new interests</u> which is at the core of Level 9—Develop New Hobbies.

Related Triggers: Boredom can come from many directions, but often from not having "Fun" as well as Loneliness. It can activate other triggers such as Depression, desire to Escape, Loneliness, and feeling Unfun/Uninteresting.

Key Defense Levels: Engage Friends and Family (play games, conversation), Join a Community (explore common interests outside of meetings), Develop New Hobbies.

★ ★

Appendix B—Web Resources

This book references numerous resources to help you Conquer Your Alcoholism. More resources are listed here. For the most up-to-date resources list, please visit http://www.conqueryouraddiction.com/key-web-resources.html.

Alcoholism General Information

- About.com (alcoholism): www.alcoholism.about.com (now www.verywell.com)
- American Medical Association: www.ama-assn.org/ama
- American Society of Addiction Medicine: www.asam.org
- Center for Disease Control (CDC): http://www.cdc.gov/alcohol/fact-sheets/alcohol-use.htm
- Cigna Substance Abuse Information and Webinars: http://www.cigna.com/healthwellness/behavioral-awareness-series/coping-with-substance-abuse
- DARA (Drug and Alcohol Asia) Web site: http://alcoholrehab.com/alcohol-rehab/
- "Science of Addiction and Recovery" www.addictscience.com
- The Mayo Clinic: *www.mayoclinic.com*
- Medhelp.org (a kind of cross between Web MD and Reddit): http://www.medhelp.org/tags/show/506/Alcoholism
- The National Council on Alcoholism and Drug Dependence: www.ncadd.org
- Web MD: www.webmd.com
- Wikipedia (general information source, particularly definitions): www.wikipedia.org

Alcoholism Support Programs (For Family and Friends)

- Al-Anon Family Groups: www.Al-anon.alateen.org
- Families Anonymous: familiesanonymous.org
- Nar-Anon Family Groups: www.nar-anon.org

Alcoholism Treatment and Related Programs

- Alcoholics Anonymous World Services: www.aa.org
- Cocaine Anonymous: www.ca.org
- Co-Dependents Anonymous World Fellowship: www.coda.org
- Do It Now: www.doitnow.org (drugs and alcohol publications at http://www.doitnow.org/pages/alcohol.html)
- Dual-Recovery Anonymous: http://www.draonline.org/
- (Over)Eaters Anonymous: http://www.oa.org/
- Faces and Voices of Recovery: www.facesandvoicesofrecovery.org
- Gamblers Anonymous: www.gambleranonymous.org

- LifeRing Secular Recovery: http://lifering.org/
- Narcotics Anonymous World Services: www.na.org
- Rational Recovery: www.rational.org
- Recovery Dynamics: http://www.kellyfdn.com/
- Salvation Army: www.salvationarmyusa.org
- Secular Organizations for Sobriety (SOS): www.sossobriety.org
- SMART Recovery: www.smartrecovery.org
- Substance Abuse and Mental Health Services Administration treatment finder: www.samhsa.gov/treatment/
- The Addiction Recovery Guide: http://www.addictionrecoveryguide.org/holistic/meditation_spirituality
- Women for Sobriety: www.womenforsobriety.org
- *Links to other "Anonymous" Programs:* http://www.ipass.net/a1idpirat/anonymousrecoverygroups.html

Anxiety, Depression and Alcohol

- Alcohol and Depression: http://www.webmd.com/depression/alcohol-and-depresssion
- Depression and Alcohol: http://alcoholism.about.com/od/depress/Depression_and_Alcohol.htm
- Depression and Alcoholism: Five Tips for Recovery— http://psychcentral.com/lib/2010/depression-and-alcoholism-five-tips-for-recovery/
- Depression and Alcoholism: http://www.learn-about-alcoholism.com/depression-and-alcoholism.html
- Depression and Alcoholism: http://www.professional-counselling.com/alcoholism-and-depression.html
- General Anxiety and Depression Information: www.anxiety-and-depression-solutions.com
- Social Anxiety Support: www.socialanxietysupport.com

Bad Habit Breakers

- (Deliberately) alienating others—http://essentialsoffabulous.com/blog/how-to-win-friends-and-stop-alienating-people/
- Attention-seeking behavior (Look at me! Look at me!)—http://www.wikihow.com/Tell-if-You-Are-Self-Absorbed
- Chronic lateness, procrastination—Lateness: http://www.webmd.com/balance/features/help-chronically-late; Procrastination: http://www.huffingtonpost.com/2013/03/20/8-tricks-to-stop-procrastinating_n_2916484.html
- Constantly complaining: http://www.lifehack.org/articles/communication/7-effective-ways-stop-complaining.html.
- Complaining (Being Argumentative): http://www.wikihow.com/Recognize-When-You%27re-Getting-Argumentative

- (Excessive) cursing—http://www.wikihow.com/Stop-Swearing
- Eavesdropping—http://everydaytipsandthoughts.com/thoughts-for-thursday-how-do-you-handle-eavesdroppers/ (this is from the person being eavesdropped on perspective)
- Freeloading—http://abcnews.go.com/GMA/MellodyHobson/friends-family-financial-freeloaders/story?id=8756440 (from the perspective of the victim)
- Gossiping—http://tinybuddha.com/blog/how-to-stop-gossiping-and-creating-drama/
- Impulsive behavior to the point of recklessness—http://www.ehow.com/how_8631725_stop-being-impulsive.html
- Interrupting—http://www.drlinaman.com/10-tips-help-stop-interrupting/
- Lying, Exaggerating—Lying: http://www.wikihow.com/Stop-Lying; Exaggerating: http://www.greatschools.org/parenting/behavior-discipline/1487-stop-exaggerating.gs (focused on stopping children from exaggerating, but good in general)
- Monopolizing the conversation— http://www.artofmanliness.com/2011/05/01/the-art-of-conversation-how-to-avoid-conversational-narcissism/
- Nitpicking, being critical and controlling—Nitpicking: https://www.ronitbaras.com/emotional-intelligence/relationships/save-your-marriage-nitpicker/ (in marriage); Being Critical and Controlling: https://www.psychologytoday.com/blog/healthy-connections/201007/help-my-controlling-behavior-is-ruining-relationships
- (Deliberate and excessive) non-conformity, often for its own sake— http://blogs.clc.co.nz/LearningStyles/archive/2011/06/24/dealing-with-non-conformist-learning-styles.aspx (on children's learning issues)
- (Not) smiling when the situation clearly calls for it—http://online.wsj.com/article/FA16266C-700C-43A2-9754-16BB0E6F7A5D.html#!FA16266C-700C-43A2-9754-16BB0E6F7A5D; Learning to smile: http://www.wikihow.com/Smile-Naturally
- Whining—http://childparenting.about.com/od/behaviordiscipline/a/Child-Discipline-How-To-Stop-Whining-In-Children.htm (about children)

Blogs, Forums, Chats and Other Alcoholism Information Sources

- About Alcoholism: http://alcoholism.about.com (now www.verywell.com)
- Alternatives for Alcohol: http://www.alternatives-for-alcoholism.com/alcoholism-test.html
- Binge Drinking: http://www.cdc.gov/alcohol/fact-sheets/binge-drinking.htm
- eHow Health: http://www.ehow.com/ehow-health/
- Med Help: http://www.medhelp.org/
- Sober Recovery: www.soberrecovery.com
- The Fix (about Addiction and Recovery): www.thefix.com

Drug Abuse Information

- Drug Abuse General Info: www.drugabuse.com
- Substance Abuse and Mental Health Services Administration treatment finder: www.samhsa.gov/treatment/

Hobby Information

- Conventional Hobbies: http://www.buzzle.com/articles/list-types-of-hobbies/

- Finding others who share your interests: www.meetup.com

- Pets and stress relief: http://www.today.com/health/5-ways-pets-can-ease-your-stress-6C10423970

- Unusual Hobbies: http://www.buzzle.com/articles/list-of-hobbies-interests.html

Inpatient Rehab Centers

- A General Index of Treatment Centers: www.theagapecenter.com/Treatment-Centers/index.htm

- Betty Ford Center: www.bettyfordcenter.org

- Drug and Alcohol Rehab Asia: http://dararehab.com/

- Harvey House: http://www.addictionadvisor.co.uk/Clinic/Harvey#.UYKejLQo43s

- Hazelden: www.hazelden.org

- Promises Addiction Treatment Center: www.promises.com

- Recovery Connection (a Rehab Finder service essentially): www.recoveryconnection.org

- Schick Shadel Hospital: www.schickshadel.com

- Silver Hill Hospital: www.silverhillhospital.org

Intervention Approach Information

- Assistance In Recovery Intervention Model: www.a-i-r.com

- The Community Reinforcement Approach and Family Training (CRAFT) intervention: http://www.robertjmeyersphd.com/craft.html

Outpatient Treatment Resources (Resource links below may include some Inpatient information/links to Inpatient Centers)

- New York State OASAS (Office of Alcoholism and Substance Abuse Services): https://www.oasas.ny.gov/

- Oxford House: www.oxfordhouse.org

- Rehab Treatment Centers by State (majority are outpatient): www.theagapecenter.com/Treatment-Centers/index.htm

Therapy Resources

- Association for Behavioral and Cognitive Therapies: www.abct.org

- Therapy Styles Overview: http://alcoholrehab.com/alcohol-rehab/rehab-therapist-styles/

Miscellaneous Websites and Resources:

- Alcoholic Drink.net (Non-alcoholic drink receipes): http://www.alcoholicdrinks.net/Non-Alcoholic-Recipes-2.htm

- Drink Focus (Interesting facts about alcohol: NOT an anti-drinking site): drinkfocus.com

- History of Alcoholic Beverages: potsdam.edu/hansondj

- International Alliance for Responsible Drinking: icap.org

- Wikipedia articles: www.Wikipedia.com.

About the Author

D.H. Williams is the author of *How to Conquer Your Alcoholism- Made Simple!* and the original breakthrough book *How to Conquer Your Alcoholism*. He is also the creator and President of *ConquerYourAddiction.com*, a website dedicated to *The Conquer Program* and more generally helping people in their fight against alcoholism and other addictions. In addition to advocating *The Conquer Program* through this book and other forums, Mr. Williams is a contributor to *TheFix.com*, an online journal for addiction professionals and the greater recovery community.

For over 20 years, Mr. Williams "moonlighted" as an alcoholic while working in the technology and management consulting fields. By the time he finally conquered his alcoholism, his life was a wreck and he had developed life-threatening health problems. Among the many "benefits" he earned as an alcoholic: foreclosure, bankruptcy, divorce, unemployment, and major health problems. He began to develop *The Conquer Program* during a major medical scare and perfected it over several years, including a great deal of personal testing against a wide variety of alcohol temptations and attacks. _All_ have been successfully rebuffed.

ENDNOTES

Preface
[1] http://www.amazon.com/How-Conquer-Your-Alcoholism-Reference/dp/0692361898
[2] https://itunes.apple.com/us/book/how-to-conquer-your-alcoholism/id967898406?mt=11

Introduction
[1] It is the author's opinion that while there are certain fields where actual "field" experience is not needed to be a good professional, addiction treatment, is *not* one of them. This means that at a minimum such professionals need to have direct experience with addicts, either in treating them one-on-one, and/or have a close family member who is an addict, so they can see up close what the addict has to go through on a day-by-day, hour-by-hour basis. Actually having been an addict is not an absolute necessity.
[2] Discussed in a separate forthcoming book for non-alcoholics titled *Why Alcoholics Drink, and Why They Can't Stop,* Conquer Your Addiction LLC

The Ten Keys to Understanding Your Alcoholism
[1] The transparent connecting tube in Figure 4 is intended to illustrate how all Levels are connected/integrated in a central defensive core around the alcoholic.

Level 1—Admit You Have an Addiction to Alcohol
[1] NIAAA. "Alcohol Use Disorders." Accessed April 20, 2017. http://www.niaaa.nih.gov/alcohol-health/overview-alcohol-consumption/alcohol-use-disorders. The NIAA does not put these cornerstones in any sort of process or even in order of occurrence; all process diagrams were created by the author.
[2] In *How to Conquer Your Alcoholism*, considerable time is spent in analyzing why alcoholics drink as it relates to the effect. In particular it describes 4 types of Blood Alcohol Content (BAC) "effects" that alcoholics can "strive" for: "Rush"—The desire for the initial "rush" of Euphoria[2] that comes with that first drink; "Buzz"—The desire for an ongoing "buzz" of Euphoria; "Numb"—The desire to "numb" yourself so you don't have to think about things troubling you; and "Checkout"—The desire to "checkout" of the world so to speak so you don't have to think about *anything*.
[3] Hopequestgroup.org. "Short Michigan Alcohol Screening Test." Accessed January 9, 2017. https://hopequestgroup.org/wp-content/uploads/2011/09/SMAST-Short-Michigan-Alcohol-Screening-Test.pdf.
[4] National Institute on Health. "Diagnosis Treatment". Accessed April 4, 2017. https://www.drugabuse.gov/Diagnosis-Treatment/DAST10.html.
[5] There is even a geriatric version that is similarly subjective if not more so, and fairly insulting (asking if drinking helps decrease your tremors, or makes it hard for you to remember parts of the day). Plus, these "tests" haven't been updated in a while; the geriatric version copyright was in 1991, and the original one years earlier.

Level 2—Know Your Triggers
[1] A link to the Amazon page for this (first) book is at https://www.amazon.com/How-Conquer-Your-Alcoholism-Reference/dp/0692361898. That book is NOT a prerequisite for this book. The key difference is the first book has much more detail on nearly every topic and Level, as well as supplemental and related topics. This more comprehensive book is best for treatment professionals, non-alcoholics wanting to better understand alcoholism, or alcoholics who enjoy reading and/or are willing to invest extra time in understanding their disease. This more simplified book is for alcoholics who just want to cut to the chase of getting sober.
[2] AlcoholRehab.com. "Alcohol Induced Anxiety." Accessed March 30, 2017. http://alcoholrehab.com/alcohol-rehab/alcohol-induced-anxiety/.
[3] There are exceptions to every rule, and if you search long enough you will find exceptions to the denial and Fear of Quitting rules. But they are very rare in my experience.
[4] Sources of Fear of Quitting testimonials: first testimonial: anonymous; second: sarahtroy, mdjunction.com; third: uppitywoman, mdjunction.com; fourth: anonymous, mdjunction.com; fifth: Jacobs, alcoholism.about.com. All accessed in December 2014 timeframe.

Level 3—Listen to Your Body!
[1] The early 1990s is my best guess when I crossed the alcoholism line, e.g. when I had accumulated at least 12 points on The Conquer Quiz in Level 1.
[2] I had sores all over my back and lower legs, which *never* healed when I was drinking. They healed when I finally stopped. Unfortunately, I still have some scarring.
[3] *Guest wifeofdrinker, alcoholism.about.com*
[4] Pinterest. Accessed April 3, 2017. Saved from siakhenn.tripod.com. https://www.pinterest.com/pin/468304061224742011/.
[5] NCBI. "Treatment of Alcoholic Liver Disease." Accessed April 25, 2017. http://www.ncbi.nlm.nih.gov/pmc/articles/PMC3036962/.
[6] Anonymous. Many such postings are anonymous.

[7] DARA Thailand. "Alcoholic Liver Disease." Accessed April 3, 2017. http://alcoholrehab.com/alcohol-rehab/alcoholic-liver-disease/.

[8] Liver Foundation. "Alcohol-Related Liver Disease". Accessed May 23, 2017. http://www.liverfoundation.org/abouttheliver/info/alcohol/.

[9] *Grace724, medhelp.org*

[10] DARA Thailand. "Liver Transplants for Alcoholics." Accessed April 3, 2017. http://alcoholrehab.com/alcoholism/liver-transplants-for-alcoholics/.

[11] *Zippy, alcoholism.about.com*

[12] *(Name redacted), alcoholism.about.com*

[13] Discussed more in the main book, but in a nutshell it refers to the following: the first drink of alcohol creates an initial period of excitement (the "rush" of pleasure in the rush/buzz/numb/checkout continuum) lasting for a short time. As we continue to drink, we progress to the state of being "buzzed" (a felling ranging from light-headedness to solidly drunk. Then if we drink enough getting to point of being "numb" (being very drunk, and "numb" to the world around us to a significant degree, and eventually checking out (e.g., passing out, either in sleep form or being totally oblivious to the outside world).

[14] For those of you who have never played Monopoly, this is where you get sent back to start the game at the beginning spot on the board ("Go") without the usual benefit of collecting money when you do so.

[15] The desire for the buzz/rush/numb/checkout feelings that alcohol can provide either lurks in the background of many triggers, or it is front and center for others—particularly "Fun"—but also others like Escape (numb/checkout), Extreme Emotions (checkout), Guilt (numb), Insomnia (checkout), Peer Pressure (buzz/rush), Powerlessness (numb, checkout), and Zest/Zeal (rush).

[16] Alcoholrehab.com. "White Knuckle Sobriety." Accessed April 26, 2017. http://alcoholrehab.com/addiction-recovery/white-knuckle-sobriety/.

[17] Notre Dame Office of Alcohol and Drug Education. "What is Intoxication?" Accessed April 26, 2017. http://mcwell.nd.edu/your-well-being/physical-well-being/alcohol/what-is-intoxication/.

[18] The main book provides a detailed discussion of various forms of tolerance.

[19] Wikipedia. "Euphoria." Accessed April 27, 2017. http://en.wikipedia.org/wiki/Euphoria.

[20] Dysphoria is defined (also from Wikipedia.org) as: *a state of feeling unwell or unhappy; a feeling of emotional and mental discomfort as a symptom of discontentment, restlessness, dissatisfaction, malaise, depression, anxiety or indifference*. **In effect it is the opposite of Euphoria**.

[21] Admitting you are an alcoholic to your doctor will likely be very difficult, and embarrassing in particular. However, for this Level to really be useful, you MUST admit to how much, and how often, you drink. Do NOT "under-report" your volume and frequency.

[22] This is why in Level 5—Detox, it is strongly encouraged for alcoholics go to inpatient treatment centers for medically-supervised detoxification. If this is not possible, the backup is to at least go to your doctor for a "pre-sobriety" checkup, including fully admitting the extent of your alcohol intake and frequency.

Level 4—Engage Friends and Family

[1] This might seem counterintuitive, but it is true. If you are trying to get sober to "please" someone else, like a partner, it will likely fail. Why? For a number of reasons. First, it implies that you truly have not admitted to yourself that you have an addiction. That alone means any treatment will fail. Second, if you are not self-motivated to get sober, you may lack the wherewithal to get you through the toughest paRTs of sobriety. Third, any change in your relationship with whomever it is you are trying to please by getting sober puts your sobriety at risk. Therefore to succeed, you must get sober for yourself.

[2] *Malvern Institute, cryingoutnow.com*

[3] The impact of alcoholism on friends, family, and loved ones is not addressed much in this book because of its brevity. However, another book due out in 2017 specifically focuses on it: *Why Alcoholics Drink, and Why They Can't Stop*, due July 2017, Conquer Your Addiction LLC.

[4] Catharsis – *"the purification and purgation of emotions—especially pity and fear"* (Wikipedia.org)

[5] NBC News. "Death of 'True Blood' Actor Nelsan Ellis Spotlights Risk in Detoxing Alone". Accessed July 12, 2017. http://www.nbcnews.com/health/health-news/actor-s-death-spotlights-risks-detoxing-alone-n781906.

[6] Make sure you fully understand your privacy policies and settings on whatever online forum you use. Facebook, for example, seems to take perverse delight in changing them every few months. They have a vested interest in making your information as public as possible – that is how they make their money! But they (grudgingly) have controls that will make your posts difficult to see by non-friends. But as far as Facebook's own monitoring people and software, as well as advertisers – forget it. They will see what you post.

[7] If possible, have them read the original book. This is not an attempt to double-sell you on the books. The best rule of thumb is that the original book is best for treatment providers, non-alcoholics, or alcoholics that really want to get into all aspects of alcoholism. *This* book is for cutting-to-the-chase of how to get and stay sober, with all the bells-and-whistles stripped away. In any event, skimming this book will likely not be enough to overcome their skepticism—they will need to invest some time in reading the full book.

Level 5—Detox

[1] There are an amazing amount of "definitions" about detoxification from alcohol. Many of which I think are full of crap. For instance, Wikipedia has it as: *"the abrupt cessation of alcohol intake coupled with substitution of cross-tolerant drugs that have effects similar to the effects of alcohol in order to prevent alcohol withdrawal. As such, the term "detoxification" is somewhat of a misnomer since the process does not in any way involve the removal of toxic substances from the body."* I have

so many problems with this so-called definition that I consider it in total to be complete and absolute bullshit. An excellent example of don't-believe-everything-you-see on the Internet.

[2] Addiction Advisor. "Chapter One: Are You Physically Addicted to Alcohol?" Accessed April 6, 2017. http://www.addictionadvisor.co.uk/stay-sober/alcohol-help_a104.shtml#.UgZdoG2qm5g.

[3] Described in great detail in How to Conquer Your Alcoholism.

[4] In my view, "serious" means not drinking for at least two weeks. Many inpatient treatment programs (which may or may not include detox) last four weeks (28 days). In theory, it only takes a few (2-5) days to remove all alcohol from your body. Of course, your body and mind will continue to react to its absence for quite some time—ranging from weeks to months to even years, depending on the person and their post-drinking activities (e.g., diet, exercise, et al.).

[5] This is another reason to do a professional detox program, and not do-it-yourself: it is harder to quit a program if there are external factors involved—3rd parties, money, even just embarrassment of being seen as a "quitter".

[6] Fishman, alcoholism.about.com

[7] Burning Tree. "What are the Dangers of Detoxing Yourself from Alcohol?" Accessed February 26, 2014. http://www.burningtree.com/dangers-detoxing-alcohol/. (Link not working as of 4/6/17)

[8] Like in a regular hospital, your rooming arrangements will vary by hospital and the terms of your insurance. In my case, while I was put in a room with someone else for the very first hours of my detox, he was removed once his DTs symptoms started to appear. In general I would encourage you to seek a private room if at all possible—the noise and smell of others can become quite disturbing.

[9] Wikipedia. "Delirium tremens." Accessed April 6, 2017. http://en.wikipedia.org/wiki/Delirium_tremens.

[10] Some medically supervised detox programs are done in "traditional" hospitals, whereas others are done in dedicated substance-abuse facilities with full or part-time medical staff and associated equipment, which often call themselves hospitals. I have no opinion as to which are generally better—it will depend on the specifics of each individual facility.

[11] Before 2014, when this book was first published, any assumption of insurance for substance abuse services (in the U.S.) was a big one on two fronts: 1) in assuming you had insurance at all, and 2) that it covered substance abuse rehabilitation. The Affordable Care Act (ACA) made this simple (and much better for alcoholics) in that it enabled (relatively) low cost insurance, excluded preexisting conditions (alcoholism included), and mandated substance abuse coverage. However the extent of the coverage will vary by insurance carrier/plan, what facilities are covered in the plan/are in network and the type of treatment desired (inpatient, outpatient, medical intensity, etc.).

[12] In a short-duration detox, you are primarily focused on how terrible you feel, and not really interested in drinking after an initial period of physical craving. However, in longer-term rehab, once you completely have alcohol out of your system you start to feel good (known as "Pink Cloud") and may start to be tempted to drink again (particularly due to the Overconfidence trigger). You may also make some "friends" who for whatever reason can't wait to drink again, and do anything including sneak out of the campus to get some alcohol. All around it is best not to have the enabler in the form of an available car.

[13] It can be astonishing what alcoholics will drink, particularly when they are detoxing and desperate for a drink.

[14] This is not a simple yes or no, you are their voluntarily or not. While some will be there under court order (or spousal threat), patients are not under arrest nor any other truly involuntary arrangement, and can usually request to leave without immediate consequence (except perhaps financially). More broadly, though while they may be there "voluntarily", for the most part they may be just be killing time so they can get that part of their sentence out of the way, with no real commitment to sobriety. It is not at all unusual for such persons to try and sneak drink and/or drugs into the facility. It is a rare rehab/detox when a person is not kicked out after being caught doing this.

[15] Suicide is generally not a high risk for alcoholics in detox, but is a significant one for drug users.

[16] This was synthesized from numerous sources, including my own. Your experience may be very different, particularly in how structured your entire day is and what restrictions you have (or don't have) in terms of activities like working, exercise, and outside contact, as well as wakeup and bed-time/lights out (no that is not a joke—they may literally turn off the lights in your room).

[17] This kind of free time is much more likely to occur in Rehab (e.g., after you have fully detoxed). During detox you are much more likely to spend that time sleeping, reading, or just vegetating in general.

[18] If you skip these meetings anyway and are generally uncooperative they are well within their rights to kick you out, and they will (I've seen it done) often at a cost to you financially.

Level 6—Rehab and Therapy

[1] All Rehabilitation programs want you to be detoxed before you start their programs. As discussed in Level 5, some (but not all) inpatient programs offer Detox services. Therapy can occur before, during, and/or after Detox. Many alcoholics are introduced to meetings such as Alcoholics Anonymous during inpatient Detox or in Rehab.

[2] Narconon. "Grim Statistics on Repeated Drug Treatment Admissions Reveal Importance of Asking Right Questions before Rehab." http://news.narconon.org/repeated-drug-treatment-admissions/. Accessed May 4, 2014 (link not working April 28, 2017).

[3] While I am not a lawyer, I strongly suspect that if you are kicked out of Rehab and were under a court order to be there in the first place, you would be in violation of that order and would incur the consequences.

[4] The fact that AA meetings have so permeated rehabilitation programs and assumed a significant role as the "leading" type of alcoholism treatment is a major bone of contention for me. As you will see in Level 7—Join a Community, while being part of community support group is strongly encouraged in the Conquer Program, AA itself as a standalone program is vastly overrated, to the point of being a disservice to alcoholics by assuming a level of success by nonalcoholics that is just not supported by the facts.

[5] I'm not about to pretend it will be easy to take sick time for alcohol rehabilitation without other people at work knowing. Indeed it may be impossible. The good news nowadays is there is far less a stigma than it used to be, and cannot be used in itself as a reason for dismissal under federal law. If you have exhausted your vacation or sick time, check into taking a leave of absence using Family Medical Leave Act (FMLA), discussed later in this Level.

[6] Remember the caution mentioned in Level 5 (Detox) about befriending other patients. However, this is less a cause for concern the farther into rehab you and your fellow patients get. Still, be wary, as you do get a strange cast of characters sometimes. Also some will be under court-order to be there—hardly a character recommendation.

[7] *Tracy, alcoholism.about.com*

[8] The New York Times. "In Russia, Harsh Remedy For Addiction Gains Favor." Accessed April 20, 2017. http://www.nytimes.com/2011/09/03/world/europe/03russia.html?pagewanted=1.

[9] *Boo, alcoholism.about.com*

[10] *anonymous, alcoholism.about.com*

[11] With Mental Health Parity Rules, cost and day limits aren't allowed unless those limits are also on other types of illnesses.

[12] Some of you might notice that a premise about this program is that the so-called "expe**RT**s," (certified or otherwise) are not enough to get you sober. So why bother with certification? First, certification can separate the competent from the quacks, and second it is not because they are bad; it is because by themselves the knowledge they impart are not enough long-term.

[13] I have already been attacked by such people.

[14] Adapted from Serenity Lane. "How To Select a Treatment Center for Alcohol & Other Drug Dependencies." Accessed April 20, 2017. http://www.serenitylane.org/articles/treatment_selection.html.

[15] Other than the fact that I did not stop drinking. But again, I believe that was because I was expecting the treatment to be the one and only defense I would ever need, which, if you really think about it, is a ridiculous expectation to have.

[16] GoodTherapy.org. "Types of Therapy." Accessed April 10, 2017. http://www.goodtherapy.org/learn-about-therapy/types.

[17] NHS (National Health Services of UK). "Pros and Cons of CBT." Accessed April 10, 2017. http://www.nhs.uk/conditions/cognitive-behavioural-therapy/Pages/Introduction.aspx#prosandcons

[18] SAMHSA National Registry of Evidence Based Programs and Practices. "Alcohol Behavioral Couple Therapy." Accessed April 20, 2017. https://www.samhsa.gov/treatment.

[19] Learn-About-Alcoholism. "Types of Alcoholism Therapy." Accessed April 20, 2017. http://www.learn-about-alcoholism.com/types-of-alcoholism.html.

[20] About.com. "Cognitive Behavior Therapy for Addiction." Accessed April 20, 2017. http://alcoholism.about.com/od/relapse/a/cbt.htm.

[21] NIH. "Treatment for Alcohol Problems: Finding and Getting Help." Accessed April 11, 2017. https://pubs.niaaa.nih.gov/publications/treatment/treatment.htm.

[22] Learn-About-Alcoholism. "Types of Alcoholism Therapy." Accessed April 20, 2017. http://www.learn-about-alcoholism.com/types-of-alcoholism.html.

[23] NIAAA. "Motivation Enhancement Therapy Manual." Accessed April 20, 2017. http://pubs.niaaa.nih.gov/publications/ProjectMatch/match02.pdf.

[24] Learn-About-Alcoholism. "Types of Alcoholism Therapy." Accessed April 20, 2017. http://www.learn-about-alcoholism.com/types-of-alcoholism.html.

[25] Wikipedia. "List of 12-Step Groups." Accessed April 11, 2017. https://en.wikipedia.org/wiki/List_of_twelve-step_groups.

[26] There are even other categories, like "psychiatric nurse" that have their own practices. It can get confusing.

[27] Like showing the patient gruesome images of terrible car crashes caused by drunken drivers.

[28] Team Lib. "The Essential Handbook of Treatment and Prevention of Alcohol Problems." Page 12. Accessed April 20, 2017. http://robinsteed.pbworks.com/w/file/fetch/52176344/TreatmentAndPreventionOfAlcoholProblems.pdf.

[29] Web MD. "Disulfiram." Accessed April 20, 2017. http://www.webmd.com/a-to-z-guides/disulfiram.

[30] Psychology Today. "What Does Hypnosis Really Feel Like?" Accessed April 20, 2017. http://www.psychologytoday.com/blog/hypnosis-the-power-trance/200907/what-does-hypnosis-really-feel.

[31] Alcoholrehab.com. "Hypnosis As An Addiction Treatment." Accessed April 20, 2017. http://alcoholrehab.com/alcohol-rehab/hypnosis-as-an-addiction-treatment/.

[32] AltMD. "Meditation for Addiction-What is Meditation?" Accessed March 10, 2014. http://www.altmd.com/Articles/Meditation-for-Addiction. (Not working as of 4/20/17). Similar: Psychology Today. "Mindfulness Meditation & Addiction." Accessed April 20, 2017. https://www.psychologytoday.com/blog/the-wise-open-mind/201004/mindfulness-meditation-addiction.

[33] Spiritual Healing For You. "Types of Meditation." Accessed March 20, 2017. http://www.spiritual-healing-for-you.com/types-of-meditation.html.

[34] The overview of the five categories of meditation comes from: Spiritual Healing For You. "Types of Meditation." Accessed April 20, 2017. http://www.spiritual-healing-for-you.com/types-of-meditation.html.

[35] AltMD. "Meditation for Addiction." Accessed March 10, 2014. http://www.altmd.com/Articles/Meditation-for-Addiction. . (Not working as of 4/20/17). Similar: Psychology Today. "Mindfulness Meditation & Addiction." Accessed April 20, 2017. https://www.psychologytoday.com/blog/the-wise-open-mind/201004/mindfulness-meditation-addiction.

[36] Gaiam Life. "Mediation and Visualization." Accessed April 20, 2017. http://life.gaiam.com/article/meditation-and-visualization.

[37] From SalvationArmyUSA.org. "Addiction Recovery (Adult Rehabilitation Centers)." Accessed April 20, 2017. http://centralusa.salvationarmy.org/usc/rehabilitation: "In some areas programs have developed that serve women with addictions, but for the most part the ARC ministry is focused on men dealing with alcohol and drug addictions."

---

[38] Adapted from Wikipedia.org. "The Salvation Army." Accessed April 20, 2017.
http://en.wikipedia.org/wiki/The_Salvation_Army.

[39] Most rehab programs have some level of trigger-related discussions (though not nearly as comprehensive and structured as this program), which will allow you an opportunity to explore deeper into some of them, such as the rehab favorite H.A.L.T. (Hungry, Angry, Lonely, Tired).

[1] Measuring the success rates of addiction treatment programs can be very complex and incredibly subjective. It mainly depends on three factors: 1) When a person is considered to have "entered" the program; 2) How long after that he or she is "measured"; and 3) The definition of "success" (and by implication "failure").

For example, if a person has entered a program and is still there a year later, is that a "success?" Would they still be a success if they drank or relapsed during that time but kept coming to meetings? How often or consistently would they have to come to be considered to still be "in the program?" Would or should they have to complete a certain number of steps (or some specific steps) to be considered to have "tried" the program? It can get pretty muddled pretty quickly when you get into the details. The vast majority of people in programs such as AA drop out within a year (95% according to AA!), with "dropping out" apparently just meaning they don't go to meetings anymore (there is no additional detail). So the assumption is those who have been there at least a year have been successful at stopping their drinking (does it also presume they have "completed" all the steps in that time? Still use their sponsor?). If you only measure people who have "been in the program" (however that is defined) for at least a year, you are going to have far higher "success rates" than if you counted ALL people starting from Day

Level 7—Join A Community

[1] In a nutshell, when calculating "success rates" it is critical to identify all key variables and keep as many of them as constant as possible—something very difficult to do with AA. For example, is a person a "success" if he/she continues to attend meetings? How many meetings are a "requirement"? What if they are drinking and attending meetings? What if they quit before they finish the 12 Steps? Or are the 12 Steps even relevant (e.g. is just attending a certain amount of meetings without drinking enough for "success"? What if no sponsor? What is the time period before labeling someone a "success": 3 months? 6 months, 2 years? It gets pretty complicated pretty quickly.

[2] The history of AA and its writings shed significant light on its criticisms today, two of which are it seeming "stale" and to some somewhat sexist—both tracing its roots back to the mid 1930s. For example, at that time (and for decades afterwards), it was thought only men could be alcoholics!. For a balanced view of AA issues and potential solutions see https://www.thefix.com/case-change-alcoholics-anonymous (written by the author).

[3] The Wall Street Journal. "Why She Drinks: Women and Alcohol Abuse." Accessed April 20, 2017.
http://online.wsj.com/article/SB10001424127887323893504578555270434071876.html.

[4] Wikipedia. "Alcoholics Anonymous." Accessed April 20, 2017.
http://en.wikipedia.org/wiki/Alcoholics_Anonymous#Program.

[5] Wikipedia. "Rational Recovery." Accessed March 18, 2014. Last updated April 20, 2017.
http://en.wikipedia.org/wiki/Rational_Recovery.

[6] SOS Sobriety. "SOS Principles." Accessed April 20, 2017.
https://static1.squarespace.com/static/576740f45016e10f9510a056/t/5768d296893fc08c1a44efc4/1466487450589/SOS_Principles.pdf

[7] Women for Sobriety. "WFS "New Life" Acceptance Program." Accessed April 20, 2017.
http://womenforsobriety.org/beta2/new-life-program/13-affirmations/.

[8] That lying is a cause of alcoholism I believe is idiotic, but in my research I found more than one "expert" who seemed to truly believe it.

[9] Be careful of course; many of these people are blithering idiots, but even they might give you some ideas.

Level 9—Develop New Hobbies

[1] Planning your alcohol purchases is a question in the Conquer Quiz in Level 1.

[2] This way of "disguising" your alcohol purchases is also part of The Conquer Quiz in Level 1.

[3] To a certain degree it did, as I never bought more than I planned on drinking (e.g., a quart of vodka towards the end), because if I did I would probably drink that as well. But buying on a real-time basis as it were probably tacked on at least 30 minutes a day to my total.

[4] Depression activities ideas drawn from Healthtalk.org. "Depression – Distraction, Activities, and Creativity." Accessed April 21, 2017. http://www.healthtalk.org/peoples-experiences/mental-health/depression/distraction-activities-and-creativity.

[5] Promises Treatment Centers. "Pets: Natural Stress Relievers." Accessed April 20, 2017.
http://www.promises.com/articles/therapy/pets-natural-stress-relievers/.

[6] Financial Planning can be a good way of calming yourself when the future is causing you all kinds of issues, including Anxiety and Change concerns. It can even help in Boredom, as it can be both complex and (counter-intuitively boring—in essence cancelling out your Boredom with a different kind of boredom.

[7] The New York Times. "Yes, Running Can Make You High." Accessed April 20, 2017.
http://www.nytimes.com/2008/03/27/health/nutrition/27best.html?_r=0.

[8] Talentspace. "Ten Creative Ways to Help Employees Relieve Stress at Work." Accessed April 20, 2017.
http://www.halogensoftware.com/blog/10-creative-ways-to-help-employees-relieve-stress-at-work.

[9] Anxiety activities drawn from Healthy Place. "Ten Ways to Get Rid of Generalized Anxiety Symptoms." Accessed April 20, 2017. http://www.healthyplace.com/blogs/anxiety-schmanxiety/2012/05/ten-activities-to-get-rid-of-anxiety/

[10] Daily Mail. "Cheers! Drinking DOES Release The Feelgood Factor In Our Brains." Accessed April 28, 2017. http://www.dailymail.co.uk/health/article-2085320/Drinking-DOES-make-feel-happy-Alcohol-triggers-endorphins-brain.html

[11] While I was convalescing from surgery, I "bowled" many games on the WII U SpoRTs Club game. It is surprising good exercise. There are a number of other active-type games and, of course, regular fitness programs available on most game systems, though WII with its special controller seems to have the most.

Level 10—Consider Spirituality

[1] Even if they are only a fraction of those that try AA.

[2] Wikipedia. "Religion and Alcohol." Accessed April 22, 2017. http://en.wikipedia.org/wiki/Religion_and_alcohol.

[3] My Recovery. "The Double-Edged Sword of Religion and Alcoholism." Accessed April 22, 2017. http://www.myrecovery.com/Spirituality-in-Recovery/david-briggs-the-doubled-edged-sword-of-religion-and-alcoholism.html.

[4] Attitudes can vary depending on whether the addiction is alcohol or drugs, with alcohol generally being treated less harshly.

[5] Of course, if you are set in your specific religion, and there is only one church in your area, you are kind of stuck.

[6] Huffington Post. "The Double-Edged Sword of Religion and Alcoholism." Accessed April 22, 2017. http://www.huffingtonpost.com/david-briggs/charlie-sheen-circus-and-_b_836934.html.

[7] Exception: I did attend several sessions of Strawberry Ministries near where I live. I went into those sessions extremely skeptical, having lived in Texas during the Evangelistic hell of the '80s and '90s. But I found them to be very well done, effectively blending spirituality themes, biblical teachings, sophisticated presentations, and even interactive visual aids and music to deliver some very good teachings on dealing with addiction from a spiritual perspective.

[8] AlcoholRehab.com. "Spirituality and Rehab." Accessed April 22 2017. http://alcoholrehab.com/alcohol-rehab/spirituality-and-rehab/.

[9] Wikipedia. "Higher Power." Accessed April 24, 2017. https://en.wikipedia.org/wiki/Higher_Power.

[10] *anonymous*

[11] Adapted from AlcoholRehab.com. "Higher Power In AA." Accessed April 24, 2017. http://alcoholrehab.com/alcohol-rehab/higher-power-in-aa/.

[12] That is the primary downside of this section—that it can require a good deal of effort on your part.

[13] I'm sure I'm going to upset a lot of people by saying that, but that's sure what it looks like to me, an "outsider."

[14] I only cite this link since it seems to do a reasonable job of doing a high-level comparison of different religions/spiritual approaches. My guess is the authors' beliefs are skewed in a particular direction, but it is not obvious from the chart.

[15] This is a phrase meaning that in times of extreme stress or fear, such as in war, all people will believe in, or hope for, a higher power. Its origin is from World War II or possibly WWI (it is not clear), where soldiers would dig holes in the ground to take cover in during bombings (to avoid shrapnel from nearby hits) or gun battles.

[16] AlcoholRehab.com. "Spirituality and Rehab." Accessed April 22 2017. http://alcoholrehab.com/alcohol-rehab/spirituality-and-rehab/.

[17] *Louise, alcoholism.about.com*

[18] *Anonymous4, examiner.com*

[19] As a feeling - *an experience of sudden and striking realization*; in religion - *the appearance of a deity to a human* (source: Wikipedia.org)

[20] *Rocky L., alcoholism.about.com*

[21] *nick K., alcoholism.about.com*

[22] Guest Ask for Gods Help, alcoholism.about.com. Accessed December 2014.

[23] If God exists, these guys better hope to hell that He has a sense of humor.

[24] 1hourataT9, alcoholism.about.com. Accessed December 2014.

[25] Newsweek. "Proof of Heaven: A Doctor's Experience With the Afterlife." Accessed April 22, 2017. http://www.newsweek.com/proof-heaven-doctors-experience-afterlife-65327.

[26] If you really want to inject great humor into the topic of spirituality, there are a number of general fiction titles that do this. One is *"Lamb"* by Christopher Moore, which takes an extremely funny look at what Jesus' life might have been before he started preaching. I've always wondered what Jesus did in his first 30 years, and this book is as good a take as any while being absolutely hilarious. I hope He has a sense of humor, otherwise people like Moore and his readers (including me) are in deep trouble.

Level 11—Make Yourself Sick of Alcohol

[1] Again, the author is **not** responsible for anything you do or experience from executing any aspect in The Conquer Program, particularly Levels 11 and 12. I can't repeat this enough, particularly in the opinion of my lawyers.

[2] Wikipedia. "Ivan Pavlov." Accessed April 26, 2017. http://en.wikipedia.org/wiki/Ivan_Pavlov.

[3] Of course you don't have to have colon problems to do this, but (in my opinion) you *do* need some sort of recent agonizing pain. The "problem" with physical pain is that the mind does not retain a memory of it, which normally is obviously a good thing but works against this kind of approach—hence the pain needs to be still lingering in your memory (or better yet, still occurring. This is the point of Level 12—The Last Detox).

[4] One interesting side effect is that I can detect the words "liquor" "wine" or "beer" in any sign on a street or in a store without trying.

[5] For me it was Southern Comfort and Gin. I was violently ill from both—SC in college when I drank a whole bottle, and gin the first time I ever tried it. I've never touched either again even when nothing else was available.

[6] Mayo Clinic. "Food Allergies: Understanding Food Labels." Accessed April 26, 2017. http://www.mayoclinic.com/health/food-allergies/AA00057.

[7] It may be that this whip-sawing back and forth between concentrated heavy drinking and detoxes is what helped me finally achieve my aversion to alcohol—I have absolutely no way of knowing. As far as I know, this rapid-fire get drunk/detox/repeat has never been tried before, at least in a clinical setting. A great research topic!

[8] I also became "sick" of wine—particularly the smell and taste of white wine—many years earlier. But in that case I believe it was from the sheer volume of drinking. I don't remember exactly when or how it happened, but one day after one of my usual very heavy consumption of wine the night before, the smell and taste started making me sick to my stomach. I rarely had more than a glass or two after that. Unfortunately I switched to vodka for the heavy alcoholic lifting.

[9] Of course there were many times when I had these effects *individually*, but not very often all at the *same* time. Perhaps experiencing these multiple times in a relatively short period are one of the reasons this approach worked for me—again, I just don't know.

[10] Approximately 3 years after this first "test," I decided to see if my "aversion" was still "active", and drank several shots of vodka and a couple of beers. I became very nauseated, with my disgust for alcohol renewed. I recognize this as being a very dangerous, even stupid thing to do, but I felt an obligation to test the longevity of my approach, since I was writing about it (if not necessarily advocating doing it). I was very pleased at the results, but do NOT suggest you do any of these "tests" yourself.

[11] There are very few hospitals/clinics providing this kind of "formal" treatment program. The testimonials I found were hospital specific (naming names), so I do not cite them here for legal liability reasons. Some people said it was very effective, others not so much. One prominent advocate is Pat O'Day, a prominent broadcaster and announcer in the U.S. Pacific Northwest who is the key spokesman for Schick Shadel Hospital (Source: Wikipedia. "Pat O'Day." Accessed April 26, 2017. http://en.wikipedia.org/wiki/Pat_O'Day).

[12] *Frank, eborg2.com*

Level 12—The LAST Detox

[1] Level 11 was optional and its effectiveness depends greatly upon the individual. If you tried making yourself physically sick along the lines of how the author did it, it may or may not have worked—it was far from guaranteed. Another possibility is that it *partially* worked; you now find that you are less tempted to drink than you were before, but you are still doing it (perhaps drinking less, avoiding certain kinds of drinks, or even drinking a bit reluctantly). In that case, Level 12 may help complete the aversion process you started.

[2] Why not just jump to this Level? Because there are very significant risks associated with *any* detox, and those who have never done it before may not have any idea how their mind and body will react – which may in some cases be dangerous and even be life-threatening (hence doing medically supervised detox is *highly* recommended).

[3] And yes, the pain medications they gave me for my colon problems didn't hurt in taking my mind off detox in the rare instances when I thought about it. And no, I did not become addicted to those medications. If you are worried about becoming addicted to pain meds, I strongly urge you to express this concern (and your drinking history) to your doctor, who will then take extra special care in prescribing them. See also a very specific discussion on the potential for other addictions in Level 9.

[4] Delirium tremens—See Level 5 for more information. Obviously this assumes your doctor *knows* you are an alcoholic. If not, tell him/her. NOW. Pick up the phone NOW.

[5] Being "remote" with medical assistance "close by" may or may not be easy. Some states such as Texas have "dry counties" where alcohol is not allowed to be sold (sometimes even in restaurants), yet medical facilities are close by.

[6] I would imagine that this is effective only your alcoholic beverage of choice was something much stronger, and you didn't really care for beer. But that is just a guess; other scenarios are possible. Perhaps "tapering off" to a beverage (regardless of alcohol content) that you hated, like some gross wine? You could then possibly tie it to some of the lessons of Level 11, making you sick of alcohol in the process.

[7] A perfect illustration of if at first you don't succeed: try, try again! Applicable for detox, certainly. However his definition of a successful detox might leave something to be desired if he had to try again and again. But I believe he was trying to say he fully detoxed without drinking and stayed sober for at least some meaningful amount of time.

[8] I found numerous testimonials about tapering, about 50/50 in terms of success. But this most likely refers to only a narrow detox time window; as an alcoholic they very likely subsequently ratcheted their drinking back up shortly thereafter. Source of testimonial: *Guest jd, alcoholism.about.com.*

[9] I have no idea if any of this has a medical basis for avoiding shakes or vomiting. Whatever works though! Source of testimonial: *Guest Wine lover, alcoholism.about.com*

[10] *Guest J, alcoholism.about.com*

[11] The main *How to Conquer Your Alcoholism* book discusses drugs that can help with withdrawal. Two good additional sources of information can be found at https://www.uptodate.com/contents/management-of-moderate-and-severe-alcohol-withdrawal-syndromes and https://www.drugs.com/condition/alcohol-withdrawal.html.

[12] I found numerous testimonials describing a wide range of drugs for anxiety (such as Librium) that were prescribed (and seemed effective), so there are apparently many options. What might work for you, of course, will need to be determined by your doctor.

[13] *Drinker06798, alcoholism.about.com*

[14] Juicing seems to emphasize detoxing as a big part of its sales pitch. I don't know how true that is, but it should certainly help with any potential vitamin deficiencies, a common problem with alcoholics. Source of testimonial: *Guest Jazmine, alcoholism.about.com*

Level 13—Develop Your Defense Progressions

[1] The five senses. I wouldn't even rule out a "sixth sense".

[2] Smart Football. "Teaching a Quarterback Where To Throw the Football." Accessed May 2, 2014. Smart Football. "Teaching A Quarterback Where To Throw The Ball." Accessed April 28, 2017. http://smartfootball.com/quarterbacking/reading-grass-versus-reading-full-coverages-or-keying-specific-pass-defenders.

[3] It bears repeating that "Stress" in the Conquer Program denotes a specific kind of physical stress. Other kinds of "stress" are most likely other triggers such as Job stress, Relationship stress, etc.

[4] It was not fixable while I was living with my eX. However, once on my own I came to realize how important keeping the house clean, making my bed, etc. was to my peace-of-mind, particularly when I came home from work.

[5] My experience also illustrates a sometimes complicating factor in separating a major trigger from a related one: when what is now a Related Trigger used to be a major trigger in the past, or vice versa. In fact, it is very possible for the same trigger to be both "major" or "related" over the course of your alcoholism life.

[6] I've had a great deal of intestinal issues, including 2 near-deaths, with both extremely painful. The shock/wear on my remaining "systems" from drinking again would almost assuredly cause a 3rd episode that I am unlikely to survive.

[7] In the main *How to Conquer Your Alcoholism* book (and to some degree on www.ConquerYourAddiction.com), a full set of tips are included for every trigger (and is the primary reason the main book is so long).

[8] In the main How To Conquer Your Alcoholism book, Level 2 by itself was longer than *this* book.

[9] See Appendix B for all the checklists.

[10] This is in contrast to floor triggers, where you want your most effective floor trigger last—as in last resort.

[11] My personal arch-nemesis.

[12] *Terri, alcoholism.about.com*

[13] Murphy's Law: What *can* go wrong *will* go wrong.

[14] *anonymous*

[15] The New York Times. "Robin Williams, Oscar-Winning Actor, Dies at 63 In Suspected Suicide." Accessed April 28, 2017. http://www.nytimes.com/2014/08/12/movies/robin-williams-oscar-winning-comedian-dies-at-63.html?hp&action=click&pgtype=Homepage&version=LargeMediaHeadlineSumCentered&module=photo-spot-region&region=photo-spot&WT.nav=photo-spot&_r=0 .

Conclusion

[1] Anonymous after a meeting in Missouri sometime in 2012.

[2] One Crafty Mother. "In Which I Answer The Question I Get Most." Accessed May 24, 2014. http://www.onecraftymother.com/2011/06/in-which-i-answer-question-i-get-most.html, final two paragraphs. Link not functional as of 3/29/17—Domain for sale.

Appendix A

[1] *Robot The Human, socialanxietysupport.com*

[2] Listen to books on tape while commuting. This can drain away Job-related and physical stress, and combined with driving can be very relaxing.

Made in United States
Orlando, FL
16 November 2021